Fuzzy Data Matching with SQL
Enhancing Data Quality and Query Performance

Jim Lehmer

Beijing · Boston · Farnham · Sebastopol · Tokyo

Fuzzy Data Matching with SQL

by Jim Lehmer

Published by O'Reilly Media, Inc., 1005 Gravenstein Highway North, Sebastopol, CA 95472.

O'Reilly books may be purchased for educational, business, or sales promotional use. Online editions are also available for most titles (*https://oreilly.com*). For more information, contact our corporate/institutional sales department: 800-998-9938 or *corporate@oreilly.com*.

Acquisitions Editor: Andy Kwan	**Indexer:** BIM Creatives, LLC
Development Editor: Angela Rufino	**Interior Designer:** David Futato
Production Editor: Gregory Hyman	**Cover Designer:** Karen Montgomery
Copyeditor: Kim Wimpsett	**Illustrator:** Kate Dullea
Proofreader: James Fraleigh	

October 2023:   First Edition

Revision History for the First Edition
2023-09-28:   First Release

See *http://oreilly.com/catalog/errata.csp?isbn=9781098152277* for release details.

978-1-098-15227-7

[LSI]

To my father and mother, Lou and Barb, whose gentle encouragement and support has been with me my entire life; and my wife Leslie and daughter Erin, who had to listen to me talk about this book non-stop for months and still somehow feigned interest...usually.

Table of Contents

Part II.   Various Data Problems

Part III.   Bringing It Together

Preface

This book contains the patterns, practices, techniques, and tricks I've picked up over the decades, usually around the problem of "Is *this* list of data related to anything in *that* table?" The canonical example is a cold-call list pulled from…"somewhere" (we'll be kind), and now Marketing (it's always Marketing) wants you to match this list they probably paid for against the company's existing customer database. Why? There are lots of reasons, but these are the chief two:

Identify new prospects
> Filter out existing customers from the list and send the new prospects down a low-cost, standardized route with perhaps a cold call, mailing list, etc. Think *Glengarry Glen Ross*.

Upsell and cross-sell existing customers
> Filter out new prospects, and if an existing customer shows up at a trade show and expresses interest, perhaps they're not aware of your entire product offering or haven't been "touched" in a while to determine their needs. Get a salesperson in front of them with some incentives, pronto.

There are other reasons, of course. Two companies merging and wanting to combine their customer relationship management (CRM) systems and eliminate duplicates is another common reason. Often the same types of techniques are used to de-duplicate even within a single dataset, like a CRM database. Or when someone comes to you with data found on the "dark web" attributed to your company. Is it yours? Is it complete? Accurate? Current?

Don't deal with data about humans? The second case study, covered in Chapter 13, will show the same techniques used to do some impact analysis on code—that is, treating source code as data to be fuzzy-matched against. I have also used the patterns in this book to parse text-based log files. You may be asked to do work in any or all of these areas and more.

For the purposes of this book, I will typically refer to "your customer data" or "your CRM data" as meaning something like your production dataset that presumably is in decent shape in terms of schema design, data quality, etc. (decent, not perfect—we will cover that). I will then talk about the "incoming data" or "imported data" as the data you are being asked to match against the customer data. In your world, "customer data" could be "patient data" or "subject data" or some such, but most of this book will cover aspects of matching human demographic attributes such as name, address, and phone number. The general techniques are useful across other areas, but you will have to do your own cognitive mapping if your data deals with something like products or pandemics.

What Problems Are We Trying to Solve?

This book answers (or attempts to answer) the following questions:

- How do I *prepare* datasets for import, for merging, and for better analysis?
- How do I *clean* the data, wherever it is? How do I help achieve data quality? (Elusive!)
- How do I *query* with pure SQL to keep the technology stack simple and "close to the data"?
- How do I *identify* the duplicates in my corporate/production/study/import data?
- How do I *remove* the duplicates in my corporate/production/study/import data?
- How do I *match* between datasets? How do I know how strong the matches are?
- How do I *report* results? How do I best get the information in front of those who need it?

By the time you are finished reading, you should have a good understanding of how to answer each question, and others besides.

What Will We Cover?

Most of the examples in the book cover how to match data between two disparate datasets. The following are the high-level steps:

Normalize
> Handle common data representation and quality problems so that the chances of successful matching are good. (For details on my usage of the term *normalized* and other terms that frequently appear in this book, please refer to the Glossary.)

Score
> Determine how well the two datasets match.

Present
> Analyze and report on the results.

To accomplish all that, this book will look at the following topics.

Part I: Review

The first part is a quick review of some SQL elements heavily used in this book. You can skip this part if you know SQL well:

- Chapter 1, "A SELECT Review", contains a quick review of the SELECT statement and joins. You are expected to be familiar with SQL—this will not be a primer, but more tips I find useful.

- Chapter 2, "Function Junction", contains the SQL functions that will be heavily used in the rest of the book.

Part II: Various Data Problems

The second part will help us with matching later in the book by covering how to "normalize" and clean up a variety of common data problems:

- What can I say about Chapter 3, "Names, Names, Names"? Names are hard (*https://oreil.ly/jPYKn*). People's names (even before we get to suffixes). Company names. Your name. My name (most people struggle at pronouncing "Lehmer" correctly, because most people don't speak German).

- Chapter 4, "Location, Location, Location", shows that addresses are hard, too (*https://oreil.ly/ZgNDc*).

- Chapter 5, "Dates, Dates, Dates", covers dates of birth and other irrelevant events. Ever seen a birth date in the future? I have. *Of course* in production! "Time has no meaning" to a person entering a date. And that's not even counting the fact that dates and time are hard, too (*https://oreil.ly/Tgmsi*). And time zones (*https://oreil.ly/ZmIe_*).

- Chapter 6, "Email", covers the fact that with tax IDs/Social Security numbers being private (and for good reason), an email address can be as close to a unique identifier as we get in the real world. Almost. But we still have to check it for validity. You'd be surprised how little is needed to comprise a "valid" email address.

- Chapter 7, "Phone Numbers", covers what to do about data like "555-555-1234 Aunt Judy's #" in your phone numbers. It's in your *production* database? No worries. We'll talk about it.

- Chapter 8, "Bad Characters", covers bad characters, and we're not talking about in your customer base. Datatypes. Character sets. Character encoding.

Nonbreaking spaces. Invisible characters besides spaces and tabs that TRIM may not know about.

- Chapter 9, "Orthogonal Data", discusses "orthogonal data." These are fancy words for people cramming 10 pounds (or kilos, your choice) of "stuff" in a 5-pound (or kilo) bag. We'll talk about it, including how to attack it, parse it, and maybe make some sense of it.

Part III: Bringing It Together

The third part covers core concepts of the book, scoring matches and tuning the results:

- Chapter 10, "The Big Score", discusses how to add it all up and decide, "Does this match?" This chapter is the core of the book, showing how to take our cleaned, normalized data and decide how strongly it matches.
- Chapter 11, "Data Quality, or GIGO", covers data quality. The quality of data in your production system. The quality of the data you're matching against. What you can do to protect yourself against less than perfect (that is, "real") data. And ultimately, how you work around it, which is often the reason behind the word *Fuzzy* in the title.
- Chapter 12, "Tying It All Together", presents a case study bringing together all the techniques used in the book so you can see how they work in concert.
- Chapter 13, "Code Is Data, Too!", is the final chapter. In case human demographic data isn't your thing, how about SQL (code) generating SQL (code) to search all types of source code and other textual artifacts for specific object names? We'll talk about what that means and why it is a "real-world" example of how to automate impact analysis and save hundreds of person-hours in the process.

Appendix

The Appendix covers the data "model" used in the book.

Needless to say, this book deals with fuzzy data matching in a very limited area, mostly human demographic data. But the techniques used can apply across a variety of datasets. Parsing a string is parsing a string, and regardless of the "meaning" of the string, the approach is often the same. Another universal aspect of data covered in the book is "Did a human enter it? Was it imported from another system?" Then it probably has data quality issues that need to be dealt with before matching can even begin, and we will talk about that, too.

Who Is This Book For?

My intended audience is people who know SQL—you can wield SELECT statements to get decent reports or to return data to your programs, you understand a WHERE clause, etc. But maybe you have never been called upon or had the need to do complex, "fuzzy" matching between two heterogeneous data sources. Data scientists, programmers, business analysts, systems integrators, and students will all find these techniques helpful.

If you wield SQL on a daily basis and know SQL functions such as TRANSLATE and DATEDIFF, you can jump right to Chapter 3, where we dive into the main content of the book. You may need a review if the idea of nesting SQL functions like this (explained later) is unknown or unreadable to you:

```
DECLARE @FullName VARCHAR(100)
SET @FullName = 'Mortimer Snedley'
SELECT
    @FullName [Full Name],
    -- LEFT for first name
    LEFT(@FullName,
        CHARINDEX(' ', @FullName) - 1) [First Name],
    -- Substring to extract the last name
    SUBSTRING(@FullName,
            CHARINDEX(' ', @FullName) + 1,
            PATINDEX('%, %', @FullName) -
            CHARINDEX(' ', @FullName) - 1) [Last Name],
    -- RIGHT to grab the suffix
    RIGHT(@FullName,
        LEN(@FullName) - 1 - PATINDEX('%, %', @FullName)) [Suffix];
```

If the preceding code seems "obscure" (if not outright obfuscated, which I guarantee it is not), then I suggest you read Chapter 1 to review the SELECT statement and Chapter 2 to review all the SQL functions used in this book.

Why SQL?

In modern data science, it is popular to pull all the data from disparate data sources into memory using something like Python or R and do all the work there. When dealing with heterogeneous data, this approach has many advantages.

However, often in business you are dealing with pure "rectangular" data—rows and columns—whether represented in a relational database system as tables, an Excel spreadsheet, or a CSV file. The first is how most businesses already represent their production business data, and the latter two can be easily imported into a SQL database table with a variety of tools. Once there, the true power of a modern relational database server comes into play almost automatically, including the following features:

- Rich set-based processing with SQL
- Automatic query optimization and parallelization
- Efficient I/O and memory utilization
- Scalability
- Large library of functions
- Stored procedures and user-defined functions
- Variety of vendors, versions, and platforms (also a trap!)
- Wide availability of cross-platform tools and query environments
- Bindings for almost every programming language

Often, if the work is to extract, transform, and load (ETL) something, then why lift it off the database server and send it across the network (latency) to be loaded into memory and processed and filtered on another server (more latency) that then sends the results back across the network into another table (still more latency)? "The fastest I/O is the one you don't do." If you are processing against very popular tables, a SQL engine may already have most of the rows cached in memory and ready anyway.

Again, there are good reasons to pull the data out of a variety of places and process it in-memory using custom code. But if everything is already in a SQL database or easily imported there, a powerful variety of techniques become available "for free." I believe that if you are manipulating a vast amount of data and can fit within a relational database server's constraints of rows and columns, then SQL often gives you as much or more power for data transformation, especially with sets of data at real scale, not available in more conventional programming languages and models. Of course, I also "drop to code" quite often! I believe in picking the right tool for the right job. And for the subject at hand, SQL is often the right tool.

Warning! Opinions Ahead!

This book is the result of decades of working with SQL, from IBM DB2 1.2 in the 1980s to Sybase SQL Server and then Microsoft SQL Server starting in the 1990s through today. At the same time I was often tasked with answering the question, "Can you tell us if these two completely different sets of data have anything in common?" Those two aspects together ended up making me a nice career. I didn't plan it, but I am grateful for it.

However, I grew up learning SQL "on the streets," so many of the things I present here work, but they may not be the best way to do things. However, they are often a "good enough" way to do them when you don't have much more than SELECT access into an environment.

Finally, I always feel like it is better to learn from someone with strong opinions instead of the wishy-washy, "Well, you could do it this way, or you could do it that way, or this third way as well." Sure, I know all that, but if I think someone is an expert on a topic, I want to know what they do, and why. If I want to compare and contrast, I'd rather talk to two knowledgeable people with different approaches to the domain space instead of trusting one to have an objective view of both. So, I don't necessarily claim to be an expert on this topic, but I *am* going to tell you what I think! There are others who will do things differently. Find them and learn from them, too. Synthesize it all together and become your own expert!

Typographical Conventions Used in This Book

The following typographical conventions are used in this book:

Italic

Indicates new terms, URLs, email addresses, filenames, and file extensions. In addition, if I am giving the name of a SQL object (database, table, view, column), then I will use italics, e.g., *crm.Customer*.

`Constant width`

Used for program listings, as well as within paragraphs to refer to program elements such as variable or function names, databases, datatypes, environment variables, statements, and keywords.

Inline code in the book looks like this: `SELECT * FROM crm.Normalized Customer`. If I am referring to a SQL or other programming language keyword, it will look like `COUNT(*)`.

Block SQL code in the text appears as follows:

```
SELECT * FROM sys.databases;
```

This element signifies a general note.

This element indicates a warning or caution.

Additional Information on the Book's Conventions

In all the book's SQL code examples, comments are meant to be read along with the code. Sometimes I will explain the query in great detail in the text following the query, but often I leave it to the comments to discuss what is going on. SQL comments look like this:

```
/*
    Comments can be between C-style delimiters
    and span multiple lines.
*/
SELECT TOP 10      /* Only get 10 rows */
    *
FROM Customers;

-- The other style of comments simply comment everything
-- out until the end of the line. Obviously these can
-- cover multiple lines, too.
SELECT TOP 10      -- Only get 10 rows
    *
FROM Customers;
```

I admit it can look a little like COBOL; maybe it's Stockholm Syndrome, but I like it and can parse it easily and quickly, yet it is not covered with "square bracket spew" like many tools generate. Don't call my baby ugly! Also, there will be times when I break lines or align keywords in a way I would never do in real life but will here to help make the parts of a complicated example stand out clearer.

 I tend to favor -- comments in real life, mostly just from muscle memory. However, the connectivity used to develop this book collapses all newlines out of SQL, such that the latter example of SELECT TOP 10 yields an error from resolving to the following:

```
SELECT TOP 10 -- * FROM CUSTOMERS
```

So, in this book I will mostly use the C-style comments.

Working SQL examples are in code blocks, with their output following, like this:

```
SELECT TOP 10
    LastName,
    FirstName
FROM crm.NormalizedCustomer
ORDER BY LastName, FirstName;
```

	LastName	FirstName
0	NULL	NULL
1	NULL	NULL
2	NULL	NULL
3	Abdallah	Johnetta
4	Acey	Geoffrey
5	Acuff	Weldon
6	Adkin	Barbra
7	Agramonte	Fausto
8	Ahle	Delmy
9	Albares	Cammy

Taking this apart, we see the SQL SELECT statement in a code block. Having run it, we also now have an output table containing the result set of 10 rows of 2 columns, *LastName* and *FirstName*. Note that the rows are numbered 0–9; this will be helpful when referring to specific output rows.

Structured, not Standard

One other thing about the examples in this book: "SQL" stands for *Structured* Query Language, and not *Standard* Query Language. While I have made a good attempt to ensure most queries in this book will run on most relational database servers, limiting output to something like 10 rows is one of those places where you have to pick a way, and I chose Microsoft SQL Server's Transact-SQL (T-SQL) way, since that is muscle memory for me. Hence, throughout this book, you will see lines like this:

```
SELECT TOP 10 * FROM crm.NormalizedCustomer
```

In some other SQL dialects, the same limitation of output rows in a query is made like this:

```
SELECT * FROM crm.NormalizedCustomer LIMIT 10
```

Similarly, the T-SQL function for extracting parts of a date is, understandably enough, called DATEPART. The equivalent IBM DB2 SQL function is, understandably enough, called DATE_PART. Both have some of the same names for various date parts, such as YEAR. However, there are also date parts that are available only on one or the other or that are named differently between the two. For example, T-SQL has these:

```
SELECT
    DATEPART(dayofweek, '2023-04-01') [Day of Week],
    DATEPART(iso_week, '2023-04-01') [ISO Week #]
```

DB2, by contrast, has these:

```
SELECT
    DATE_PART(DOW, '2023-04-01') [Day of Week],
    DATE_PART(EPOCH, '2023-04-01') [UNIX Epoch]
```

Rather than have awkward and space-wasting examples of both everywhere I use `TOP`
`10` or `DATEPART`, I just bring such things to your attention here and trust you will
translate them to your SQL dialect appropriately.

Often in the examples I won't go to the trouble of doing a full `SELECT` against a table
but will instead simply set up a SQL variable or variables with some exemplar data
and go. Like this, explained in Chapter 5:

```
DECLARE @CustomerDOB DATETIME = '1990-04-01T12:53:49.000'
DECLARE @IncomingDOB DATE =     'April 1, 1990'
SELECT
    CASE
        WHEN CAST(@CustomerDOB AS DATE) = @IncomingDOB
            THEN 'Match!'
        ELSE 'No Match!'
    END [Do They Match?];
```

Do They Match?
Match!

Finally, you may notice I use some words repeatedly throughout the book. Refer to
the Glossary for the definitions of frequently used terms.

The Data "Model"

I use a simple set of tables and views throughout this book. It isn't a "model" per se
but represents an extremely simplified environment with just a few datasets to keep
the examples from getting bogged down in some "real-world" scenario that wouldn't
apply to your life anyway. The main table and view are shown next. The complete set
of tables is shown in the Appendix.

Environment Layout

The database has the following schemas besides *dbo*:

crm
> The production CRM system for our examples

ref
> "Reference" data, such as postal code cross-reference tables

staging
> Where imported data to be checked against the production customer data is stored

student
> Used in a single example

Customer Table

This is our base Customer table as represented in our *crm* system (see Table P-1):

```
SELECT TOP 10 /* Just sniff 10 rows for data sanity.*/
    *
FROM crm.Customer
ORDER BY id;
```

"Normalized" View

This view is for data-matching uses later, where we will normalize the imported data as well as compare "apples to apples." For example, it takes all the punctuation and spaces out of phone numbers. It also CamelCases the column names (see Table P-2):

```
SELECT TOP 10
    *
FROM crm.NormalizedCustomer
ORDER BY LastName;
```

Table P-1. Customer

id	first_name	last_name	company_name	address	city	county	state	zip	country	phone1	phone2	email	web_address
1	NULL	NULL	Acme Corp	123 Snell Ave	Jefferson City	Cole	MO	65101	U.S.A.	NULL	573-555-3256	NULL	www.acme.test
2	NULL	NULL	Foo, Inc.	457 Prairie View St	Boulder	Boulder	CO	80301	US	NULL	303-555-5623	NULL	www.foo.test
3	NULL	NULL	Snedley & Sons, L.L.C.	443 Arroyo Rd	Raton	Colfax	NM	87740	U.S.	NULL	575-555-0956	NULL	www.snedley.test
4	Johnetta	Abdallah	NULL	1088 Pinehurst St	Chapel Hill	Orange	NC	27514	United States	919-555-9345	919-555-3791	johnetta_abdallah@example.com	NULL
5	Geoffrey	Acey	NULL	7 West Ave #1	Palatine	Cook	IL	60067	USA	847-555-1734	847-555-2909	geoffrey@example.com	NULL
6	Weldon	Acuff	NULL	73 W Barstow Ave	Arlington Heights	Cook	IL	60004	U.S.A.	847-555-2156	847-555-5866	wacuff@example.com	NULL
7	Barbra	Adkin	NULL	4 Kohler Memorial Dr	Brooklyn	Kings	NY	11230	US	718-555-3751	718-555-9475	badkin@example.com	NULL
8	Fausto	Agramonte	NULL	5 Harrison Rd	New York	New York	NY	10038	U.S.	212-555-1783	212-555-3063	fausto_agramonte@example.com	NULL
9	Delmy	Ahle	NULL	65895 S 16th St	Providence	Providence	RI	02909	United States	401-555-2547	401-555-8961	delmy.ahle@example.com	NULL
10	Cammy	Albares	NULL	56 E Morehead St	Laredo	Webb	TX	78045	USA	956-555-6195	956-555-7216	calbares@example.com	NULL

Table P-2. The Normalized View (the "left" side)

	LastName	First Name	Company	Address1	City	County	State	Postal Code	Country	Mobile Phone	HomePhone	Email	Web
0	NULL	NULL	Acme Corp	123 Snell Ave	Jefferson City	Cole	MO	65101	U.S.A.	NULL	5735553256	NULL	www.acme.test
1	NJLL	NULL	Foo, Inc.	457 Prairie View St	Boulder	Boulder	CO	80301	US	NULL	3035553623	NULL	www.foo.test
2	NULL	NULL	Snedley & Sons, L.L.C.	443 Arroyo Rd	Raton	Colfax	NM	87740	U.S.	NULL	5755550956	NULL	www.snedley.test
3	Abdallah	Johnetta	NULL	1088 Pinehurst St	Chapel Hill	Orange	NC	27514	United States	9195559345	9195553791	johnetta_abdallah@example.com	NULL
4	Acey	Geoffrey	NULL	7 West Ave #1	Palatine	Cook	IL	60067	USA	8475551734	8475552909	geoffrey@example.com	NULL
5	Acuff	Weldon	NULL	73 W Barstow Ave	Arlington Heights	Cook	IL	60004	U.S.A.	8475552156	8475555866	wacuff@example.com	NULL
6	Adkin	Barbra	NULL	4 Kohler Memorial Dr	Brooklyn	Kings	NY	11230	US	7185553751	7185559475	badkin@example.com	NULL
7	Agramonte	Fausto	NULL	5 Harrison Rd	New York	New York	NY	10038	U.S.	2125551783	2125553063	fausto_agramonte@example.com	NULL
8	Ahle	Delmy	NULL	65895 S 16th St	Providence	Providence	RI	02909	United States	4015552547	4015558961	delmy.ahle@example.com	NULL
9	Albares	Cammy	NULL	56 E Morehead St	Laredo	Webb	TX	78045	USA	9565556195	9565557216	calbares@example.com	NULL

Some may object to my use of the word *normalized* in this sense, as perhaps being confusing with the concept of data model normalization in relational databases (e.g., third-normal form, aka 3NF). My use is more in the sense that we are correcting or overcoming inconsistencies in the data representation. Thinking about it further, I would also argue that in many cases we are simply compensating for data that was improperly normalized in the data modeling sense. If phone numbers were split into area code, exchange, number, and extension fields; if names were properly split into last name and suffix fields; if addresses were correctly split between street number, name, directions, street type, ZIP, the +4 part of the ZIP, and so on; then very little of the work in this book would need to happen. But most systems don't store the data that way because they would constantly be reassembling it back into a valid phone number to display to a user or robodial a customer. So instead we must compensate for all of this ourselves.

Meet the Snedleys

"Smedleys?" I've been asked. No, "Snedleys." I don't know how I came up with that name; I've joked it was to "further anonymize the data," but it may have just been an early typo that stuck. Anyway, the Snedleys will come up in various places in the book, handling apparent duplicates being one reason.

Everyone likes user stories and personas, so let me introduce them:

Mortimer Snedley
   Nicknamed "Mort." Family patriarch, recently deceased.

Blanche Snedley
   "The Widow Snedley."

Mortimer Snedley, Jr.
   Goes by "Junior" within the family, but he abhors it. From his address he apparently still lives in Mom's basement. We wonder what game he is currently playing down there.

Clive Snedley
   The prodigal son, who fled to Canada in the 1960s upon receiving a letter from the President of the United States beginning with "Greetings." The family hasn't seen him since.

Snedley & Sons, L.L.C.
    The family company. "& Sons" was only aspirational after Clive left.

Mortimer Snedley Trust
    A trust set up to take care of Blanche and Junior after Mort passed.

Mortimer Snedley Estate
    Another "person-like" entity set up after Mort's demise.

Using Code Examples

Supplemental material (code examples, exercises, etc.) is available for download at *https://oreil.ly/fuzzy-data-matching-w-sql-code*.

If you have a technical question or a problem using the code examples, please send email to *support@oreilly.com*.

This book is here to help you get your job done. In general, if example code is offered with this book, you may use it in your programs and documentation. You do not need to contact us for permission unless you're reproducing a significant portion of the code. For example, writing a program that uses several chunks of code from this book does not require permission. Selling or distributing examples from O'Reilly books does require permission. Answering a question by citing this book and quoting example code does not require permission. Incorporating a significant amount of example code from this book into your product's documentation does require permission.

We appreciate, but generally do not require, attribution. An attribution usually includes the title, author, publisher, and ISBN. For example: "*Fuzzy Data Matching with SQL* by Jim Lehmer (O'Reilly). Copyright 2024 Jim Lehmer, 978-1-098-15227-7."

If you feel your use of code examples falls outside fair use or the permission given above, feel free to contact us at *permissions@oreilly.com*.

O'Reilly Online Learning

O'REILLY®   For more than 40 years, *O'Reilly Media* has provided technology and business training, knowledge, and insight to help companies succeed.

Our unique network of experts and innovators share their knowledge and expertise through books, articles, and our online learning platform. O'Reilly's online learning platform gives you on-demand access to live training courses, in-depth learning paths, interactive coding environments, and a vast collection of text and video from O'Reilly and 200+ other publishers. For more information, visit *https://oreilly.com*.

How to Contact Us

Please address comments and questions concerning this book to the publisher:

> O'Reilly Media, Inc.
> 1005 Gravenstein Highway North
> Sebastopol, CA 95472
> 800-889-8969 (in the United States or Canada)
> 707-829-7019 (international or local)
> 707-829-0104 (fax)
> *support@oreilly.com*
> *https://www.oreilly.com/about/contact.html*

We have a web page for this book, where we list errata, examples, and any additional information. You can access this page at *https://oreil.ly/fuzzy-data-matching-w-sql*.

For news and information about our books and courses, visit *https://oreilly.com*.

Find us on LinkedIn: *https://linkedin.com/company/oreilly-media*

Follow us on Twitter: *https://twitter.com/oreillymedia*

Watch us on YouTube: *https://youtube.com/oreillymedia*

Acknowledgments

I have had the great luck to have some close personal friendships over the years. How do I know they are true friendships? Because some of those friends helped with this book, reviewing early drafts and being enthusiastic about the subject matter. One was Ken Astl, who I met when the database connectivity company I worked for (Micro Decisionware, or MDI) was bought by Sybase in 1994, and I transferred to their Connectivity Products Group in Emeryville, California. Mark Price is actually my cousin, and I often quip my parents' favorite between the two of us. Mark spent a long career in public service keeping the world safe for democracy—by being a webmaster for a large public library system, for one. Margaret Devere is a professional tech writer and editor extraordinaire who also happens to have a very good grasp of SQL and was a tech reviewer for this book. It is better for every sentence she read and every SQL statement she inspected. She also was one of the people who interviewed me for my first software engineering job at MDI in 1991. Thanks, Margaret! In addition to

Margaret, there were two other tech reviewers to whom I owe my thanks. Levi Davis and Atilla Toth both found many errors, corrected my wording so I wouldn't look foolish in public, and prodded me to do better. I appreciated every comment, if not at the first reading ("But those are my words! My jokes! My code!"). Thank you all! As "they" say, any errors, omissions, or unclear wordings that remain are mine and mine alone.

I must also thank my wife, Leslie, and my daughter, Erin, who have now lived with me through the writing of two books. They listened to me natter for months about this subject while feigning interest. I don't know if that's love or Stockholm Syndrome, but thank you both! Finally, my father, Lou, passed while I was writing this book. Along with my mother, Barb, my parents' love and encouragement has always been rock steady in everything I have done, including this. It is good being surrounded by love—I recommend it!

PART I
Review

## CHAPTER 1

A SELECT Review

This chapter represents a very quick review of SQL elements used throughout this book. In particular, we will cover the following topics:

- Simple SELECT statements (see the next section)
- Common table expressions (see page 6)
- In CASE of emergency (see page 10)
- Joins (see page 15)

These will all be used in examples in the remainder of the book, so let's take some time and get used to them here.

Simple SELECT Statements

In the beginning was the word, and the word was SELECT. To get anything out of a relational database table, you need SELECT. Here it is in its simplest form (to save space, only the first 10 rows are shown in the result set, and we're counting DC as a state):

```
SELECT * FROM crm.CustomerCountByState;
```

	State	Total
0	AK	6
1	AL	0
2	AR	1
3	AZ	9
4	CA	72
5	CO	9

	State	Total
6	CT	5
7	DC	1
8	DE	0
9	FL	28

That gives us a "raw" dump of all the columns in the table (the *), in whatever order the rows may happen to be stored in the database table (*database order*).

Now we will switch to a bit "wider" dataset with more columns. Let's take the top 10 by whatever states happen to sort first in the customer dataset. We're also going to be choosy about which columns we want and not just grab them all:

```
SELECT TOP 10    /* Because we only want 10          */
      LastName,
      FirstName,
      City,
      State
FROM crm.NormalizedCustomer
ORDER BY State; -- This is the filter for the TOP 10
```

	LastName	FirstName	City	State
0	Campain	Roxane	Fairbanks	AK
1	Ferencz	Erick	Fairbanks	AK
2	Giguere	Wilda	Anchorage	AK
3	Kitty	Gail	Anchorage	AK
4	Paprocki	Lenna	Anchorage	AK
5	Weight	Penney	Anchorage	AK
6	Deleo	Carin	Little Rock	AR
7	Borgman	Keneth	Phoenix	AZ
8	Eschberger	Christiane	Phoenix	AZ
9	Kannady	Regenia	Scottsdale	AZ

Let's stop and take a look at all of that. First, refer to the SQL SELECT itself. I tend to always break up my SQL statements in this manner. It makes understanding the different clauses easier. I am able to quickly scan the "pattern" of this style. Then we should see a table with the 10 rows of 4 columns we asked for.

Let's keep going. How many customers do we have in each state? The following code is a common pattern—I use it all the time while doing exploratory data analysis (EDA) (*https://oreil.ly/gm1Br*). This example may not count true unique customers if there are duplicates in our data (often likely, even in a production CRM system), but this will be close enough for our example:

```
SELECT TOP 10
    State,
    COUNT(*) Total   /* "Total" is the name assigned to the column */
FROM crm.NormalizedCustomer
GROUP BY State       /* Required for aggregate functions      */
ORDER BY 2 DESC, 1; -- States with most customers first
```

	State	Total
0	CA	72
1	NJ	52
2	NY	46
3	TX	32
4	PA	29
5	FL	28
6	OH	22
7	MD	17
8	IL	15
9	MI	14

In most examples, I am going to use something like SELECT TOP 10 to limit the resulting output, as shown here.

In this type of distribution query, we are looking at one (or more) columns and doing a COUNT(*) on the number of rows for each group (we will cover COUNT in Chapter 2 on useful SQL functions). Note we can give the output of the COUNT a column name in the results, in this case *Total*.

The results show us a nice distribution with a "long tail" of 1s in the *Total* column. The GROUP BY is required and needs to contain all columns that aren't part of the aggregation (more on that in a moment).

The ORDER BY is interesting. Here I am sorting the total of the most common states first (2 DESC specifies the second column in the result set, in descending order) and then the first column in the result set (the 1). Normally, using column ordinals in this clause is frowned on in production code because if the column list changes, you often have to go and rework the ORDER BY. Remove a column and suddenly your ordinal may be out of range, causing an error. But we aren't doing production code in this book. I often use this shorthand form to save typing when using the pattern:

```
SELECT Foo, COUNT(*) Total FROM Bar GROUP BY Foo ORDER BY 2 DESC, 1;
```

Many dialects support using ordinals in the GROUP BY as well. Again, I don't think using them is a good idea for anything that might be pushed into production.

If I didn't want to use ordinals, I would do the following. This is the same query, but I am not using ordinals, and I am giving meaningful names to the result columns:

```
SELECT TOP 10
    State    [Top 10 States],   /* You can put spaces in column names to make */
    COUNT(*) [Total Customers]  /* the results more readable (and if you do,  */
                                /* surround the name with square brackets).   */
FROM crm.NormalizedCustomer
GROUP BY State
ORDER BY COUNT(*) DESC, State;  -- Note using the COUNT function again
```

	Top 10 States	Total Customers
0	CA	72
1	NJ	52
2	NY	46
3	TX	32
4	PA	29
5	FL	28
6	OH	22
7	MD	17
8	IL	15
9	MI	14

Common Table Expressions

That second COUNT(*) brings up another point. We can use functions in other places, such as the WHERE or ORDER BY clause. What if instead of the top 10, we simply want all states with *10 or more* customers? We wouldn't know that answer in advance, so we couldn't use it in a SELECT TOP 10 (or LIMIT 10) clause. Here is one way to do it, using common table expressions (CTEs), aka the WITH statement:

```
/*
    Think of a CTE as a temporary "view,"
    although it isn't as performant. In
    this case the CTE name is CustomerCountByState.
*/
WITH CustomerCountByState
AS
(
    SELECT
        State,
        COUNT(*) Total
    FROM crm.NormalizedCustomer
```

```
    GROUP BY State
)
/*
    Now we can use our CTE.
*/
SELECT
    State [States w/More Than 10 Customers],
    Total [# in State]
FROM CustomerCountByState
WHERE Total > 9                 /* Or >= 10, your choice */
ORDER BY Total DESC, State;
```

	States w/More Than 10 Customers	# in State
0	CA	72
1	NJ	52
2	NY	46
3	TX	32
4	PA	29
5	FL	28
6	OH	22
7	MD	17
8	IL	15
9	MI	14
10	MA	12
11	WI	11
12	TN	10

CTEs aren't efficient. If you use them in multiple places in a query, they act more like a macro expansion, not a true view. But I like them because they allow me to build up queries in an orderly manner that others can understand. There are *many* ways to solve the preceding problem in SQL. A subquery would get us to the same place but in my opinion isn't as readable. Basically you can think of a CTE as lifting the subquery in the following SELECT out and predefining it and giving it a name. I have aliased the subquery *CustomerCountByState* so that the similarity to the preceding CTE is explicit:

```
SELECT
    State [States w/More Than 10 Customers],
    Total [# in State]
FROM
(
    SELECT
        State,
        COUNT(*) Total
    FROM crm.NormalizedCustomer
```

```
      GROUP BY State
) CustomerCountByState    /* Gotta give the subquery an alias.
                             It can be anything. I often use "A"
                             for simple queries like this, but am
                             naming it the same as the CTE to be
                             explicit. */
WHERE Total > 9
ORDER BY Total DESC, State;
```

	States w/More Than 10 Customers	# in State
0	CA	72
1	NJ	52
2	NY	46
3	TX	32
4	PA	29
5	FL	28
6	OH	22
7	MD	17
8	IL	15
9	MI	14
10	MA	12
11	WI	11
12	TN	10

In many cases I will use CTEs during EDA and then, as I get closer to rolling something into production, change them into proper views with the same names. Hence:

```
-- This:
WITH Foo
AS
(
    SELECT * FROM Bar WHERE Status = 'Foo'
)
SELECT * FROM Foo;

-- Becomes this:

CREATE VIEW Foo
AS
(
    SELECT * FROM Bar WHERE Status = 'Foo'
)
```

The query can remain unchanged (presuming it is running in the default schema), and the view can be used in other queries as well:

```
SELECT * FROM Foo;
```

The interesting thing about CTEs is I often chain them in a row, each building and filtering on the one before it:

```
WITH CustomerCountByState
AS
(
    SELECT
        State,
        COUNT(*) Total
    FROM crm.NormalizedCustomer
    GROUP BY State
),
CitiesInTopStates
AS
(
    SELECT
        City,
        State,
        COUNT(*) Total
    FROM crm.NormalizedCustomer
    WHERE
        /*
            States with more than 4 (or >= 5) customers.
        */
        State IN (SELECT State FROM CustomerCountByState WHERE Total > 4)
    GROUP BY City, State
)
SELECT
    City,
    State,
    Total
FROM CitiesInTopStates
/*
    Cities with 5 or more (or > 4) customers.
*/
WHERE Total >= 5
ORDER BY Total DESC, City, State;
```

	City	State	Total
0	New York	NY	14
1	Philadelphia	PA	8
2	Chicago	IL	7
3	Miami	FL	6
4	Raton	NM	6
5	Baltimore	MD	5
6	Gardena	CA	5
7	Milwaukee	WI	5
8	Orlando	FL	5

	City	State	Total
9	Phoenix	AZ	5
10	San Francisco	CA	5

Note in the following example that a CTE can be a nice way to get you away from using ordinals or SQL functions in your ORDER BY clause, but I wouldn't recommend using them only for that:

```
WITH TopTenStates
AS
(
    SELECT
        State,
        COUNT(*) Total
    FROM crm.NormalizedCustomer
    GROUP BY State
)
SELECT TOP 10
    State [Top 10 States],
    Total [Total Customers]
FROM TopTenStates
ORDER BY Total DESC, State;
```

	Top 10 States	Total Customers
0	CA	72
1	NJ	52
2	NY	46
3	TX	32
4	PA	29
5	FL	28
6	OH	22
7	MD	17
8	IL	15
9	MI	14

In CASE of Emergency

I use the CASE expression a lot. It is basically an expression form of a *switch* statement in a C-syntax programming language. Remember your ancient history, like this example:

```
/* Ye olde C-style switch statement - brought to you by K&R. */
switch(foo) {
    case 0:
        bar = "It was zero.";
        break;
```

```
        case 1:
            bar = "It was one.";
            break;
        default:
            bar = "Dunno what it was.";
            break;
    }
```

You can achieve similar results in SQL as follows:

```
SELECT
    CASE foo
        WHEN 0 THEN 'It was zero.'
        WHEN 1 THEN 'It was one.'
        ELSE 'Dunno what it was'
    END bar
FROM xyzzy;
```

In this book, you will see me use all three of the styles used in the following code block for varying reasons, including mood and the space available to show an example (including whether I am emphasizing the CASE or something else in the query).

Consider this simple table:

City	USPSCity
O'Fallon	OFallon

How do we check if the two cities are "the same"? The following code shows how. I expand upon this technique later in the book; this example is instead to show three styles of CASE expressions all checking for the same thing:

```
/*
    We will cover this example in depth in Chapter 3.
*/
WITH NormalizeCities
AS
(
    SELECT
        City,
        USPSCity,
        REPLACE(TRANSLATE(City,    '.,-''()[]`', '         '),
                ' ', '') NormCity,
        REPLACE(TRANSLATE(USPSCity, '.,-''()[]`', '         '),
                ' ', '') NormUSPSCity
    FROM Foo
)
SELECT
    City,
    USPSCity [USPS City],
```

```
/*
    Single-line CASE statement.
*/
CASE City WHEN USPSCity THEN 'Match!' ELSE 'No Match!' END [Match?],
NormCity [Norm. City],
NormUSPSCity [Norm. USPS City],
/*
    Multi-line CASE with expression test after the CASE.
*/
CASE NormCity
    WHEN NormUSPSCity THEN 'Match!'
    ELSE 'No Match!'
END [Do Normalized Match?],
/*
    Multi-LINE CASE with expression test in the WHEN. Note "=".
*/
CASE
    WHEN NormCity = NormUSPSCity THEN 'Match!'
    ELSE 'No Match!'
END [Still?]
FROM NormalizeCities;
```

City	USPS City	Match?	Norm. City	Norm. USPS City	Do Normalized Match?	Still?
O'Fallon	OFallon	No Match!	OFallon	OFallon	Match!	Match!

Gee, that's a lot! Let's take that apart piece by piece. The WITH statement creating the *NormalizeCities* CTE is simply making the example SELECT query CASE statements simpler (the REPLACE and TRANSLATE functions will be explained in Chapter 2).

The SELECT is working completely with the SQL variables—no table, view, or CTE required. We are simply looking at different ways to express the CASE expression, so that's what I want to emphasize here. The four columns in the SELECT dumping out the various forms of the city are obvious. So we will look at the three CASE expressions in order. All are basically a simple "if…then…else" expression—if a match occurs, then return "Match!", else "No Match!" For something as simple as this, see also the IIF SQL function in Chapter 2.

The first CASE is expressed all in a line:

```
CASE City WHEN USPSCity THEN 'Match!' ELSE 'No Match!' END [Match?]
```

You can read it like this: "In the CASE of the value in *City*, WHEN it is equal to *USPSCity* THEN return the value 'Match!', ELSE return the value 'No Match!', and name the result (the column in the result set) *Match?*"

The next one varies only in adding new lines and indentation to make the syntactic elements more obvious to the script reader (that's you). It returns a column named *Do Normalized Match?*:

```
CASE NormCity
    WHEN NormUSPSCity THEN 'Match!'
    ELSE 'No Match!'
END [Do Normalized Match?],
```

The third is of more interest:

```
CASE
    WHEN NormCity = NormUSPSCity THEN 'Match!'
    ELSE 'No Match!'
END [Still?]
```

In this case (ahem) there is no value following the CASE. Instead, the WHEN has the test clause in it, followed by the THEN.

Think of it like this: "In the following CASEs, WHEN the value of *NormCity* is equal to the value of *NormUSPSCity*, THEN return the value 'Match!', ELSE return the value 'No Match!' and name the result *Still?*"

This is often the preferred form, because it allows more complexity. See the next example.

As mentioned, the SQL function IIF does a similar job (as can COALESCE or ISNULL), so why go to all the complications of a CASE expression? For something like this, I wouldn't. However, let's change the city and see how we can use CASE to handle a much more complicated subject. We will only use the last style of CASE expression for this so we can look at each test line by line:

```
DECLARE @City VARCHAR(50) = 'St Louis'          /* How we store it              */
DECLARE @ImportCity VARCHAR(50) = 'Saint Louis'  /* How Marketing receives it */
SELECT
    @City City,
    @ImportCity [Imported City],
    CASE
        /*
            Really crude approach, but effective. Note trailing spaces in each
            match term to make sure and not find embedded "st" instances, for
            example.
        */
        WHEN REPLACE(@City, 'St ',   'Saint ') =  @ImportCity THEN 'Match!'
        WHEN REPLACE(@City, 'St. ',  'Saint ') =  @ImportCity THEN 'Match!'
        WHEN REPLACE(@City, 'Ste ',  'Sainte ') = @ImportCity THEN 'Match!'
        WHEN REPLACE(@City, 'Ste. ', 'Sainte ') = @ImportCity THEN 'Match!'
```

```
                /*
                      And so on, and so forth...however many CASEs you got...
                */
                ELSE 'No Match!'
            END [Result?];
```

City	Imported City	Result?
St Louis	Saint Louis	Match!

Even that's not too exciting, since it could be replaced by a single IIF function (explained in Chapter 2):

```
SELECT
    @City City,
    @ImportCity [Imported City],
    IIF(REPLACE(@City, 'St ',   'Saint ') = @ImportCity
        OR REPLACE(@City, 'St. ',  'Saint ') = @ImportCity
        OR REPLACE(@City, 'Ste ',  'Sainte ') = @ImportCity
        OR REPLACE(@City, 'Ste. ', 'Sainte ') = @ImportCity,
        'Match!', 'No Match!') [Result?];
```

That then brings us back to why we should use CASE over something simpler like IIF. How about this? The LEN, LEFT, and RIGHT functions will also be explained in Chapter 2.

```
DECLARE @City VARCHAR(50) = 'Ste Genevieve'       /* How we store it             */
DECLARE @ImportCity VARCHAR(50) = 'St Genevieve'  /* How Marketing receives it */
SELECT
    @City City,
    @ImportCity [Imported City],
    CASE
        /*
            WHENs can actually check all variety of tests.
        */
        WHEN REPLACE(@City, 'St ',   'Saint ') = @ImportCity THEN 'Match!'
        WHEN REPLACE(@City, 'St. ',  'Saint ') = @ImportCity THEN 'Match!'
        WHEN REPLACE(@City, 'Ste ',  'Sainte ') = @ImportCity THEN 'Match!'
        WHEN REPLACE(@City, 'Ste. ', 'Sainte ') = @ImportCity THEN 'Match!'
        WHEN LEFT(@ImportCity, LEN('St ')) = 'St '
            AND RIGHT(@ImportCity, LEN('Genevieve')) = 'Genevieve'
            THEN 'Chauvinist!'
        WHEN LEFT(@ImportCity, LEN('St. ')) = 'St. '
            AND RIGHT(@ImportCity, LEN('Genevieve')) = 'Genevieve'
            THEN 'Chauvinist!'
        ELSE 'No Match!'
    END [Result?];
```

City	Imported City	Result?
Ste Genevieve	St Genevieve	Chauvinist!

Here, we were checking beyond simple tests of equality to look and see if there are any underlying data quality issues, which we politely call out (since the town and person are both of French origin and Genevieve is feminine, the proper title is "Sainte," not "Saint").

Joins

We've covered simple SELECT statements. Let's look at joins next. Like belly buttons, there are basically two types: INNER and OUTER. There are also LEFT and RIGHT joins, but for our purposes I always use LEFT. Let's look at an INNER JOIN first. For every row in the customer data, find the corresponding "friendly" state name in the postal reference table. You may not know it using the SQL INNER JOIN syntax; you may know it simply as a correlated SELECT:

```
SELECT TOP 10
    C.LastName [Last Name],
    C.FirstName [First Name],
    C.City,
    A.StateOrProvince State
/*
    Both tables are in the FROM
*/
FROM crm.NormalizedCustomer C,
     ref.PostalAbbreviations A
WHERE
    C.State = A.Abbreviation
ORDER BY C.LastName, C.FirstName;
```

	Last Name	First Name	City	State
0	NULL	NULL	Jefferson City	Missouri
1	NULL	NULL	Boulder	Colorado
2	NULL	NULL	Raton	New Mexico
3	Abdallah	Johnetta	Chapel Hill	North Carolina
4	Acey	Geoffrey	Palatine	Illinois
5	Acuff	Weldon	Arlington Heights	Illinois
6	Adkin	Barbra	Brooklyn	New York
7	Agramonte	Fausto	New York	New York
8	Ahle	Delmy	Providence	Rhode Island
9	Albares	Cammy	Laredo	Texas

We can also use the INNER JOIN...ON syntax to be more explicit about our intentions:

```
SELECT TOP 10
    C.LastName [Last Name],
    C.FirstName [First Name],
    C.City,
    A.StateOrProvince State
FROM crm.NormalizedCustomer C
INNER JOIN ref.PostalAbbreviations A ON
    C.State = A.Abbreviation
ORDER BY C.LastName, C.FirstName;
```

	Last Name	First Name	City	State
0	NULL	NULL	Jefferson City	Missouri
1	NULL	NULL	Boulder	Colorado
2	NULL	NULL	Raton	New Mexico
3	Abdallah	Johnetta	Chapel Hill	North Carolina
4	Acey	Geoffrey	Palatine	Illinois
5	Acuff	Weldon	Arlington Heights	Illinois
6	Adkin	Barbra	Brooklyn	New York
7	Agramonte	Fausto	New York	New York
8	Ahle	Delmy	Providence	Rhode Island
9	Albares	Cammy	Laredo	Texas

Note the two result sets are identical. I will tend to use explicit JOIN syntax throughout this book.

The thing to remember with inner joins is *if there isn't a match between the two, then a row doesn't get sent to the result set.* INNER is like "intersection" if you remember sets from math. For example, our customer data contains only United States states plus the District of Columbia. If there were a customer from the Canadian province of New Brunswick, then that customer's data would *not* be included in the preceding results.

One thing that's new in both examples is we've given each table an alias: "C" for *NormalizedCustomer* and "A" for *PostalAbbreviations*. This helps distinguish which columns we are talking about when they both share the same name: is it the column in the customer data or the one in the reference data? When there are no columns with the same names between the two tables, the aliases aren't needed, but I find them good practice to always use them on joins, again to be explicit about my intentions. Notice we also gave more user-friendly column names in the result set, with spaces in *Last Name* and *First Name* instead of just *CamelCase*, e.g., *LastName*.

Also, on a JOIN the ON is not a complete replacement for the WHERE clause. In fact, trying to make it so can lead to some surprising results.

A Diversion into NULL Values

Check this out: we have NULL values in our CRM data in some name fields:

```
SELECT LastName, FirstName from crm.NormalizedCustomer WHERE LastName IS NULL;
```

	LastName	FirstName
0	NULL	NULL
1	NULL	NULL
2	NULL	NULL

We also have them in our import dataset:

```
SELECT LastName, FirstName from staging.Customers ORDER BY LastName, FirstName;
```

	LastName	FirstName
0	NULL	NULL
1	NULL	NULL
2	NULL	NULL
3	Abdallah	Johnetta
4	Acey	Geoffrey
5	Acuff	Weldon
6	Adkin	Barbra
7	Agramonte	Fausto
8	Ahle	Delmy
9	Albares	Cammy

So why don't they get found in a JOIN?

```
SELECT
        SC.LastName,
        SC.FirstName
FROM staging.Customers SC
INNER JOIN crm.NormalizedCustomer NC ON
        SC.LastName = NC.LastName
        AND SC.FirstName = NC.FirstName
ORDER BY SC.LastName, SC.FirstName;
```

	LastName	FirstName
0	Abdallah	Johnetta
1	Acey	Geoffrey
2	Acuff	Weldon
3	Adkin	Barbra
4	Agramonte	Fausto
5	Ahle	Delmy
6	Albares	Cammy

"Wait!" you exclaim. "I remember something about ANSI_NULLS." Let's try that:

```
SET ANSI_NULLS OFF;
SELECT
        SC.LastName,
        SC.FirstName
FROM staging.Customers SC
INNER JOIN crm.NormalizedCustomer NC ON
        SC.LastName = NC.LastName
        AND SC.FirstName = NC.FirstName
ORDER BY SC.LastName, SC.FirstName;
```

	LastName	FirstName
0	Abdallah	Johnetta
1	Acey	Geoffrey
2	Acuff	Weldon
3	Adkin	Barbra
4	Agramonte	Fausto
5	Ahle	Delmy
6	Albares	Cammy

Hmmm…still missing those NULL rows. Why? Because it is working as designed; as the documentation (*https://oreil.ly/YWwqF*) says, "SET ANSI_NULLS ON affects a comparison only if one of the operands of the comparison is either a variable that is NULL or a literal NULL. If both sides of the comparison are columns or compound expressions, the setting does not affect the comparison." This is where you have to use a WHERE clause instead, and something like EXISTS:

```
SELECT
        SC.LastName,
        SC.FirstName
FROM staging.Customers SC
WHERE EXISTS (SELECT LastName, FirstName FROM crm.NormalizedCustomer)
ORDER BY SC.LastName, SC.FirstName
```

	LastName	FirstName
0	NULL	NULL
1	NULL	NULL
2	NULL	NULL
3	Abdallah	Johnetta
4	Acey	Geoffrey
5	Acuff	Weldon
6	Adkin	Barbra
7	Agramonte	Fausto
8	Ahle	Delmy
9	Albares	Cammy

So, be aware when joining tables if any of the join columns have NULLs in them, or you will have to change your approach.

OUTER JOINs

Now for an OUTER JOIN. This is not a "real" example but is useful for our limited data so far. What states do we *not* have customers in? A left outer join will have NULL for any values in the "right-side" table (in the following *dbo.PotentialMatches*) that don't have a match from the "left-side" table:

```
SELECT TOP 10
    A.StateOrProvince State,
    P.last_name [Last Name],
    P.first_name [First Name],
    P.company_name Company,
    P.City
FROM ref.PostalAbbreviations A
/*
    Attempt to join against our import data.
*/
LEFT OUTER JOIN dbo.PotentialMatches P ON
    A.Abbreviation = P.State
ORDER BY A.StateOrProvince;
```

	State	Last Name	First Name	Company	City
0	Alabama	NULL	NULL	NULL	NULL
1	Alaska	NULL	NULL	NULL	NULL
2	Arizona	NULL	NULL	NULL	NULL
3	Arkansas	NULL	NULL	NULL	NULL
4	California	Hamilton	Charlene	NULL	Santa Rosa
5	California	Rochin	Xuan	NULL	San Mateo
6	California	Waycott	Kanisha	NULL	L.A.

	State	Last Name	First Name	Company	City
7	Colorado	NULL	NULL	Foo, Inc.	Boulder
8	Connecticut	Layous	Ma	NULL	North Haven
9	Delaware	NULL	NULL	NULL	NULL

Those first four rows with NULL values in the import data indicate there were four states found in the *ref.PostalAbbreviations* table (left) that had no matches within the import data (right).

Now we can add the WHERE clause using this fact:

```
SELECT TOP 10
    A.StateOrProvince [1st 10 States Not In Import File]
FROM ref.PostalAbbreviations A
/*
   Join against our customer data.
*/
LEFT OUTER JOIN dbo.PotentialMatches P ON
    A.Abbreviation = P.State
WHERE
    P.State IS NULL     /* Where no match in import data */
ORDER BY A.StateOrProvince;
```

	1st 10 States Not In Import File
0	Alabama
1	Alaska
2	Arizona
3	Arkansas
4	Delaware
5	District of Columbia
6	Georgia
7	Idaho
8	Illinois
9	Iowa

If the "left" and "right" seems confusing, think of the SELECT as all on one line, reading from left to right:

```
SELECT * FROM lefttable l LEFT OUTER JOIN righttable r ON l.somecol = r.somecol
```

In a *left* OUTER JOIN, the columns from the *right* table will have NULLs in the result set if there wasn't a match.

The preceding is a bit contrived and may not be useful, however. There could be lots of states without *potential* customers. Here's a better question: What states do we not have *current* customers in? Where do we need to concentrate our sales efforts?

```
SELECT TOP 10
    A.StateOrProvince [State Not In Import File]
FROM ref.PostalAbbreviations A
/*
    Join against our customer data.
*/
LEFT OUTER JOIN crm.NormalizedCustomer C ON
    A.Abbreviation = C.State
WHERE
    C.State IS NULL     /* Where no match in customer data */
ORDER BY A.StateOrProvince;
```

	State Not In Import File
0	Alabama
1	Delaware
2	Vermont
3	West Virginia

Of course, we could have gotten the same result with a sub-SELECT. Which is clearer? I will let you decide:

```
SELECT
    StateOrProvince [State Without Customers]
FROM ref.PostalAbbreviations
WHERE
    Abbreviation NOT IN (SELECT State FROM crm.NormalizedCustomer)
ORDER BY StateOrProvince;
```

	State Without Customers
0	Alabama
1	Delaware
2	Vermont
3	West Virginia

Obviously the reverse is useful, too, and actually the more common case:

```
SELECT
    COUNT(DISTINCT A.StateOrProvince) [# States With Customers]
FROM ref.PostalAbbreviations A
LEFT OUTER JOIN crm.NormalizedCustomer C ON
    A.Abbreviation = C.State
WHERE
    C.State IS NOT NULL;  -- At least 1 match in customer data
```

States With Customers
47

Let's go back to the import data. It wasn't useful to ask what states weren't in it; it could be many. It wasn't useful to do a join to ask what states were in it; we can just extract that with a SELECT DISTINCT or a GROUP BY State. But import data is noisy. Are there any records in the import data that aren't from a valid United States state or the District of Columbia? For once I will show a RIGHT OUTER JOIN, just to keep the tables in the SELECT in the same order:

```
SELECT
    P.State [Invalid State In Import File]
FROM ref.PostalAbbreviations A
/*
    Join against our customer data.
*/
RIGHT OUTER JOIN dbo.PotentialMatches P ON
    A.Abbreviation = P.State
WHERE
    A.Abbreviation IS NULL      /* Where no match in left dataset */
ORDER BY P.State;
```

	Invalid State In Import File
0	NULL
1	NB

We see the import file has at least one missing state (not unusual) and one for "NB". What's that?

```
SELECT
    P.country,
    P.state [Invalid State In Import File]
FROM ref.PostalAbbreviations A
/*
    Join against our customer data.
*/
RIGHT OUTER JOIN dbo.PotentialMatches P ON
    A.Abbreviation = P.state
WHERE
    A.Abbreviation IS NULL      /* Where no match in left dataset */
ORDER BY P.state;
```

	Country	Invalid State In Import File
0	U.S.	NULL
1	Canada	NB

Ah, "NB" is in Canada, so it is New Brunswick! One mystery solved, another opened. What are we going to do with it? In many cases you will have to ask "The Business" how to deal with this. For regulatory reasons you may not be able to deal with someone in Canada. Do you "drop the record on the floor" or send it somewhere so a

"We're sorry" communication can be sent? Or does it need to be routed to a subsidiary or parent company in that country? That is beyond the scope of the book but does show some of the issues you will have to deal with. But you know how to identify the person in any case:

```
SELECT
    last_name [Last Name],
    first_name [FirstName]
FROM dbo.PotentialMatches
WHERE state = 'NB'
```

Last Name	FirstName
Snedley	Clive

Again, outer joins are useful when you know data on one "side" (I typically choose the right) could be missing or not matched when trying to join with data from the other side, in this case the left. In other words, if you think of the canonical list of *all* states as being in the reference table on the "left," there may or may not be customers from all those states in the CRM table on the right, and hence when joining, you can expect NULL values in result rows for the right-side columns where there is a row in the left with no match on the right.

Finding the Most Current Value

Consider the following "real-life" scenario.

A loan may move from an opportunity in a CRM system to a loan application in the loan origination system. Being different applications, these are different tables in different databases. Then perhaps the loan origination system moves the loan from the application phase to underwriting and the processing phase, which moves it to another table, too. Perhaps it then goes to a servicing table after the loan is signed by the customer and booked. That table may in fact be in another application database as well, as part of the banking "core" system. In all four of those tables across three applications will be a value for the total loan amount, which may naturally change along the way with the normal back-and-forth of getting a loan and then paying it off over time. So, the question becomes, "Regardless of the state of the loan—opportunity, application, processing, or servicing—what is the *current* loan amount?"

Behold the COALESCE expression and its beauty (see also Chapter 2), which returns the first non-NULL value in a list of values. Also notice how I naturally include the use of outer joins and their utility, too. Sneaky:

```
SELECT
    COALESCE(L.LoanAmount, P.LoanAmount,
        A.LoanRequestAmount, O.OpportunityAmount) LoanAmount
```

```
FROM
    crm.Opportunity O
LEFT OUTER JOIN loan.LoanApplication A ON
    O.CustomerId = A.CustomerId
LEFT OUTER JOIN loan.LoanProcessing P ON
    O.CustomerId = P.CustomerId
LEFT OUTER JOIN core.Loan L ON
    O.CustomerId = L.CustomerId
WHERE O.CustomerId = 12345;
```

First, we know the preceding is unreal because there is *no way* three disparate systems would share the same customer IDs, let alone have the same column names for them. We will cover how those types of joins are done across applications that don't know about each other in later chapters, especially Chapter 9. But looking beyond that, we start the SELECT with the *Opportunity* table, because that's where any deal is going to start—with a loan officer opening an opportunity and filling in a few details. The LEFT OUTER JOIN clauses then bring in the rows from the other applications, *if they exist*.

Since the flow of the loan is from opportunity to application to processing to servicing, we can see that in reverse order in the COALESCE, a dashboard or report will typically want the "most current" information, so we start by looking at the core system's *L.LoanAmount* field. If it is not NULL, the loan has booked, and the core's loan accounting system will have the currently calculated daily loan balance. If that is NULL, however, then the other columns are examined, left to right, until a non-NULL value is found, with *O.OpportunityAmount* being the guaranteed stop-gap (and also the fuzziest value when you think about it, since it will almost certainly be subject to change over the life of the loan process).

If the previous COALESCE had been expressed as either a CASE expression or an IIF function, it would have been much more complicated and ugly!

Final Thoughts on SELECT

To do anything "in real life" that I discuss in this book, you will need at least SELECT access to the tables and views under investigation. In Microsoft SQL Server, this can be easily granted with the *db_datareader* role on the database, but since that is a database-level role, it may not be appropriate to your environment if you work in a highly secured industry. You will need to be granted *at least* the following or equivalent on every table you will be accessing:

```
GRANT SELECT ON Foo.Bar TO YourLogin;
```

YourLogin can obviously be a database role or group in which your ID is a member. Of course, if you created the database(s), you are *db_owner* and can do what you want.

I discussed the utility of CTEs (see "Common Table Expressions" on page 6). I use them a lot in my work but can't emphasize enough that they are not a panacea. If a query is going to get run repeatedly, it is better to create a view for it and let the SQL optimizer do its job. CTEs behave basically like macros, that is, "expanding in place" where they are referenced, and can be very slow if you create complicated chains of them. However, sometimes in a consulting job all you have is SELECT granted and no Data Definition Language (DDL) access to CREATE a view. Then you have to do what you have to do, and CTEs are often "good enough."

In case you missed it, I find the CASE expression flowing out of my fingertips almost every time I am doing matching or mapping of data. I find it much more readable than the IIF function, even if it is a bit more typing:

```
-- This?
SELECT IIF(Foo = 1, 'Foo', 'Unfoo') [Foo?] FROM Xyzzy;

-- Or this?
SELECT CASE WHEN Foo = 1 THEN 'Foo' ELSE 'Unfoo' END [Foo?] FROM Xyzzy;
```

In this case (I promise, that's the last pun), they are equivalent, and the choice is a matter of personal taste. However, as so often happens, requirements change, and suddenly you may find yourself wanting to do the following:

```
-- No. Just no. This way lies (t)error!
SELECT IIF(Foo = 1, 'Foo',
       IIF(Bar = 1, 'Bar', 'Unbarrable')) [Foo or Bar?] FROM Xyzzy;

-- But this approach adapts pretty easily.
SELECT
    CASE
        WHEN Foo = 1 THEN 'Foo'
        WHEN Bar = 1 THEN 'Bar'
        ELSE 'Unbarrable'
    END [Foo or Bar?]
FROM Xyzzy;
```

You can see that the IIF approach will get ugly pretty fast as the tests to be checked multiply.

We've now seen that the absence of data, such as NULLs returned from LEFT OUTER JOIN queries, can be as interesting as its presence and that, in fact, missing data is the first level of "fuzzy." Let's move on to Chapter 2 and look at some useful SQL functions to add to our SELECT statements to start dealing with all that fuzzy data out there!

Function Junction

Now that we've looked at SELECT, we can look at adding various SQL functions to it to help us "slice and dice" the data, deal with data quality issues, and transform it to the shape we need. We've seen COUNT already, so we'll start with it and the rest of the aggregate functions that often help during EDA to understand some simple statistics. In this chapter, we will cover the following topics:

- Aggregate functions (see page 28)
- Conversion functions (see page 31)
- Cryptographic functions (see page 34; we won't be using them in the way you think, though!)
- Date and time functions (see page 35)
- Logical functions (see page 37)
- String functions (see page 38)
- System functions (see page 51)

You will get very used to reading, and ideally very good at using, SQL functions by the end of this book. I take a highly functional approach to the problems presented, so something like the following will become a common sight to you:

```
SELECT
    LEFT(REPLACE(REPLACE(StreetAddress, ' ', ''), '.', ''), 10) AddressPrefix
FROM crm.CustomerAddress
```

Always read functions calling functions from the inside out. The previous code should read to you as follows:

1. Replace all spaces in the results from the first REPLACE, also with an empty character.

2. Replace all period (full-stop) characters in the value from the column *Street Address* with an empty character.

3. Take the left 10 characters of *that* result and return that truncated value in a column labeled *AddressPrefix*.

To illustrate most functions, we will use the *crm.CustomerCountByState* view as a simple test dataset to "keep the data out of the way of the functions." The dataset looks like this:

```
SELECT TOP 10
    State,
    Total
FROM crm.CustomerCountByState
ORDER BY Total DESC, State;
```

	State	Total
0	CA	72
1	NJ	52
2	NY	46
3	TX	32
4	PA	29
5	FL	28
6	OH	22
7	MD	17
8	IL	15
9	MI	14

Note that some states have zero customers, which may be important in terms of running statistics.

Aggregate Functions

These functions are used to "do what they say" across a dataset. The examples use the view *crm.CustomerCountByState* as a simple test dataset.

MAX

Finds the maximum numeric value in a column:

```
SELECT
    MAX(Total) [Highest # of Customers in Any State(s)]
FROM crm.CustomerCountByState;
```

Highest # of Customers in Any State(s)
72

However, you usually want attributes associated with that maximum count, and I tend to prefer something like this:

```
SELECT TOP 1
    State [Top State],
    Total [# of Customers]
FROM crm.CustomerCountByState
ORDER BY Total DESC;
```

Top State	# of Customers
CA	72

MIN

The opposite of MAX:

```
SELECT
    MIN(Total) [Lowest # of Customers in Any State(s)]
FROM crm.CustomerCountByState
WHERE Total > 0; -- Only where we actually have customers
```

Lowest # of Customers in Any State(s)
1

COUNT

If you just want a quick count of the number of rows (or aggregated rows), you can use COUNT(*):

```
SELECT
    COUNT(*) [# of States and Districts in State Table]
FROM ref.PostalAbbreviations;
```

# of States and Districts in State Table
51

But you can also use COUNT with a column name, which will give you the number of non-NULL rows that match your search criteria:

```
SELECT COUNT(company_name) [# of Non-NULL Company Names]
FROM crm.Customer;
```

# of Non-NULL Company Names
5

Finally, note that you can add DISTINCT to the column name in COUNT, which then returns the number of distinct values in that column:

```
SELECT COUNT(DISTINCT state) [# of Distinct State Values]
FROM crm.Customer;
```

# of Distinct State Values
47

Since there are 50 states plus the District of Columbia in our postal reference table, we now know we don't have customers in at least four of them:

51 – 47 = 4 (states missing customers)

SUM

Sums the values in a numeric column:

```
SELECT
    SUM(Total) [Total Customers]
FROM crm.CustomerCountByState;
```

Total Customers
508

AVG

Gives the average of a numeric column:

```
SELECT
    AVG(Total) [Average Customers Per State]
FROM crm.CustomerCountByState;
```

Average Customers Per State
9

SQL has other aggregate functions; for more info, you can check the documentation (*https://oreil.ly/Ea0Yl*).

Conversion Functions

The following two functions both convert a given value to a new datatype. There is also PARSE, but I rarely use it, or the TRY_* variants to all three. These others aren't useless functions; I often just don't remember they exist and find other ways!

CAST and CONVERT

The SQL Server documentation (*https://oreil.ly/hvCg1*) treats these two together, and I will, too. I tend to use CAST except when I need CONVERT's *style* parameter.

First, CAST and a common use case: left-padding zeros. In this table, `zip` was brought in as an INT column (it happens—we will talk about it in Chapter 7):

```
SELECT TOP 10
    RIGHT('00000' + CAST(zip AS VARCHAR), 5) [Short ZIP Codes]
FROM dbo.USFakeDemoData
WHERE zip < 10000
ORDER BY 1;
```

	Short ZIP Codes
0	01581
1	01602
2	01602
3	01603
4	01742
5	01887
6	02128
7	02138
8	02210
9	02346

What are we doing here? We are taking a string of five zeros, '00000', and concatenating the ZIP code to the right of that. But in SQL the + operator is overloaded, and SQL doesn't know whether to add zero to the ZIP code or concatenate the two values. By explicitly doing a CAST of the ZIP code to VARCHAR, SQL takes the hint and does concatenation. It then takes the rightmost five digits of the result. Note that while the WHERE clause is not strictly necessary, this type of technique is often used in data quality exercises across millions of rows, and there is no need to have SQL do the processing of concatenating and then taking the right five digits for ZIP codes that are already five digits long.

By the way, we can do the same thing with FORMAT, which is more concise. In the following code, the '00000' parameter is a format string instruction FORMAT to return the value as a five-digit string padded with leading zeros (on the left) as needed to reach five characters:

```
SELECT TOP 10
    FORMAT(zip, '00000') [Short ZIP Codes]
FROM dbo.USFakeDemoData
WHERE zip < 10000
ORDER BY 1;
```

	Short ZIP Codes
0	01581
1	01602
2	01602
3	01603
4	01742
5	01887
6	02128
7	02138
8	02210
9	02346

CONVERT is often used to format the various DATE and TIME (and DATETIME and TIME STAMP) datatypes into well-known formats, the handiest of which for data matching purposes is ISO 8601 (*https://oreil.ly/2ybXE*). Here is how to use CONVERT to get the ISO 8601 form of the current date and time. See the documentation (*https://oreil.ly/6UwRo*) for more details.

```
/*
    This one always reads somewhat backwards to me:
    "CONVERT to VARCHAR(25) from GETDATE() using
    style 126" (SQL Server's designation for ISO
    8601 timestamp format).
*/
SELECT CONVERT(VARCHAR(25), GETDATE(), 126) [Date/Time in ISO 8601];
```

Date/Time in ISO 8601
2023-07-27T09:54:37.330

COALESCE

While actually an expression and not a function, COALESCE looks like a function, and I tend to think of it that way. Since it returns the first non-NULL value in a series of arguments, it is often useful for converting NULL values to something else—say, a zero, or an "unknown" value, like this:

```
SELECT TOP 10
    A.Abbreviation State,
    COALESCE(C.City, '_Unknown_') City
FROM ref.PostalAbbreviations A
LEFT OUTER JOIN crm.NormalizedCustomer C ON
    A.Abbreviation = C.State
ORDER BY COALESCE(C.City, '_Unknown_'), A.Abbreviation;
```

	State	City
0	AL	_Unknown_
1	DE	_Unknown_
2	VT	_Unknown_
3	WV	_Unknown_
4	MD	Aberdeen
5	KS	Abilene
6	KS	Abilene
7	TX	Abilene
8	TX	Abilene
9	NJ	Absecon

One place COALESCE can be handy is in merging new values from an import dataset. Let's say we get an updated customer feed update every day and that we trust the data source explicitly in terms of data quality. We know both sides have a customer key to join on. Each row in the import dataset will have a non-NULL customer key plus one or more columns of non-NULL data to update the customer table with. Anything that hasn't changed is set to NULL in the import data. This approach is used instead of sending back all the unchanged values in the import dataset to avoid upsetting field-level audit tracking. If a field really didn't change, you don't want an audit record showing that it was changed but both the old and new values were the same.

This is the pattern you'd use:

```
SELECT
    COALESCE(I.LastName,  C.LastName)  LastName,
    COALESCE(I.FirstName, C.FirstName) FirstName,
    COALESCE(I.Company,   C.Company)   Company,
    -- and so on...
    COALESCE(I.Email,     C.Email)     Email
```

```
FROM crm.Customer C
INNER JOIN staging.ImportCustomer I ON
    C.CustomerId = I.CustomerId
```

TRY_CONVERT

If you call CONVERT on data that cannot be validly converted to another datatype, an error will occur. You can get around the error by using TRY_CONVERT, which returns NULL if a successful cast cannot take place. One place TRY_CONVERT comes in handy is when parsing hexadecimal constants into a valid integer. If you are not given a valid constant, you can COALESCE the resulting NULL to 0:

```
SELECT
    COALESCE(TRY_CONVERT(VARBINARY(50), '0xFFFF', 1), 0) [Valid Hex Constant],
    COALESCE(TRY_CONVERT(VARBINARY(50), '0xFFFG', 1), 0) [Invalid Cast To 0];
```

Valid Hex Constant	Invalid Cast To 0
65535	0

TRY_CONVERT takes three parameters. The first is the datatype to attempt converting to (VARBINARY(50) in our example). The second parameter is the value to cast (in our trivial case just a couple of strings). The third is a *style* parameter, and for that you should consult the SQL documentation for CONVERT, which uses the same values. For the previous, from the SQL Server documentation (*https://oreil.ly/vmBw0*), a style of 1 means the following:

> For a binary *data_type*, the expression must be a character expression. The *expression* must have an *even* number of hexadecimal digits (0, 1, 2, 3, 4, 5, 6, 7, 8, 9, A, B, C, D, E, F, a, b, c, d, e, f). If the *style* is set to 1, the expression must have 0x as the first two characters. If the expression contains an odd number of characters, or if any of the characters is invalid, an error is raised.

Since in the first example we passed in a valid hexadecimal string according to those rules, *0xFFFF*, it gets converted successfully to binary, and upon selection SQL then converts that to its decimal representation, i.e., *65535*. The second string is not a valid hexadecimal constant, so TRY_PARSE yields NULL, and COALESCE sets that to *0*.

Cryptographic Functions: HASHBYTES

SQL comes with many cryptographic functions, but we will be using only one of them. We won't be encrypting or decrypting anything in this book, but sometimes these functions come in handy for other reasons, especially hashes.

We will actually use this in a special case in Chapter 10. The HASHBYTES function takes the passed-in value and returns a VARBINARY hash based on the algorithm chosen. MD5 is deprecated but is fine for our noncryptographic needs:

```
SELECT HASHBYTES('MD5', 'A value to be hashed.') [Hashed Value];
```

Hashed Value
b'\x93\x1c]î\xb9C\xb5{z\x84K\xe1My\x10\t'

Wanna see that a little prettier?

```
SELECT
    CAST
    (
        HASHBYTES('MD5', 'A value to be hashed.')
        AS BIGINT
    ) [Hashed Value As BIGINT];
```

Hashed Value As BIGINT
8828264600592519168

Date and Time Functions

We will use a lot of these, because dates like birth dates are often useful for matching.

GETDATE

Gets the current date and time:

```
SELECT GETDATE() [Right Now, As I Am Writing This];
```

Right Now, As I Am Writing This
2023-07-27 09:54:40.120000

In the following examples, I use GETDATE() to represent any valid date/time value in a column in a table, and that includes valid date/time string values such as 'July 19, 2023' or '2023-07-19T13:15:17.018'.

DATEADD

What is 100 years from today? The yyyy date part parameter specifies to do the math in years:

```
SELECT GETDATE() Today, DATEADD(yyyy, 100, GETDATE()) [100 Years From Today];
```

Today	100 Years From Today
2023-07-27 09:54:40.653000	2123-07-27 09:54:40.653000

That's pretty trivial. How about 100 *days* from today? That's a bit tougher to calculate in our head usually. The dd indicates to use days:

```
SELECT GETDATE() Today, DATEADD(dd, 100, GETDATE()) [100 Days From Today];
```

Today	100 Days From Today
2023-07-27 09:54:41.213000	2023-11-04 09:54:41.213000

You can "go forward into the past!" How about 29 months ago? Yes, mm means months. Note the negative number passed as the number of months. Just like in sixth grade where you learned that subtracting was just adding with negative numbers:

```
SELECT GETDATE() Today, DATEADD(mm, -29, GETDATE()) [29 Months Ago];
```

Today	29 Months Ago
2023-07-27 09:54:41.910000	2021-02-27 09:54:41.910000

DATEDIFF

If DATEADD lets you travel forward and backward in time, DATEDIFF can tell you how far you went:

```
SELECT
    GETDATE() Today,
    DATEDIFF(yyyy,
            '1966-09-08T20:30:00.000',
            GETDATE()) [Years Since Star Trek Debuted];
```

Today	Years Since Star Trek Debuted
2023-07-27 09:54:42.543000	57

DATEPART

Lets you extract various pieces of a date (see the documentation: *https://oreil.ly/DUwFo*). DATEADD and DATEPART use the same abbreviations for specifying the time interval desired. Note that this parameter is not a string and requires no quote delimiters:

```
SELECT DATEPART(yyyy, GETDATE()) [Current Year];
```

Current Year
2023

The preceding is the same as using the YEAR function (there are also DAY and MONTH functions that do what you think):

```
SELECT YEAR(GETDATE()) [Current Year];
```

Current Year
2023

Unlike C's date functions, SQL considers months of the year to be 1-relative like right-thinking people:

```
SELECT MONTH('2020-01-01') [What Ordinal For January?];
```

What Ordinal For January?
1

ISDATE

A very handy function indeed. You can't match on someone's date of birth, say, if the date on one or the other side of the comparison isn't even a valid date. ISDATE lets you check when a date is coming in as a textual value (a numeric string or as the date written in words). It is not useful when the date is already in a SQL DATE-compatible datatype (in which case it is either a valid date or NULL). ISDATE returns 1 if the passed-in value is a valid date, or 0 otherwise:

```
SELECT
    ISDATE('1990-01-01') [YYYY-MM-DD],     /* Valid format.                    */
    ISDATE('January 1, 1990') [Textual],   /* Text is valid as long as correct! */
    ISDATE('1 JAN 1990') [Abbreviated],    /* And can be in many formats,       */
    ISDATE('Januwary 1, 1990') [Misspelled Date], /* Not a valid date.          */
    ISDATE('-9999/01/01') [Too Early],     /* Outside SQL Server's date range.  */
    ISDATE('99999/01/01') [Too Late]       /* Ditto.                            */
```

YYYY-MM-DD	Textual	Abbreviated	Misspelled Date	Too Early	Too Late
1	1	1	0	0	0

Logical Functions: IIF

The one I use the most is IIF, although for reasons already explained, I tend to use the CASE expression more.

The `IIF` function evaluates an expression and returns the second parameter if true; otherwise, it returns the third parameter. The resemblance to the traditional `if...then...else` of other programming languages is intentional:

```
/*
    If January or February warn the reader!
*/
SELECT
    CONVERT(VARCHAR(25), GETDATE(), 23) [Today Is],
    IIF((DATEPART(mm, GETDATE()) < 3), 'Cold - Brrr!', 'Nice!') [Bundle Up?];
```

Today Is	Bundle Up?
2023-07-27	Nice!

String Functions

This book concentrates heavily on string manipulation, and the following functions all get used. Learn them, love them.

CHARINDEX and PATINDEX

We will be using `CHARINDEX` and `PATINDEX` a lot. `CHARINDEX` returns the index of the first occurrence of a specified character in a *1-relative string* (programmers used to 0-relative strings, beware!), or 0 if it is not found:

```
SELECT
    CHARINDEX('-', '800-555-1234') [Where Is First Dash?],
    CHARINDEX('(', '800-555-1234') [Where Is First Paren?];
```

Where Is First Dash?	Where Is First Paren?
4	0

`PATINDEX` does the same but looks for a wildcarded pattern using SQL's % (percent sign) as the universal wildcard (typically * or the asterisk in other languages):

```
SELECT
    PATINDEX('%555%', '800-555-1234') [Where Is First '555'?],
    PATINDEX('%Ext%', '800-555-1234') [Where Is First 'Ext'?];
```

Where Is First '555'?	Where Is First 'Ext'?
5	0

`CHARINDEX` and `PATINDEX` get interesting when combined with `LEFT`, `RIGHT`, and `SUBSTRING`.

I find the parameter order of these two functions confusing, in that most other string functions take the string to be searched or manipulated (typically a column name) as the first parameter, with other parameters following to control the behavior. However, CHARINDEX and PATINDEX take the value to be searched *for* first and then the string (name of the column) *to be searched*.

Consider:

```
LEN(foo)
    RIGHT(foo, 10)
SUBSTRING(foo, 4, 3)
TRANSLATE(foo, '123', 'abc')
CHARINDEX('A', foo)
```

It just seems backward to me, and I always have to remember to "reverse" the parameters on these two "index" functions. I am bringing it up here to help you remember, too.

LEN

Returns the length of a string, that is, a count of all the characters (not necessarily bytes) in a string, including whitespace:

```
/*
    Note embedded doubled single quotes for escaping
    a single single quote character in the sentence
    (got that?). Also the + for string concatenation.
*/
SELECT
    LEN('This is a really long sentence ' +
        'and would be hard to count its ' +
        'characters by hand, don''t you think?') [Sentence Length?],
    LEN('') [Empty String Length?],
    LEN(NULL) [NULL Length?];
```

Sentence Length?	Empty String Length?	NULL Length?
98	0	NULL

Note that the length of NULL is NULL. So just like we discussed how to deal with NULLs when checking for equality, if you are going to check for the length of strings that could be NULL and treat them as zero-length strings, you have to be prepared to do the extra work using something like COALESCE to get the NULL replaced with a 0.

LEFT, RIGHT, and SUBSTRING

LEFT returns the given number of characters from the left (beginning) of a string:

```
SELECT LEFT('65201-0256', 5) [5-Digit ZIP]
```

5-Digit ZIP
65201

LEFT (and RIGHT) will return the entire string if it is shorter than the length requested:

```
SELECT LEFT('12345', 10) [ZIP+4]
```

ZIP+4
12345

NULL simply returns NULL, as usual:

```
SELECT LEFT(NULL, 5) [NULL Is NULL...Again]
```

NULL Is NULL...Again
NULL

Surprising to no one except a Pythonista, perhaps, negative lengths yield an error. This will come up in an example a bit later and can happen when you are dynamically computing the lengths to take from a string and aren't guarding against zero or negative lengths in your calculations:

```
SELECT LEFT('65201-0256', -5) [Ooops! Miscalculated Length!]

*   mssql+pyodbc://{os.environ["DEMO_UID"]}:***@TestDB
        (pyodbc.ProgrammingError) ('42000', '[42000] [Microsoft][ODBC SQL
Server Driver][SQL Server]Invalid length parameter passed to the left function.
(536) (SQLExecDirectW)')
        ...
```

Note that if dynamically calculating the length to take with LEFT or RIGHT, a value of 0 returns an empty string, ''.

Then, RIGHT. We've already seen a good use for it, left-padding zeros on "numbers" that should be strings. This is quite common when importing CSVs with ZIP codes or Social Security numbers with no formatting that often get converted into integers. The string "05436" gets interpreted as the number 5436 and so on:

```
SELECT
    0   [One Digit],
    500 [Three Digits],
    RIGHT('00000' + CAST(0 AS VARCHAR), 5)   [Five Digits],
    RIGHT('00000' + CAST(500 AS VARCHAR), 5) [Also Five Digits];
```

One Digit	Three Digits	Five Digits	Also Five Digits
0	500	00000	00500

Finally, there is SUBSTRING for pulling out the "middle" of a string, using a 1-relative starting character and a length:

```
SELECT SUBSTRING('800-555-1234', 5, 3) [Phone # Exchange];
```

Phone # Exchange
555

SUBSTRING can be used to extract the left or right parts of a string as well. I tend to use LEFT and RIGHT for those purposes to make my reasoning explicit, but some people like the "one tool" approach of simply using SUBSTRING for all three. Do what makes you feel good.

LEFT, RIGHT, and SUBSTRING are interesting and all...as long as you know the fixed location of something you want to parse out. But what if you don't? Remember, LEN, CHARINDEX, and PATINDEX? Behold! The following is a common problem—receiving a "full name" that is simply a person's name all in one box (think "contest sign-up sheets"):

```
WITH NamesToBeParsed
AS
(
    /*
        Pretend all names are "first<space>last<optional comma, space & suffix>"
        Here we're just synthesizing a name to look like that.
    */
    SELECT FirstName + ' ' + LastName [FullName]
    FROM crm.NormalizedCustomer
    WHERE LastName = 'Snedley, Jr.'
)
SELECT
    FullName [Full Name],
    /*
        LEFT for first name
    */
    LEFT(FullName,
        CHARINDEX(' ', FullName) - 1) [First Name],
    /*
        SUBSTRING to extract the last name
    */
    SUBSTRING(FullName,
            CHARINDEX(' ', FullName) + 1,
            PATINDEX('%, %', FullName) -
            CHARINDEX(' ', FullName) - 1) [Last Name],
    /*
        RIGHT to grab the suffix
    */
    RIGHT(FullName,
```

```
        LEN(FullName) - 1 - PATINDEX('%, %', FullName)) [Suffix]
FROM NamesToBeParsed;
```

Full Name	First Name	Last Name	Suffix
Mortimer Snedley, Jr.	Mortimer	Snedley	Jr.

There's a lot going on in that query. First, we declare and populate the @FullName variable to simulate a column name in the rest of the example. Let's pick the rest apart with a lot of comments. Consider the "Full Name" string first and where everything is in terms of position in the data (the numbers under the name represent character positions—the "S" in "Snedley" is in position 10, for example):

```
Mortimer Snedley, Jr.
0        1        2
123456789012345678901
```

We can see the first space is at 1-relative position 9, and the ", " (comma and space) start at position 17. Got that? So:

```
LEFT(FullName,
     CHARINDEX(' ', FullName) - 1) [First Name],
```

For the length of characters to take for the first name, we calculate the index of the first space found using CHARINDEX, which returns nine; then we subtract one from that to not count the trailing space in the results. That gives eight, and when we look at the data, we see that "Mortimer" is indeed eight characters long:

$9 - 1 = 8$

This evaluates to the following and yields "Mortimer":

```
LEFT(FullName, 8)
```

The suffix works *somewhat* similarly, with a few more calculations:

```
RIGHT(FullName,
      LEN(FullName) - 1 - PATINDEX('%, %', FullName)) [Suffix];
```

Here, PATINDEX finds the location of the ", " (comma and space) starting at position 17. RIGHT wants a length, but we have a position, so we have to calculate the length by taking the entire length of the string with the LEN function and subtracting the PAT INDEX location from that, and we then subtract an extra one to account for the space in the "space and comma" pattern. Our overall string length is 21, and the pattern starts at 17; hence, we have this:

$21 - 17 - 1 = 3$

This evaluates to the following and yields "Jr.":

```
RIGHT(FullName, 3)
```

Finally, we get to that SUBSTRING. What the heck is going on there? Well, actually, not much more than we've already seen, just feeding the peculiar needs of SUBSTRING needing both a starting location *and* a length of characters to take:

```
SUBSTRING(FullName,
          CHARINDEX(' ', FullName) + 1,
          PATINDEX('%, %', FullName) -
          CHARINDEX(' ', FullName) - 1) [Last Name],
```

Let's just take it one at a time. SUBSTRING takes the text to be searched, *FullName* here, and then wants a starting location and a length. The starting location is defined by CHARINDEX(' ', FullName) + 1. In this case, we find the first space (at 9) and then jump past it (the + 1) to get to the start of the last name at 10, which looking back is indeed the starting location of "Snedley." Great. Easy. Just like determining the end of first name, but adding a 1 to jump forward (right), rather than subtracting 1 (moving back left) to get past that space:

$9 + 1 = 10$

But now we need a length! Well, we know that the last name is separated by a suffix with the pattern ", " (comma and space). So that's the end of last name (if it exists; more in a bit). Hence, we find the starting location of that comma-and-space pattern (17), then subtract the starting location of last name (the first space) from that (9), and finally again subtract an extra 1 to account for and remove the trailing comma:

```
Mortimer Snedley, Jr.
0        1        2
1234567890123456789012

CHARINDEX(' ', FullName) -- yields 9
PATINDEX('%, %', FullName) -- yields 17
```

$17 - 9 - 1 = 7$

Hence, we have the following:

```
SUBSTRING(FullName, 10, 7)
```

This of course yields "Snedley."

One last thing. What if there is no suffix? Do these patterns still work?

```
WITH NamesToBeParsed
AS
(
    /*
```

```
        No "Jr." suffix in the LastName field this time.
        So what will PATINDEX find?
    */
    SELECT FirstName + ' ' + LastName [FullName]
    FROM crm.NormalizedCustomer
    WHERE LastName = 'Snedley'
        AND FirstName = 'Mortimer'
)
SELECT
    FullName [Full Name],
    /*
        LEFT for first name
    */
    LEFT(FullName,
        CHARINDEX(' ', FullName) - 1) [First Name],
    /*
        SUBSTRING to extract the last name
    */
    SUBSTRING(FullName,
            CHARINDEX(' ', FullName) + 1,
            PATINDEX('%, %', FullName) -
            CHARINDEX(' ', FullName) - 1) [Last Name],
    /*
        RIGHT to grab the suffix
    */
    RIGHT(FullName,
        LEN(FullName) - 1 - PATINDEX('%, %', FullName)) [Suffix]
FROM NamesToBeParsed;

*  mssql+pyodbc://{os.environ["DEMO_UID"]}:***@TestDB
        (pyodbc.ProgrammingError) ('42000', '[42000] [Microsoft][ODBC SQL
Server Driver][SQL Server]Invalid length parameter passed to the LEFT or SUB-
STRING function. (537) (SQLExecDirectW)')
        ...
```

Alas, no! We get:

```
Invalid length parameter passed to the LEFT or SUBSTRING function.
```

 Depending on your query environment, the error message you get may look differently. For example, the (pyodbc.Programming Error) ('42000', '[42000] [Microsoft][ODBC SQL Server Driver][SQL Server] before the error message is produced by the Python call stack in Jupyter, which was used to produce this book.

The LEFT function should be fine; it is looking for the first space and using the length of the whole string, and both exist. The SUBSTRING function is the culprit. If PATINDEX returns 0, then that ends up being as follows:

$$0 - 9 - 1 = -10$$

Ooops!

And indeed, −10 is an invalid length parameter for SUBSTRING. We can fix that and a related but not fatal problem with the *Suffix* logic, using the IIF logical function we've already seen:

```
WITH NamesToBeParsed
AS
(
    SELECT FirstName + ' ' + LastName [FullName]
    FROM crm.NormalizedCustomer
    WHERE LastName LIKE 'Snedley%'
        AND FirstName = 'Mortimer'
)
SELECT DISTINCT
    FullName [Full Name],
    LEFT(FullName,
        CHARINDEX(' ', FullName) - 1) [First Name],
    SUBSTRING(FullName,
            -- Starting position is still the first space.
            CHARINDEX(' ', FullName) + 1,
            -- If a "comma and space" is found...
            IIF(PATINDEX('%, %', FullName) > 0,
                -- ...then use the original calculation to extract last name.
                PATINDEX('%, %', FullName) - CHARINDEX(' ', FullName) - 1,
                -- Else use this calculation instead.
                LEN(FullName) - CHARINDEX(' ', FullName))) [Last Name],
    -- If a "comma and space" is found...
    IIF(PATINDEX('%, %', FullName) > 0,
        -- ...then use the original calculation to extract suffix.
        RIGHT(FullName, LEN(FullName) - PATINDEX('%, %', FullName) - 1),
        -- Else just send back an empty string (no one likes NULLs).
        '') [Suffix]
FROM NamesToBeParsed;
```

Full Name	First Name	Last Name	Suffix
Mortimer Snedley	Mortimer	Snedley	
Mortimer Snedley, Jr.	Mortimer	Snedley	Jr.

Perfect! It solves both variants in the data.

The only thing that changed was adding two IIF functions, one to calculate the length for SUBSTRING and the other to do the same for RIGHT. In both cases, the IIF looks to see if the ", " (comma and space) pattern exists, and if so, it uses our original calculation for determining the length for SUBSTRING and otherwise returns an empty string for a missing suffix. IIF works nicely here because it is terse and the conditions it is checking are simple and won't change. You could also use CASE expressions to solve this. I leave that as an exercise for the reader.

It all looks complicated, but if you take each piece apart into its components, you can understand what is going on. Draw a sample string, number the positions, and play around with extracting various pieces from the left, right, and middle. Here again is our first sample:

```
Mortimer Snedley, Jr.
0         1         2
123456789012345678901
```

We will cover more of this technique later (with REVERSE—and not just to play around but to solve a problem).

 Similar simple parsing patterns are useful in any programming language that offers LEFT, RIGHT, and SUBSTRING style functions, or even just a single "substring" function, since you can usually emulate the "left" and "right" functions with it. However, if you are programming in languages like C# or Python and have access to real "parse" or "split" functions, use them! Sometimes I will write small custom programs just to handle this kind of parsing before importing the data into a relational database. While this book focuses on a SQL-only approach, it is not saying, "Only use SQL!" Use whatever tools you have available, when and where it is easiest to use them.

LTRIM, RTRIM, and TRIM

Originally there was only LTRIM and RTRIM—TRIM came later. They all basically do the same thing: remove spaces (by default—you can now specify which characters to remove, but only in the newest version of SQL Server) from the "edges" of a string. LTRIM removes leading (left) spaces, RTRIM removes trailing (right) spaces, and TRIM removes both. "Back in the day" before TRIM was available, it could be emulated with LTRIM(RTRIM(LastName)). Given all that, we'll just look at TRIM:

```
DECLARE @PaddedData VARCHAR(50) = '   Text surrounded by spaces.   '
--                                 0         1         2         3
--                                 1234567890123456789012345678901234
SELECT
    LEN(@PaddedData) [LEN Ignores Trailing Spaces],
    DATALENGTH(@PaddedData) [DATALENGTH Does Not],
    LEN(TRIM(@PaddedData)) [Length After TRIM];
```

LEN Ignores Trailing Spaces	DATALENGTH Does Not	Length After TRIM
30	34	26

Some interesting points. First, LEN ignores trailing spaces! DATALENGTH does not, but it doesn't return a count of true "characters" in the string, but instead the number of *bytes*. That for our purposes here is fine, but with multibyte character sets is not what you probably want. Either way, there were four leading and four trailing spaces in our example:

$$34 - 4 - 4 = 26$$

and that's our length after TRIM.

LOWER and UPPER

LOWER and UPPER do what it says on the tin:

```
SELECT
    LOWER('Mortimer Snedley') Lowercase,
    UPPER('Mortimer Snedley') Uppercase;
```

Lowercase	Uppercase
mortimer snedley	MORTIMER SNEDLEY

This is not generally useful since SQL comparisons are case insensitive by default. If you do end up working with a case-sensitive database, you can do either of the following:

Ignore case.
> Manually choose a case-insensitive collation for all compares using COLLATE (covered in Chapter 8).

Use UPPER or LOWER.
> Pick one and force everything you're comparing into either uppercase or lowercase on both sides and move on.

I tend to use COLLATE instead of LOWER and UPPER because it forces some other character representation issues into a uniform representation and not just whether all characters are being compared in the same case.

REPLACE and TRANSLATE

I use REPLACE all the time, for things like the following, expanded here to make it easier to understand. Read from the "inside out":

```
SELECT TOP 10
    phone1 [Mobile Phone],
    /*
        Get rid of normal punctuation found in phone numbers.
    */
    REPLACE
    (
```

```
        REPLACE
        (
            REPLACE
            (
                REPLACE
                (
                    phone1, '-', ''  /* All hyphens with empty string    */
                ), ' ', ''           /* All spaces with empty string     */
            ), '(', ''               /* All open parens with empty string  */
        ), ')', ''                   /* All close parens with empty string */
    ) [Just Digits Now]              /* The order of REPLACEs is unimportant */
    FROM crm.Customer
    WHERE phone1 IS NOT NULL
    ORDER BY phone1;
```

	Mobile Phone	Just Digits Now
0	201-555-1553	2015551553
1	201-555-1638	2015551638
2	201-555-2514	2015552514
3	201-555-2989	2015552989
4	201-555-3967	2015553967
5	201-555-4168	2015554168
6	201-555-4924	2015554924
7	201-555-5688	2015555688
8	201-555-6245	2015556245
9	201-555-7810	2015557810

This is a good place to notice that the output of a function can be the input to another function, whose output can be the input to another, and so on, and this can include the same function repeatedly. Always work "from the inside out." In this case *phone1* is having any dashes converted to an empty string. Then that output has any spaces REPLACEd with an empty string. Finally, replace all open parentheses and all close parentheses with empty strings as well.

You can do the same thing with TRANSLATE…almost. It looks at a string of "from" characters and changes each one found in the input to the corresponding character *in the same location* (offset) in the string of "to" characters. It is easier to see an example than explain it. In the following, anywhere in *phone1* that TRANSLATE finds the characters -, (, or), it will "translate" those characters to spaces, returning the result with all other characters from *phone1* unchanged. Given "201-555-1553," it should return "201 555 1553":

```
SELECT TOP 10
    phone1 [Mobile Phone],
    TRANSLATE(phone1, '-()', '   ') Translated
```

```
      /* "From" offsets: 123    123 <-- "To" offsets */
FROM crm.Customer
WHERE phone1 IS NOT NULL
ORDER BY phone1;
```

	Mobile Phone	Translated
0	201-555-1553	201 555 1553
1	201-555-1638	201 555 1638
2	201-555-2514	201 555 2514
3	201-555-2989	201 555 2989
4	201-555-3967	201 555 3967
5	201-555-4168	201 555 4168
6	201-555-4924	201 555 4924
7	201-555-5688	201 555 5688
8	201-555-6245	201 555 6245
9	201-555-7810	201 555 7810

With TRANSLATE we can't translate to an empty string as in REPLACE, because it is replacing one character at a time from the input value, and there is no such thing as an "empty character." So we must translate to something, and I chose spaces. Note there are three characters in the "from" string: -, (, and). There are therefore three spaces in the "to" string. Anywhere in *phone1* where a character in the "from" string is found, it will be replaced with the corresponding character at the same offset in the "to" string (which in this case is all spaces). This is an important function for the rest of this book, so make sure you understand it.

Perhaps an easier way to see it is to return the ordinal of the first nine letters in the alphabet:

```
SELECT
    TRANSLATE('DEAD BEEF',    /* Silly example input string */
              'ABCDEFGHI',    /* First nine letters         */
              '123456789')    /* Ordinals for those letters */
    [Letter Position]
```

Letter Position
4514 2556

REPLACE can change any *string* to any other *string*, including an *empty string*. TRANSLATE can replace any *character* with any other *character*. We couldn't take the preceding simple sample to do the ordinals for all the alphabet, because we'd need to start using *strings* for the number "10" and above as we went past the *character* "I."

We can combine the two functions and achieve a slightly shorter version than using all REPLACE functions. Since TRANSLATE can look for and change multiple characters at once, we can use it as a single "inside" call and then pass that to REPLACE to change the spaces output by TRANSLATE into empty strings:

```
SELECT TOP 10
    phone1 [Mobile Phone],
    REPLACE
    (
        TRANSLATE(phone1, '-()', '    '), ' ', ''
    ) [Translated and Replaced]
FROM crm.Customer
WHERE phone1 IS NOT NULL
ORDER BY phone1;
```

	Mobile Phone	Translated and Replaced
0	201-555-1553	2015551553
1	201-555-1638	2015551638
2	201-555-2514	2015552514
3	201-555-2989	2015552989
4	201-555-3967	2015553967
5	201-555-4168	2015554168
6	201-555-4924	2015554924
7	201-555-5688	2015555688
8	201-555-6245	2015556245
9	201-555-7810	2015557810

Which technique is better? I have never measured performance between REPLACE and TRANSLATE, and for this type of work, that usually doesn't make much difference. If you are trying to change a lot of characters at once, TRANSLATE would seem to be better because it is one function call, and combining it with REPLACE typically makes it a shorter SQL expression (and shorter and less complex is easier to debug).

REVERSE

Reverses a character string (we will see a cheap parlor trick with it later—intrigued?):

```
SELECT REVERSE('123ABC') [Reversed!];
```

Reversed!
CBA321

STRING_AGG

The SQL Server documentation (*https://oreil.ly/kiD1Q*) says STRING_AGG "concatenates the values of string expressions and places separator values between them. The separator isn't added at the end of string." It is easiest to understand how to use it with an example:

```
WITH StatesWithCustomers
AS
(
    SELECT DISTINCT TOP 100
        State
    FROM crm.NormalizedCustomer
    ORDER BY State
)
SELECT
    'Boss, I am PROUD to say we now have customers in: ' +
    STRING_AGG(State, ', ') + '.' [Obsequious Self-Promoting]
FROM StatesWithCustomers;
```

Obsequious Self-Promoting

Boss, I am PROUD to say we now have customers in: AK, AR, AZ, CA, CO, CT, DC, FL, GA, HI, IA, ID, IL, IN, KS, KY, LA, MA, MD, ME, MI, MN, MO, MS, MT, NC, ND, NE, NH, NJ, NM, NV, NY, OH, OK, OR, PA, RI, SC, SD, TN, TX, UT, VA, WA, WI, WY.

We will use STRING_AGG together with GROUP BY in the discussion on scoring in Chapter 10 to concatenate together the reasons something scored as it did.

System Functions

These final two functions both check to see if a given value "is" something—either NULL or numeric. The first will be uncontroversial. The second may surprise you.

ISNULL

ISNULL checks an expression for NULL and, if it is, then replaces the NULL with the specified value. I used to use it all the time but have found COALESCE more versatile. Check it out:

```
/*
    Not setting it, so it will be NULL.
*/
DECLARE @NullableValue INT
SELECT
    ISNULL(@NullableValue, 0)    [Set to 0],
    COALESCE(@NullableValue, 0) [This Was, Too];
```

Set to 0	This Was, Too
0	0

```
/*
   Now the variable has a value.
*/
DECLARE @NullableValue INT = 2
SELECT
    ISNULL(@NullableValue, 0)   [Now Should Be 2],
    COALESCE(@NullableValue, 0) [Should Be 2, Too];
```

Now Should Be 2	Should Be 2, Too
2	2

ISNUMERIC

ISNUMERIC is a bit different. It returns 1 if a non-numeric expression (a string, typically) represents a valid number and 0 otherwise...sorta. Kinda. What do I mean?

```
SELECT ISNUMERIC('123') [Of Course It Is Numeric];
```

Of Course It Is Numeric
1

Fine. "123" is numeric, so ISNUMERIC returned a 1 (it returns 0 otherwise). There should also be no surprises in any of the following, if you understand SQL numeric datatypes:

```
SELECT
    ISNUMERIC('1E3')    [Sci Notation Is Numeric],
    ISNUMERIC('1.0')    [As Is Decimal],
    ISNUMERIC('-1.0E-3') [Neg #s and Exponents Are Numeric],
    /*
       Maybe this one is surprising to you? It originally was to me!
    */
    ISNUMERIC('$100.00') [Currency Is, Too];
```

Sci Notation Is Numeric	As Is Decimal	Neg #s and Exponents Are Numeric	Currency Is, Too
1	1	1	1

Now for perhaps the "surprising" part:

```
SELECT '-' [Test], ISNUMERIC('-') [Result], 'A hyphen is "numeric"' [Comment]
UNION
SELECT '.',        ISNUMERIC('.'), 'A period is "numeric"'
UNION
SELECT '+',        ISNUMERIC('+'), 'A plus sign is "numeric"'
UNION
```

```
SELECT '$',        ISNUMERIC('$'), 'A currency symbol is "numeric"'
UNION
SELECT '£',        ISNUMERIC('£'), 'Currency symbol not in my locale is numeric'
UNION
SELECT ',',        ISNUMERIC(','), 'A comma is "numeric," because Europe'
UNION
SELECT '/',        ISNUMERIC('/'), 'Binary operators are not "numeric"'
UNION
SELECT '0xABCDEF', ISNUMERIC('0xABCDEF'), 'Hex is not considered "numeric"'
UNION
SELECT '1/1/1990', ISNUMERIC('1/1/1990'), 'A date is not consider "numeric"'
--ORDER BY ;
```

Test	Result	Comment
$	1	A currency symbol is "numeric"
+	1	A plus sign is "numeric"
,	1	A comma is "numeric," because Europe
-	1	A hyphen is "numeric"
.	1	A period is "numeric"
/	0	Binary operators are not "numeric"
£	1	Currency symbol not in my locale is numeric
0xABCDEF	0	Hex is not considered "numeric"
1/1/1990	0	A date is not consider "numeric"

So take ISNUMERIC's "truth" with a grain of salt, or you may be a bit surprised if you thought it was just going to check that every character is in the range 0–9, plus maybe an optional decimal point and sign! Instead, it checks for 0–9, periods, commas, plus and minus signs, and currency symbols—together or singly. I have always thought this violates "The Principle of Least Surprise," especially since it is not noted in the ISNUMERIC documentation.

Final Thoughts on Functions

In traditional programming languages there has long been the imperative approach:

```
var a = 1;
var b = 2;

if (a == b)
{
    Console.WriteLine("Equal!");
}
else
{
    Console.WriteLine("Unequal!");
}
```

A more functional approach has been gaining ground with languages like Haskell and Lua, but also in those older imperative languages like C# that now support using lambda notation, passing anonymous functions around as arguments, etc.

In SQL, you can use an imperative approach in some dialects to write stored procedures that look a lot like traditional languages—cursors that simulate reading and writing to files, control flow, and all the rest. But that is frowned upon. Like SAS or R, SQL has a very "set-oriented" view of data processing that welcomes a more functional solution to many problems. With some versions of SQL you can even create user-defined SQL functions that can return either scalar (single) or table-based values and then use those anywhere you'd use a built-in SQL function.

It may be a bit hard to digest the "functions calling functions calling functions to get the value we want" technique at first, but I promise by the end of this book you will be used to it! It is a powerful way of thinking about data and being able to construct new data out of what you already have.

Take some time and read the documentation for *all* the SQL functions available on your RDBMS. Even if you don't see a need for them today, you may find one later. For example, we will find a use for HASHBYTES in this book and even another function not covered in this chapter—SOUNDEX—that looks to be very "fuzzy" indeed but can have a real-world use.

## PART II

Various Data Problems

## CHAPTER 3

Names, Names, Names

What can I say? Names are hard (*https://oreil.ly/37bke*). Is it James or Jim? Spell-checking is impossible: people name their kids *anything*. Add in cross-cultural differences, and it becomes very hard to do much with names; but we must try! The rest of this chapter is going to assume you're dealing with some system where your customer records are stored with fields similar to these if dealing with a human.

What's in a Name?

You've had to fill out forms with your name since kindergarten. You know the drill on how they are supposed to work. The first three are the most common:

Last name
> Or family name or surname. Maybe you have fields for matronymics and patronymics, too.

First name
> Or given name. May be optional.

Middle name
> Or middle initial or middle names. Optional.

Nickname(s)
> Optional.

Suffix
> Optional.

Titles and honorifics

Optional, and you'll learn why we'll ignore them.

Full name

Often synthesized from the others, but woe to you if your incoming data only has this; we will talk about it at the end!

Or if dealing with businesses, simply this:

Company name

While we commonly tear apart human names into their constituent parts, rarely are entity names held in more than one field. No matter the structure of the entity—corporation, partnership, trust, whatever—we jam it into one field. Except sometimes there is another field that looks like company name.

DBA

"Doing Business As," often used by an individual who hasn't established a more formal entity such as an LLC. John Smith may be doing business as "Smith Home Contracting."

Is It Relevant?

Just as honorifics and suffixes can tell us more about an individual than just their name, there are obviously an enormous number of subparts to a large corporation beyond its legal name. The most interesting is perhaps its organizational structure— a parent holding company with various companies in its portfolio, each of those having regions, divisions, departments, groups, teams; many participating in partnerships with other companies; and so on. This is a fascinating area, and if you have the data, it can allow some very sophisticated customer and competitor analysis.

The problem is that you usually don't have data that accurate about your customers or competitors. You may know Jane Doe's title is "Vice President" of the "South Sales Division" of the "Midwest Region" of Foo Corp, but without a current org chart, stock filings, and an insider telling you when Jane has been promoted or left, you really have no understanding of Jane's role or position in Foo Corp. "Vice President" means nothing—in a financial company or bank, everyone above the tellers are vice president. You need more meaningful data. Does she have direct reports? How many? How many people total report to her? Does she have budget and signature authority? How much? How do *you* know that? Is your knowledge current? How do you keep it current? Are your sources violating confidentiality and opening your company to liability for knowing them?

Multiply all that across your entire customer base and most businesses don't find value in tracking their customers on an ongoing basis at that level of corporate detail. Especially since it is in flux all the time as people get hired, fired, retired, promoted, demoted, laterally moved, new jobs elsewhere, or sick and die. That's often hard to track even in your own business, let alone another you have no direct visibility into! So this book won't deal with these data attributes, and they're probably wrong if you have them, anyway.

In the United States, you could be dealing with the issue of "person-like entities." This is my term for legal entities such as some estates, guardianships, and trusts that share the same tax ID with a person, living or dead. Some CRM systems such as Salesforce require either a person account or a company account record for recording customer information; they are different records with different schemas and must be chosen up front when creating the entry. But for tax reporting purposes often these "person-like entities" get shoved into a person account, even though they are a legal entity. So you may also be dealing with the difference between these:

- Mortimer Snedley
- Mortimer Snedley Estate

Both are in the system as "humans," both with the same tax ID, address, etc. Depending on how your company encodes them in the system, you may have some fun distinguishing between the two! The first step is knowing you have that issue in your data. You may also have the issue if data was imported into your system without enough edit checks; often companies end up as individuals or vice versa during a system migration, for example. Cleanup sometimes follows. Sometimes.

There may also be honorifics, titles, etc., but these are seldom useful (and often clutter) for data matching. Someone may be "Mrs." *and* "Dr." *and* "CEO." The same goes for suffixes, where someone may be recorded as both "Mortimer Snedley" and "Mortimer Snedley, Jr." In fact, we're going to learn "fuzzy" is the name of the game with names and that *quite* often "less is more."

Two final notes before we dive in. First, *everything you know about names is wrong.* No, really—everything. One of my best friends on the planet legally has only a single name (he's mononymic, and proud of it). His name seems like a common first name, but he claims it is his "last name," and there are famous people with it as a last name, so who can tell? It's his legal name, so he must be correct! All we can do is handle it as best we can.

Second, we will be dealing with data quality all along, and there is even a chapter about it later, Chapter 11. But realize now and on everything we talk about that the data on one side or other of the match can be *wrong*. Not just encoded differently between systems, but flat-out wrong. Often it is incorrect in production! Depending on your company's data quality maturity, it is not uncommon to have "impossible data" in the system. My favorite example, because everyone understands it, is "birth dates in the future"; if you are dealing with real customers, that's sorta hard to have in real life, but I am willing to bet you have some in your CRM system.

Anyway, names can be wrong, too; characters get left out or transposed. First names get entered in last name fields, and vice versa. Users don't follow punctuation standards; it is frankly better if there is no punctuation allowed, but then you have to stop them from entering any on something like "Jr." And what about "O'Connor," which is the customer's legal last name?

Also, *sometimes people lie*. This won't happen that often in your production system because customers may have had to supply a valid ID at some point to prove their legal name to one of your representatives. But the data that is coming in from Marketing for you to match? Was it from a trade show? Maybe entries for a drawing for some prize? Yeah, good luck with that—that data will be 50% junk if it was just a sign-up sheet and not dropping business cards in a fishbowl. That "Mickey Mouse" guy gets around.

One more thing, but first, a bad joke:

- Question: What do you call someone who speaks three languages?
- Answer: Trilingual.
- Q: And two languages?
- A: Bilingual.
- Q: And those who manage to know only one language?
- A: American.

I am guilty as charged. I know only English, and barely that, and the naming standards of English-speaking countries. I know nothing about using these ideas with right-to-left (RTL) or ideographic languages. I presume since much of what we do in the book is oriented toward dealing with punctuation, if there is Latin-based punctuation, then those techniques still work. However, I am saying up front this may not apply to your language, writing, or culture.

Last Names

We will deal first with last names, also known as *family names*, or surname, as it is called in LDAP directories like Active Directory (I match against LDAP user data a lot using SQL via the ADSI driver for SQL Server). There are so many things to talk about:

Is there punctuation?
"O'Connor" comes to mind and of course hyphenated names like "Woodsworth-Biggleson," but so does "Snedley, Jr." That leads to the next question.

Are there suffixes?
Are they combined in the last name field like in the prior bullet (a problem we'll deal with, or try to), or are they in their own field?

Are there matronymics and patronymics in there?
Are you handling them as hyphenated names or just how?

What's the length limit?
Any records nudging up against it? Did staff have to get creative to shove something in there? If so, that can make matching against the correct name harder. We can try to deal with it, or use simple truncation at least. Also, does the import data have a longer field length? Do you know what your strategy is going to be to handle possible truncations? This and other schema differences applies for all incoming fields.

Is it really the last name?
On the incoming data, a quick lookover to see if there are any obvious swaps between name fields is a good idea. There are people with the last name of "Jim," but they're much rarer than those with that first name.

Do you have business names there?
Some CRM systems encode company names in the last name field and (ideally) NULLs in the first and middle name fields. There are also those pesky "person-like entities." Do your last names contain words like "Trust" or "Estate" in them?

Punctuation

Punctuation in and of itself is not bad; they are just more characters to match, right? The following should hold true on most systems:

O'Connor = O'Connor

But often systems strip out punctuation. The US Postal Service (USPS) doesn't like it in addresses, for example, so if the data you are dealing with on one side or the other has been "normalized" to USPS standards, there may be no punctuation. City is actually a better example for this. Take O'Fallon, Missouri. The residents spell it "O'Fallon." The USPS wants it "OFallon" (or really, "OFALLON"). Besides changing the pronunciation in most people's heads, it makes it harder to match, because as you may have noticed:

O'Fallon <> OFallon

There are other similar issues. Sometimes hyphenated names are entered with spaces because the data entry system doesn't allow hyphens. There can also be inconsistencies between how your users enter the data (gasp!).

What to do about it? Simple. Remember this technique from the chapter on functions, because we're going to use it a lot:

```
SELECT TOP 10
    /*
        Note the doubled single quote counts as a single character
    */
    REPLACE
    (
        TRANSLATE(LastName, '.,-''()[]`', '          '), ' ', ''
    ) [Normalized Last Name]
FROM crm.NormalizedCustomer
WHERE LastName IN ('O''Connor')
ORDER BY LastName;
```

Normalized Last Name
OConnor

We can translate various common punctuation used in names (or found in name fields) to spaces and then replace all spaces with empty strings (which means we don't need to then wrap them in TRIM). Now it won't matter what punctuation was or was not on either side; they should be the same. Observe the following:

```
DECLARE @City     VARCHAR(50) = 'O''Fallon'  /* How we store it   */
DECLARE @USPSCity VARCHAR(50) = 'OFallon'    /* How USPS wants it */
/*
    TRANSLATE, REPLACE and compare both sides.
*/
SELECT
    @City City,
    @USPSCity [USPS City],
    CASE @City
        WHEN @USPSCity THEN 'Match!'
        ELSE 'No Match!'
    END [Do They Match?],
    REPLACE
    (
        TRANSLATE(@City, '.,-''()[]`', '          '), ' ', ''
    ) [Norm. City],
```

```
REPLACE
(
    TRANSLATE(@USPSCity, '.,-''()[]`', '             '), ' ', ''
) [Norm. USPS City],
CASE REPLACE(TRANSLATE(@City, '.,-''()[]`', '             '), ' ', '')
    WHEN REPLACE(TRANSLATE(@USPSCity, '.,-''()[]`', '             '), ' ', '')
        THEN 'Match!'
    ELSE 'No Match!'
END [Do They Match Now?];
```

City	USPS City	Do They Match?	Norm. City	Norm. USPS City	Do They Match Now?
O'Fallon	OFallon	No Match!	OFallon	OFallon	Match!

We will be using this technique on all kinds of fields, such as names, phone numbers, etc. By "normalizing" the representation of the field, you remove many permutations. For example, consider the following:

```
Snedley, Jr.
Snedley, Jr
Snedley Jr.
Snedley Jr
```

Through normalizing, they all become simply this:

```
SnedleyJr
```

That makes this a good time to talk about suffixes, eh?

Suffixes

You may be proud you're a Sr. or a Jr. or a III or Esq. or a PhD, and we're happy for you. However, when it comes to data matching, suffixes cause two problems:

- They are often in the last name field instead of their own field proper. We'll talk about this because it comes up.

- They tend to be "noisy" in that some people use them all the time, some people use them part of the time (and when legally required if it is their full legal name), and some want to acknowledge they're a "Junior" only if forced to admit it. You may have them as "Snedley, Jr." in your CRM system because that's their legal name, but everywhere else they enter their name as "Snedley." (Oh, why can't poor Junior ever be allowed to step out from behind the old man's shadow?) This is similar to titles. Are they someone who *never* puts "Dr." before their name or someone who *always* adds "JD"? There is just too much variation to be reliable, even in a book on fuzzy data!

That leads to a fundamental truth in data: *people lie.* Or more accurately, they present themselves as they want to be seen. Similar to perhaps not wanting to be a "Junior," I used to work with someone who lived in a suburb of Kansas City, Missouri, but didn't want to acknowledge it. So he always wrote "Kansas City" as his address, trusting that the ZIP code would get him his mail, and it did. "No harm, no foul" as far as he was concerned, but of course this is the kind of thing that drives any data steward crazy.

This is why I consider both suffixes and city names to be "suspect data" and tend to try to ignore them if possible in favor of more accurate "root" data: people rarely lie about their last names (except for contest entries) or their ZIP codes. Both of those fields have higher "validity" in fuzzy data matching than whether the data contains a suffix for someone when they legally have one or they entered the city correctly. We will talk about this more in both Chapters 10 and 11.

If suffixes are in their own attribute field on both sides of the data, great! You can ignore them (my preference) or treat them as another name field, *after normalizing out punctuation*. This is sometimes useful if you have a lot of related family members in your customer data and hence will have both the "Sr." and the "Jr." and will need them to help disambiguate the matches.

But if the suffixes are in your last name field? Well, now we have a bit of a problem. We can normalize punctuation and hope both sides end up with always having the suffix, or not. Not likely. You can't just take the LEFT *x* characters: what is a valid *x*? That's not a valid path to go down (it will be for some other fields later, though!).

No, we have to go in and try to parse it out somehow. If you skimmed or skipped Chapter 2, you may want to go back and review the section on LEFT, RIGHT, and SUBSTRING. We will use the SUBSTRING solution for getting out the last name, but instead of using SUBSTRING to pull it out of the middle of a full name, we will use LEFT, since we are working in the last name field itself. For simplicity's sake we're hoping staff always enters a suffix with a preceding ", " (comma and space) after the last name (that's a big hope, but you have to start somewhere and refine from there):

```
SELECT
    LastName [Last Name],
    LEFT(LastName,
        /*
            If a comma and space are found...
        */
        IIF(PATINDEX('%, %', LastName) > 0,
            /*
                ...then calculate remaining length after it.
            */
            PATINDEX('%, %', LastName) - 1,
            /*
                Else use the string length.
            */
            LEN(LastName))) [Normalized Last Name],
    RIGHT(LastName,
```

```
        /*
            If a comma and space are found...
        */
        IIF(PATINDEX('%, %', LastName) > 0,
            /*
                ...then calculate remaining length after it.
            */
            PATINDEX('%, %', LastName) - 5,
            /*
                Else there is none.
            */
            0)) [Suffix]
FROM crm.NormalizedCustomer
WHERE
    LastName LIKE 'Snedley%';
```

	Last Name	Normalized Last Name	Suffix
0	Snedley	Snedley	
1	Snedley	Snedley	
2	Snedley	Snedley	
3	Snedley	Snedley	
4	Snedley, Jr.	Snedley	Jr.

Of course, there could be other punctuation and whitespace in what's left. Let's deal with normalizing all that, too. I am going to split everything out so it is more understandable:

```
SELECT
    REPLACE(
        TRANSLATE(
            LEFT(LastName,
                /*
                    If a space is found...
                */
                IIF(CHARINDEX(' ', LastName) > 0,
                    /*
                        ...then use its location.
                    */
                    CHARINDEX(' ', LastName) - 1,
                    /*
                        Else use this calculation instead.
                    */
                    LEN(LastName)
                    )
                ),
            '.,-''()[]`', /* Translate these characters */
            '         '  /* ...into spaces            */
            ),
```

```
        /*
            Replace spaces with empty strings
        */
        ' ', '') [Normalized Last Name]
FROM crm.NormalizedCustomer
WHERE
    LastName IN ('Snedley, Jr.', 'O''Connor');
```

Normalized Last Name
0   OConnor
1   Snedley

That all looks complicated, but you've now seen each piece of it multiple times. Reading it from the "inside out" can often help. In that case we calculate the length of the last name with no suffix using the IIF, pass that to LEFT to extract just the last name, then TRANSLATE any special characters to spaces, and finally REPLACE all spaces with empty strings and return that value as the normalized last name with no suffix or punctuation. Great! But what about cultures with multiple family names in the "last name," such as "Garcia Lopez"?

```
SELECT
    REPLACE(
        TRANSLATE(
            LEFT(LastName,
                /*
                    If a space is found...
                */
                IIF(CHARINDEX(' ', LastName) > 0,
                    /*
                        ...then use its location.
                    */
                    CHARINDEX(' ', LastName) - 1,
                    /*
                        Else use this calculation instead.
                    */
                    LEN(LastName)
                    )
                ),
            '.,-''()[]`', /* Translate these characters */
            '        '    /* ...into spaces            */
            ),
        /*
            Replace spaces with empty strings
        */
        ' ', '') [Normalized Last Name]
FROM crm.NormalizedCustomer
WHERE
    LastName = 'Garcia Lopez';
```

Normalized Last Name
Garcia

That's a problem, and a harder one to solve, at least with pure SQL. Ultimately, you may have to make a decision based on your customer data and deal with it one way or another. There is an old technique called Soundex (*https://oreil.ly/RJDV1*) that may help, and SQL supports it. It converts names into four-digit numbers that can be compared to determine how "close" they sound. For example:

```
DECLARE @FirstName  VARCHAR(50) = 'Smith'
DECLARE @SecondName VARCHAR(50) = 'Smythe'
SELECT
    @FirstName            [Name #1],
    @SecondName           [Name #2],
    SOUNDEX(@FirstName)   [Soundex #1],
    SOUNDEX(@SecondName)  [Soundex #2];
```

Name #1	Name #2	Soundex #1	Soundex #2
Smith	Smythe	S530	S530

This indicates they "sound alike." Not too exciting for us, though, because making the following is a bit too fuzzy:

Smith = Smythe

But check it out:

```
DECLARE @FirstName  VARCHAR(50) = 'Snedley'
DECLARE @SecondName VARCHAR(50) = 'Snedley, Jr.'
SELECT
    @FirstName            [Name #1],
    @SecondName           [Name #2],
    SOUNDEX(@FirstName)   [Soundex #1],
    SOUNDEX(@SecondName)  [Soundex #2];
```

Name #1	Name #2	Soundex #1	Soundex #2
Snedley	Snedley, Jr.	S534	S534

Ah! Maybe we don't have to care about suffixes embedded in our last names at all, eh?

And look:

```
DECLARE @FirstName  VARCHAR(50) = 'Garcia'
DECLARE @SecondName VARCHAR(50) = 'Garcia-Lopez'
DECLARE @ThirdName  VARCHAR(50) = 'Garcia Lopez'
SELECT
    @FirstName            [Name #1],
    @SecondName           [Name #2],
    @ThirdName            [Name #3],
```

```
SOUNDEX(@FirstName)  [Soundex #1],
SOUNDEX(@SecondName) [Soundex #2],
SOUNDEX(@ThirdName)  [Soundex #3];
```

Name #1	Name #2	Name #3	Soundex #1	Soundex #2	Soundex #3
Garcia	Garcia-Lopez	Garcia Lopez	G620	G620	G620

Maybe that's the way you solve it: by adding SOUNDEX as another "score" beyond just a simple last name match. It will depend on your data.

Finally, usually you would not do this in raw queries over and over. You would take this type of logic for normalizing each field and either write a view around the table that contains it to normalize the data for you or perhaps encapsulate the logic in stored procedures or user-defined SQL functions you could then call for each column needing normalization. Of course, all of this implies you have the ability to roll such changes to production, which may not be the case. There are other ways to then handle it, each clumsier than the last. In descending order of priority:

1. Encapsulate everything in a "normalized" view:

   In the same database
   This may be hard if you don't have DDL (CREATE) access to that database, which is likely if it is a production application database.

   In another database
   Often you can end up just using "three-part names" and "four-part names" to get to everything easily. In other words, you may be able to create a view in your own database that accesses the CRM database using names like *CRMDB.crm.Customers* if on the same server, or *CRMServer.CRMDB.crm .Customers* if on another server.

2. Use ETL. This means you query into a target table (do the normalization once). Again, this can be into the same database as the original data or another, depending on needs and your level of access.

3. Use CTEs. This is not the best approach, because you have to re-specify them over and over (and they're already slower), but they are always available as long as you have SELECT access.

First Names

In many ways you would think you could treat the first name just like the last name: normalize it and hope for the best. Alas, no. Consider my name: am I James or Jim? I am both, depending on the context (but rarely Jimmy and never Jamie). I may be

"James" in your CRM system but wrote down "Jim" to win that game console in that drawing from the fishbowl:

James <> Jim

The solution? I typically punt and look only at the first initial. Of course, that doesn't help us when Anthony shortens to Tony, but it covers the previous example and Charles to Chuck or Chaz and is good enough for most name shortenings. Hence:

```
SELECT TOP 10
    LastName [Last Name],
    LEFT(FirstName, 1) [First Initial]
FROM crm.NormalizedCustomer
WHERE LastName IS NOT NULL
ORDER BY LastName;
```

	Last Name	First Initial
0	Abdallah	J
1	Acey	G
2	Acuff	W
3	Adkin	B
4	Agramonte	F
5	Ahle	D
6	Albares	C
7	Amigon	M
8	Amyot	J
9	Andreason	T

The first name field also picks up a lot of nicknames, as opposed to legal names or shortenings. For example, if someone goes by "Junior" all their life, they may write down "Junior" in a first name box or on their name tag. There is not much you can do about this, frankly. Our ultimate approach to matching will be to build up a "score," and part of that is to give some fuzziness to topics like this and still find a match.

Finally, I've seen a husband and wife named Donald and Donna. I am sure there are happily married James and Jamies, Josephs and Josephinas, and so on. For that matter, thinking about the old *Saturday Night Live* skit, there could be and are, I am sure, two Pats in matrimonial bliss (although in the skits Pat's partner was Chris). In fact, my copyeditor, Kim, pointed out that Taylor Lautner's wife is Taylor Lautner. So again, we will discuss building up a "score" later that indicates our confidence in a match, but you can see there will be many different attributes needed before the score differs for Don and Donna, Pat and Pat, or Taylor and Taylor. Name, address, home phone—all certainly not enough! Stay tuned....

Middle Name

I find first names not very useful and often middle names or initials not useful at all. Obviously, for the same reasons as first name, if I have a middle name, I will shorten it to just an initial. And replacing all punctuation is vital if the data does contain middle initials, since you don't want to be comparing "J" to "J." ("J" and a period or full stop).

One thing you should note is that in some subcultures there are limited lists of names given to infants and that often there are multiple middle names (from the same limited list) to help disambiguate each other. In those cases, middle names or initials may indeed be useful, but you will need to be able to handle multiples of them *and the data has to have them*. This is a case where you have to know your production data and do some EDA on the data you're matching against to see if a given approach will work, needs tweaking, or requires another solution entirely.

One more thing—what about those people (and there are many) who use their middle name as their informal "first" name? You *could* check for that! For simplicity's sake my fake *crm* data doesn't have middle names, so we will use three SQL variables to represent the first, middle, and last name columns:

```
DECLARE @FirstName   VARCHAR(50) = 'James'   /* Our customer first name field  */
DECLARE @MiddleName  VARCHAR(50) = 'Thomas'  /* Our customer middle name field */
DECLARE @NameToMatch VARCHAR(50) = 'Tom'     /* The incoming data to match     */
SELECT
    CASE
    WHEN LEFT(@FirstName, 1) = LEFT(@NameToMatch, 1)
      OR LEFT(@MiddleName, 1) = LEFT(@NameToMatch, 1)
        THEN 'Match!'
    ELSE 'No Match!'
END [Do They Match?];
```

Do They Match?
Match!

In my experience this approach introduces too many false positives. Instead, it is better to just let the scoring take care of it for you.

Nicknames

If your CRM system captures them, fine, but you will rarely find it on the data you want to match against. Or more accurately, they are using a nickname (not their legal name) *and not telling you*. Depending on the prevalence of nicknames in your production system it may be worthwhile to match against both first name and nickname in your production system as "first name," contravening what I just said about attempting to match first and middle name as "first name"! The reasoning is that while some small percentage of people use their middle name as their "first name" (small enough that trying to match both against first name yields too many false positives), there are a great many more who use their nickname routinely as their "first name."

Again, our sample data doesn't have a nickname column, so we will just emulate our test using SQL variables:

```sql
DECLARE @FirstName   VARCHAR(50) = 'Mortimer' /* Our customer first name field */
DECLARE @Nickname    VARCHAR(50) = 'Junior'   /* Our customer nickname field   */
DECLARE @NameToMatch VARCHAR(50) = 'Junior'   /* The incoming data to match    */
SELECT
    CASE
    WHEN LEFT(@FirstName, 1) = LEFT(@NameToMatch, 1)
      OR LEFT(@NickName, 1) =  LEFT(@NameToMatch, 1)
        THEN 'Match!'
    ELSE 'No Match!'
    END [Do They Match?];
```

Do They Match?
Match!

Don't forget you may then have to combine checking *just* the initials and also the incoming data against first, middle, and nicknames!

Company Name

Company names are easy, as long as there is a company name field. If the company name is stored in the last name field, you have a bit more work (like being able to determine a company from an individual in that system). The first thing to remember, though, is you want to normalize the company name. In fact, it is just as or more urgent to do so than individual names. Why?

- Acme Corporation
- Acme Corp.
- Acme Corp
- Acme - A Roadrunner Corporation
- Snedley & Sons
- Snedley & Sons, L.L.C.
- Snedley and Sons LLC

…and so on. Just like with individuals, your system may hold a legal name from the legal articles of incorporation whereas the data to be matched may have some more informal representation(s). That includes what some employee from one of those companies attending a conference dashed off on the entry form for the prize give-away from your Marketing department. See the problem?

There will be at some point an inspiration to "super-normalize" company names. Instead of just removing punctuation and spaces, let's get rid of "Corporation" and "Corp" and "LLC" in all their variants! Sounds great, doesn't it?

> Dick the Butcher: "The first thing we do, let's kill all the lawyers."
> —William Shakespeare, *Henry VI*, Part 2, Act IV, Scene 2

And obviously it is all those legal terms that are causing the problem! The issue then becomes false positives like "The Corpulent Corpuscle Corp." You don't want to just naively use `REPLACE(CompanyName, ' Corp', '')`, now do you? It is doubtful the resulting "ulent uscle" will be a useful match term.

The other problem with this approach is invariably you will overdo it. While on the way to getting that company name to the simplest name possible, you will be tempted to throw out things like articles such as "A," "The," and so on. What harm is there in reducing "The Gap" to "Gap" for comparison's sake? Maybe you see the problem when you come to "The Limited" and are also reducing "Limited" as part of getting rid of company legal types in the name ("Inc.", "Corp.", and so on). What about the English band The The? Surely they are some sort of corporate entity under the covers. Would they simply become an empty string in your database? And would you alphabetize them as "The The" or "The, The"? Someone at their record label had to decide, but our normalization techniques will take care of that.

Anyway, normalizing is a great technique, and you can tell I love it, but don't carry it too far, OK?

Full Name

There you sit all smug. Your data is in a nice, normalized database, each field holding just its own attribute, edit checks on everything—your production data is clean. Great!

Then in comes Marketing with their list to match against, and lo, there aren't last name and first name fields. No, there is just *FullName* in the column heading of the CSV file. Sigh.

Actually, if you go back and look at the `LEFT`, `RIGHT`, and `SUBSTRING` function discussion, you will see you already have all the tools you need. It may get more complicated, because it may be something in this format:

> Mortimer J. Snedley, Jr.

You thus have more spaces and punctuation to deal with. But it all decomposes the same. The trick is to work left to right: take off the first name using our simple LEFT trick, then work with the remainder as if it were a new string, and finally decide what is or can be the next candidate to grab with LEFT. Your biggest problem is going to be dealing with data that looks like this all coming in via *FullName*:

```
Mortimer J. Snedley, Jr.
John Smith
Snedley & Sons, L.L.C.
Acme Inc
```

Building something in pure SQL to deal with all of those is doable, but not very pretty. You may want to try other techniques to split that data apart before importing it into the database. How are your "mad code skillz"? Sometimes I will write something in C# to really quickly massage the data into a better "shape" and then proceed with that loaded into SQL.

 I use C# because that's who I am; as for SQL, there is a lot of "muscle memory" in my fingers for C#. You can use Python or R or Haskell or whatever you cool kids are doing nowadays. I may also use Excel or even mundane Windows Notepad or vi depending on my needs. Your toolbox has more than a hammer, however versatile SQL may be, so use all the tools at your disposal. I even use Excel to generate code fairly often, but that's a story for another book.

Log Files

This may seem like a weird place to bring it up, but while we're here, you can use the same techniques to import text log files into SQL and then parse out various interesting nuggets, like how many "Object reference not set to an instance of an object" errors you get in a day. Many web applications still log to text files, and these files yield to the same techniques.

But really, it's the 21st century, so either point your logging infrastructure at a SQL database as a target (almost all do that with simple configuration changes now) or use an ingestion and parsing tool like Splunk (*https://oreil.ly/snd40*) or Microsoft Log Parser (*https://oreil.ly/dMBuT*) (free) to get the logs not just into the database, but parsed and ready for consumption. (I am not affiliated with either company and get no reward for mentioning their tools.) For that matter, for such a simple query as shown previously, if you have log files and are on *IX (UNIX, Linux, BSD) or Windows with Windows Subsystem for Linux (WSL) installed, are you sure you don't just want to use grep -c (*https://oreil.ly/sfL8V*)?

"Person-Like Entities"

Finally, what about that list? What if you're getting a mix of people and companies all in one dataset, and no clear indicator which is which, but you need to filter them appropriately? There isn't a great answer, but there *is* a real-world one. You can go looking for "magic words" in the name to detect companies. Ugly? You betcha! It's terrible! (I would use `<blink>` and `<marquee>` tags here if I could.)

But here's the deal: it works *most of the time*, and "the perfect is the enemy of the good" in this business. Again, we have no *FullName* column in our dataset (you should be thankful), but we can emulate it with a SQL variable:

```
DECLARE @FullName       VARCHAR(50) = 'Snedley & Sons, L.L.C.'
DECLARE @NormalizedName VARCHAR(50)
SET @NormalizedName =
    REPLACE(TRANSLATE(@FullName, '.,-''()[]`', '          '), ' ', '')
SELECT
    @FullName       [Full Name],
    @NormalizedName [Normalized Full Name],
    /*
        Important to use normalized name here to rid us of that
        pesky punctuation first.
    */
    CASE
        WHEN RIGHT(@NormalizedName, 3)  IN ('LLC', 'INC')    THEN 'Business'
        WHEN RIGHT(@NormalizedName, 4)  IN ('CORP')          THEN 'Business'
        WHEN RIGHT(@NormalizedName, 5)  IN ('TRUST')         THEN 'Business'
        WHEN RIGHT(@NormalizedName, 6)  IN ('ESTATE')        THEN 'Business'
        WHEN RIGHT(@NormalizedName, 7)  IN ('LIMITED')       THEN 'Business'
        WHEN RIGHT(@NormalizedName, 11) IN ('CORPORATION')   THEN 'Business'
        WHEN RIGHT(@NormalizedName, 12) IN ('INCORPORATED')  THEN 'Business'
        ELSE 'Person'
    END [Contact Type];
```

Full Name	Normalized Full Name	Contact Type
Snedley & Sons, L.L.C.	Snedley&SonsLLC	Business

Final Thoughts on Names

So much can go wrong with names, even in a well-designed system with a good data schema. It starts with simple data entry errors (we'll cover data quality in Chapter 11). Then there are (often cross-cultural) encoding problems such as whether hyphenated last names or matronymics and patronymics are allowed and how they are entered. I know of at least one subculture where it is virtually impossible to determine individuals apart by name only, even at the same address, unless you are prepared to handle the *multiple* middle names that they use for disambiguation. The last pretender to the Austro-Hungarian empire was named Franz Joseph Otto Robert Maria Anton Karl

Max Heinrich Sixtus Xavier Felix Renatus Ludwig Gaetan Pius Ignatius von Habsburg. Can your system handle him? I bet not on the number of constituent names, nor perhaps on a length basis (more than 120 characters total). Like my mononymic friend, who for a while had to have a driver's license stating his first name was "NFN" ("No First Name") because the state's motor vehicle department couldn't handle the simple fact that an *H. sapiens* had chosen to go by a single name, despite the preceding and well-publicized examples of Bono, Cher, Madonna, and Prince (let alone the "love symbol" the latter then adopted).

Then add in all the rest.... Nicknames. Suffixes and people who hate to be called "Junior" even when they are one. Conversely, people who love to be called "Junior" over their given name. Those sneaky people who use their middle name as their "first" name. Legal name changes—we didn't even cover that! Does your system know *when* they married the love of their life and took or added their beloved's surname or later when they divorced that lying, cheating monster and got back their rightful old name? It may matter when trying to match them to your data!

 This brings up one of my favorite rants: the inability of many systems to adequately account for marriage and divorce and the name changes that arise from both, either by replacement, addendum, or subtraction. I know of at least one system where the users were forced—for historical audit continuity as much as the difficulty to change the underlying ID—to continue to use login names with their ex-spouse's name as part of the ID. Every. Single. Day. Don't do that to your users if you can help it!

One last thing: if you understood the approaches used in this chapter, then much of the rest of the book is simply "directed study," applying the same tools to different domains. You will soon look for and use the same patterns in other datasets as well. Most "data people" are precise, but this isn't a precise business. Don't let that make you a victim! "That list from Marketing" (clears throat) "doesn't have everything I need, but I can construct most of what I want from what's already in there. Onward."

"Fuzzy" is the name of the game!

## CHAPTER 4

Location, Location, Location

Addresses differ around the world, and while I have worked in Canada and England, I will stick with what I really know and discuss only United States addresses and their components like ZIP code. However, most of the techniques presented here are probably applicable elsewhere, perhaps with some tuning to account for differences in postal code formats and so on.

What Makes an Address?

Addresses are composed of many parts:

Street number
   "123"

Street name
   "Main"

Street type
   "St" versus "Blvd" versus "Rd" versus "Hwy"

Box, suite, lot, or apartment number
   Perhaps "Floor" and other variants.

City
   Sometimes called *locale* in schemas (or even just *l* in LDAP).

County
   Are you "data quality mature"? In your system's user interface is county a cascading drop-down list based on the state chosen or, better, the ZIP code?

State, province, or state/province abbreviation
Probably the latter.

ZIP or postal code
What about "+4" for the United States? Does your organization consistently enter and check that for data quality?

Country
Is it from a constrained drop-down list? Good. If it is a freeform text field that is hand-entered, then probably Not Good.

Latitude and longitude
Unlikely, or it is getting autopopulated by a background process and still could be wrong (hint: rural addresses, P.O. boxes, etc.). This isn't useful for address matching, so we will drop it from our discussion.

In the United Kingdom and other Commonwealth countries, perhaps you have a "House Name" field ("Snedley House"). Maybe there are other administrative units between city and county or county and state or province. There may also be "Attention" or "Attn" in one of the lines to denote who to deliver to in a large company.

Likely, many of these attributes are combined; the first three may be in a *Street1* or *Address1* column and the box or suite in *Street2* or *Address2*, as in the following CSV file:

```
LastName,FirstName,Street1,Street2,...
Snedley,Mortimer,443 Arroyo Rd,Box 22,...
```

In addition, you may be capturing multiple addresses per customer for home, billing, shipping, etc. You will need to know if you are supposed to match the incoming data against all of them or simply against some "primary" address.

You are going to start seeing some common themes appear. Certain concerns that were true for names will remain true for addresses, phone numbers, and other fields. The techniques used become "muscle memory" over time because they are so common.

Street Address

Let's cut to the chase. Most people get their street *number* correct. The rest? Is it "Mountain View" or "Mountainview"? Both streets exist in various locales. USPS and certain other entities have views about which spelling to use, which can be surprising to the locals. Is it "Rd." or "Rd" or even "Road"? Is it "US-50 Highway West," "US 50 Hwy W," or "Hwy 50 W"? (I've seen all three.) It's a problem.

My answer is going to seem a bit like "nuke it from space," but I have a reason. We are collecting lots of attributes to possibly (note the "possibly") match against. If we get a bit fuzzy on this one, there are others that will help us refine our match later. Depending on the data (I always do some EDA first to determine the "shape" of the data on both sides), I may parse out the first "word" and assume that's a street number and then take the first *x* characters of the next "word." But most often I just do the following quick and dirty trick:

```
SELECT TOP 10
    /*
        The following "10" is obviously tunable to better fit your needs.
    */
    LEFT(Address1, 10) [Only Compare 1st Part]
FROM crm.NormalizedCustomer
ORDER BY LEFT(Address1, 10);
```

	Only Compare 1st Part
0	1 Central
1	1 Century
2	1 Commerce
3	1 Garfield
4	1 Huntwood
5	1 Midway R
6	1 N Harlem
7	1 N San Sa
8	1 Rancho D
9	1 S Pine S

It's so crude. I feel ashamed. Really.

But you would be surprised how often this is good enough! And since it is rare to have a 10-digit street number, it usually catches the number and some part of the street name, as we can see by looking at the other "end" of the data:

```
SELECT TOP 10
    LEFT(Address1, 10) [Part of Address to Compare]
FROM crm.NormalizedCustomer
ORDER BY LEFT(Address1, 10) DESC; -- Let's see what's at the "bottom"
```

	Part of Address to Compare
0	99586 Main
1	9939 N 14t
2	99385 Char
3	993 Washin
4	992 Civic
5	99 Tank Fa

	Part of Address to Compare
6	99 5th Ave
7	98839 Hawt
8	987 Main S
9	985 E 6th

Box, Suite, Lot, or Apartment Number

Do you need them? Are you getting good enough matches without them? Then ignore them. Remember, unless you are the size of Amazon, your customer base may not be large enough to care. Sure, you may have two customers in the same apartment complex, but then, do they have the same names? My opinion is to ignore this if you can. If you can't, then you may have to attempt some sort of normalization to compare against on both sides and hope for the best. We have no *Address2* field in our sample data, so a SQL variable comes to the rescue to show what I mean:

```
DECLARE @Street2          VARCHAR(50) = 'Suite 500'
DECLARE @IncomingStreet2 VARCHAR(50) = 'Ste 500'
SELECT
    @Street2         [Production Street2],
    @IncomingStreet2 [Incoming Data],
    /*
        The following shows the kind of normalization you can do to
        attempt to always be comparing "apples to apples" on both
        sides. You can add as many REPLACEs as you need. Ugh.
        Pay attention to the "column names" (variables) in each
        clause to keep clear what's going on.
    */
    REPLACE
    (
        REPLACE
        (
            REPLACE(@Street2, 'Suite', 'Ste'),
            'P.O. Box', 'Box'
        ),
        'Apartment', 'Apt'
    ) [Normalized Street2],
    REPLACE
    (
        REPLACE
        (
            REPLACE(@IncomingStreet2, 'Suite', 'Ste'),
            'P.O. Box', 'Box'
        ),
        'Apartment', 'Apt'
    ) [Normalized Incoming],
    CASE
```

```
REPLACE
(
    REPLACE
    (
        REPLACE(@Street2, 'Suite', 'Ste'),
        'P.O. Box', 'Box'
    ),
    'Apartment', 'Apt'
)
WHEN
    REPLACE
    (
        REPLACE
        (
            REPLACE(@IncomingStreet2, 'Suite', 'Ste'),
            'P.O. Box', 'Box'
        ),
        'Apartment', 'Apt'
    ) THEN 'Match!'
ELSE 'No Match!'
END [Do They Match?];
```

Production Street2	Incoming Data	Normalized Street2	Normalized Incoming	Do They Match?
Suite 500	Ste 500	Ste 500	Ste 500	Match!

Don't Overdo It!

The astute observer will realize that the LEFT(Address1, 10) trick in the street address discussion attempts to circumvent the whole similar problem we just saw of "Suite versus Ste" and for a much, much larger set of words:

- Boulevard versus Blvd
- Circle versus Cir
- Court versus Ct
- Highway versus Hwy (Note that "Highway" can be all over in an address, not just a suffix. Consider "Business US-50 Highway South".)
- North versus N (You didn't think we had to worry about just road types, did you?)
- Northwest versus NW (Remember, a lot of directionals can be in the string or at the end, even past the road type.)
- Parkway versus Pkwy
- Place versus Pl (Or is that "Plaza"? Now you have two "Pl" results. Is that OK?)
- Road versus Rd

- South versus S (Beware changing all "South" to "S" unless you change "123 South St" to "123 S St," which is an entirely different thing!)

- Street versus St

…and so on and so on. The list is very large if you want to be thorough. Obviously, punctuation differences are simply normalized out, so we don't worry about "Rd versus Rd." ("Rd" plus period). Also, everything mentioned in "City" on page 86 applies to roads, when the road name is "Saint George Ave" (or is that "St. George Avenue"?).

Note if you do this type of normalization on *Address1* or *Address2* type fields, you might want to do it *before* you normalize spaces out! Let's look at some of these problems. First, our sample data:

```
SELECT
    Address1
FROM crm.NormalizedCustomer
WHERE
        Address1 LIKE '%Road%'
    OR Address1 LIKE '%South%'
    OR Address1 LIKE '%State%'
ORDER BY Address1;
```

	Address1
0	1 State Route 27
1	1844 Southern Blvd
2	3 State Route 35 S
3	3273 State St
4	33 State St
5	366 South Dr
6	51120 State Route 18
7	5384 Southwyck Blvd
8	6 S Broadway St
9	72 Southern Blvd
10	721 Interstate 45 S
11	73 Southern Blvd
12	73 State Road 434 E
13	83 County Road 437 #8581
14	85092 Southern Blvd
15	868 State St #38
16	8728 S Broad St
17	9 State Highway 57 #22
18	92 Broadway

A naive "change all" algorithm trying to normalize things like "9 State Highway 57 #22" to "9 St Hwy 57 #22" causes us pain:

```sql
SELECT
    REPLACE
    (
        REPLACE
        (
            REPLACE
            (
                REPLACE(Address1, 'Highway', 'Hwy'),
                'Road', 'Rd'
            ),
            'South', 'S'
        ),
        'State', 'St'
    ) [Naive Normalization - Ooops!]
FROM crm.NormalizedCustomer
WHERE
        Address1 LIKE '%Road%'
    OR Address1 LIKE '%South%'
    OR Address1 LIKE '%State%'
ORDER BY Address1;
```

	Naive Normalization - Ooops!
0	1 St Route 27
1	1844 Sern Blvd
2	3 St Route 35 S
3	3273 St St
4	33 St St
5	366 S Dr
6	51120 St Route 18
7	5384 Swyck Blvd
8	6 S BRdway St
9	72 Sern Blvd
10	721 InterSt 45 S
11	73 Sern Blvd
12	73 St Rd 434 E
13	83 County Rd 437 #8581
14	85092 Sern Blvd
15	868 St St #38
16	8728 S BRd St
17	9 St Hwy 57 #22
18	92 BRdway

¡No bueno! Sure, we got our "9 St Hwy 57 #22," but we also got "73 Southern Blvd" changed to "73 Sern Blvd" and "6 S Broadway St" changed to "6 S BRdway St." Doh! "Spaces," you think, "I need to check and make sure there are always surrounding spaces!" Good idea! Sorta.... First, notice how hard the problem actually is, since you can't use pattern matching or you end up where you were earlier, so you have to do something like the following:

```
SELECT
    /*
        We're going to change the highly indented style for
        this one - I know you can follow along. I'm so proud
        of you!
    */
    REPLACE(
    REPLACE(
    REPLACE(
    REPLACE(
    REPLACE(
    REPLACE(
    REPLACE(
    REPLACE(
    REPLACE(
    REPLACE(
    REPLACE(
        /*
            For each keyword, always start with the one
            surrounded by spaces on both sides.
        */
        Address1, ' Highway ', ' Hwy '),
                  ' Highway',  ' Hwy'),
                  'Highway ',  'Hwy '),
                  ' Road ',     ' Rd '),
                  ' Road',      ' Rd'),
                  'Road ',      'Rd '),
                  ' South ',    ' S '),
                  ' South',     ' S'),
                  'South ',     'S '),
                  ' State ',    ' St '),
                  ' State',     ' St'),
                  'State ',     'St ') [Better? Still Ooops!]
FROM crm.NormalizedCustomer
WHERE
        Address1 LIKE '%Road%'
    OR Address1 LIKE '%South%'
    OR Address1 LIKE '%State%'
ORDER BY Address1;
```

	Better? Still Ooops!
0	1 St Route 27
1	1844 Sern Blvd
2	3 St Route 35 S
3	3273 St St
4	33 St St
5	366 S Dr
6	51120 St Route 18
7	5384 Swyck Blvd
8	6 S Broadway St
9	72 Sern Blvd
10	721 InterSt 45 S
11	73 Sern Blvd
12	73 St Rd 434 E
13	83 County Rd 437 #8581
14	85092 Sern Blvd
15	868 St St #38
16	8728 S BRd St
17	9 St Hwy 57 #22
18	92 Broadway

That fixed "Broadway" becoming "BRdway," but we see "Broad" still becoming "BRd," and "State St" becoming "St St."

The net of all this is again why I simply take some number of characters off the left of the street before or after normalizing spaces and punctuation out and move on. Going down this rathole becomes a much larger problem than is easily conquered in pure SQL.

If you need more normalization beyond this, there are third-party address cleansing services; you may want to explore engaging one. There are also open source geolocation libraries such as GeoPy (*https://oreil.ly/soHLo*). You may want to explore both approaches, but be aware their utility can be limited if many of your addresses are like "PO Box 12." Geolocation is not really useful in those cases, since they will typically then just use some "city center" as the location. Nor can many address-cleansing solutions do much in terms of making sure such a box number is valid at a given post office.

City

Is it "Saint Charles" or "St. Charles" or "St Charles"? Worse, are you sure you have the gender right on that "Saint"? It's "Saint Louis" but "Sainte Genevieve," which may get rendered "Sainte" or "Ste." or "Ste" or even the wrong but common "St." Obviously again normalizing the name—removing spaces and punctuation—helps in the compare, but there isn't much you can do sometimes because:

    Sainte <> Ste

If I have the ZIP or postal code, then I actually consider the city name noisy data and usually drop it from the comparisons. It is rare in most cases that matching on city name adds much value, unless you are missing a postal code (that informal "fishbowl drawing" scenario again—did they just dash down "NYC" or "LA" and move on?).

County

The first question is, where are you getting this data from in your customer system? Are you sure it's correct? Is it constrained in the user interface to allow only those counties that are actually in a given state, for example? Or are users just typing in a text field? (Uh-oh.) What about data you imported into your system? Do you have an idea of how good the data quality on county was in that dataset? Are you *sure*?

Better, do you pay for a geolocation service that fills that information in for you? That is the gold standard. But if not—if county is human-entered or coming from the imported data—I consider it highly suspect and, like city, often not useful if you have something better to match against, like ZIP or postal code.

Otherwise, if you have to match on it, it is like any other name—normalize it and hope for the best, realizing there's a St. Louis County, so everything we talked about with things like "Saint" in city is true for county, too (and, as previously mentioned in street addresses, in street names like "Saint George Ave"). Also, unless the field is required in the data entry form, it is quite common for this attribute to be empty for a good percentage of the rows in a dataset, so that lowers its overall usefulness, too.

State or State Abbreviation

You will probably have the state abbreviation. If the incoming data has "California" instead of "CA," my first recommendation is to find a reference (they exist online at the USPS and other places) and create a small mapping table like *ref.Postal Abbreviations* in our samples. Then use that mapping table to cross-reference between the two or to transform the incoming data to have just the abbreviations. I would do the latter, adding a column "to the right" of the existing columns, perhaps, during one of the first ETLs.

State, especially normalized down to two-character abbreviations, doesn't have the same issues as most names—no spaces or punctuation, no variants in spelling (just misspellings or mistakes like using "AR" when you meant "AZ"). It can be a useful match, but again, if you have ZIP or postal codes, why bother? Oh, and don't forget military APO and FPO codes, if you have deployed armed services members in your customer base.

ZIP or Postal Code

A ZIP+4 nine-digit ZIP code plus a street number will just about be the best match you can get. Unfortunately, ZIP+4 is rare (or else is "80301-0000"), and likely you have only five-digit ZIP codes either in your production data or in the data you are matching against. After making sure the ZIP code is five characters long, you will find ZIP codes useful for matching. A five-digit ZIP code and a street number may not be unique, but it and those first 10 characters of the street address will most likely be. Observe the difference between the following two. With EDA we've already determined the incoming data has ZIP+4. While our production data does not, we will try to match on both the street address and just the ZIP code minus the "+4."

In the following example, we'll do a left outer join on the postal code and address. The WHERE clause is simply to limit our result set to a manageable number and make sure the addresses are not NULL:

```
SELECT
    COUNT(*) [# Matched]
FROM crm.NormalizedCustomer C
LEFT OUTER JOIN dbo.PotentialMatches P ON
    LEFT(C.PostalCode, 5) = LEFT(P.zip, 5)
    AND C.Address1 = P.address
WHERE
        C.LastName = P.last_name
    AND C.FirstName = P.first_name
    AND C.LastName = 'Snedley'
    AND C.Address1 IS NOT NULL
    AND P.address IS NOT NULL;
```

Matched
0

Remembering our discussions on street addresses, let's just take the first 10 characters of the address instead of trying to match on it exactly:

```
SELECT
    COUNT(*) [# Matched]
FROM crm.NormalizedCustomer C
LEFT OUTER JOIN dbo.PotentialMatches P ON
    LEFT(C.PostalCode, 5) = LEFT(P.zip, 5)
```

```
        AND LEFT(C.Address1, 10) = LEFT(P.address, 10)
    WHERE
            C.LastName = P.last_name
        AND C.FirstName = P.first_name
        AND C.LastName = 'Snedley'
        AND C.Address1 IS NOT NULL
        AND P.address IS NOT NULL;
```

 # Matched

10

But remember what I said about data sometimes being noisy and not needed? Check it out:

```
SELECT
    COUNT(*) [Same # Matched]
FROM crm.NormalizedCustomer C
LEFT OUTER JOIN dbo.PotentialMatches P ON
    LEFT(C.PostalCode, 5) = LEFT(P.zip, 5)
    /*
        Do we even NEED address at all? Let's comment it out
        and see what happens to our row count.
    AND LEFT(C.Address1, 10) = LEFT(P.address, 10)
    */
WHERE
        C.LastName = P.last_name
    AND C.FirstName = P.first_name
    AND C.LastName = 'Snedley'
    AND C.Address1 IS NOT NULL
    AND P.address IS NOT NULL;
```

Same # Matched

10

For the purposes of this test case and this data, perhaps street address adds no value whatsoever and can be dropped from the comparisons (and ultimately, the score). However, in general having some amount of data from the street address along with the postal code is of value.

Country

Unless you are working for a multinational conglomerate and, more importantly, with international data, then country is even less useful than county, usually, and is typically incorrect or defaulted to something like "USA" (if the system is in the United States), even if the postal code is set to something that is obviously not a valid United States ZIP code. And for that matter, is it "United States," "USA," or "US"? One system I worked on had all three in the data, even though the field *had never been*

---

exposed to user input! Let that sink in for a while. (Hint: Various automated address quality vendors, data imports, and other programmatic inputs were the culprits.)

You are going to be a sad panda if you have to use country to match on in your data. As always, apply all the techniques you've learned so far: removing punctuation and spaces and perhaps normalizing everything to a two-character or three-character ISO country code (use cross-reference tables), as shown in the following example. Of course, doing that for all the countries in the world, the variants on their spelling and abbreviations will be difficult. I suggest dividing it up by country and letting people familiar with the vagaries of each do the work and then perhaps roll all the results together afterward, if that would even be meaningful.

```
SELECT TOP 10
    Country,
    CASE
        WHEN Country IN
        (
            'United States',
            'U.S.',
            'U.S.A.',
            'US',
            'USA'
        ) THEN 'US'
        ELSE Country
    END [Normalized Country]
FROM crm.NormalizedCustomer;
```

	Country	Normalized Country
0	U.S.A.	US
1	US	US
2	U.S.	US
3	United States	US
4	USA	US
5	U.S.A.	US
6	US	US
7	U.S.	US
8	United States	US
9	USA	US

Final Thoughts on Locations

You should leave this chapter understanding that when it comes to data matching, *more attributes to match against do not necessarily lead to better results!* If there is "junk data" anywhere in your production data, I am willing to bet it is in addresses. If you have postal code, do you need city? Especially if it adds a cross-check problem, such as my former coworker claiming to live in Kansas City when he did not.

Similarly, sometimes comparing whole strings is problematic. Are you sure you have the "+4" part of the ZIP code on both sides of the comparison? Are you sure they're accurate? If not, instead of writing a lot of logic like this:

> If there are nonzero "+4" parts to both postal codes, then compare them; otherwise, only use five digits.

just truncate both sides to five digits and move on! The same is true for street addresses: don't go down the route (pun) of trying to normalize out all the various street types if you can just truncate to some fairly accurate "prefix" that makes that problem disappear entirely.

Finally, be prepared to discover that many attributes in your address data are just wrong. For businesses without a large international presence, country is often wrong and also all over the place in spelling. Latitude and longitude, if filled in by a geolocation process, may still be incorrect, especially for many rural addresses where the calculated location ends up being a pin in the center of the town with their post office. What does your geolocation software do with APO/FPO military addresses? Do you even know?

In fact, anything filled in by an automated process may be suspect—country, latitude, longitude, county, the "+4" on ZIP codes—depending on the quality of the data going into it and also how the process handles all these issues. That is why I ignore all these attributes as much as possible. Even in terms of data cleansing these processes can "get in the way." If they normalize "New York" and "NYC" to "New York City," that is great for your production data but leaves us a problem if we want to match on city and the incoming data has "NYC." Again, this is why I often simply resort to the first ten characters of the normalized address and the five-digit ZIP code.

It may seem strange to think "less is more" when it comes to data, but in the case of fuzzy matching, it often is! You will understand why when you finish Chapter 10, on scoring.

## CHAPTER 5

Dates, Dates, Dates

There are three basic problems with dates:

- They are impossibly hard (*https://oreil.ly/l-ijG*).
- They can be represented by an almost infinite number of culture formats.
- Even taking all that into account, they can be misentered.

In this chapter we'll discuss all of these problems and various approaches to handling them.

Time Is Relative

Why are dates "impossibly hard"? I used to work on a CRM system that, depending on the user's locale setting, could display to an end user a birth date a day in the future or past of what the person whose nativity it represented thought was their birthday. Why? Because it didn't force all birth dates into simply a date-only format like YYYY-MM-DD. After all (thought that system's designers), you may want to capture what *time* your customer (your patient's new child?) was born. So the birth date field was of course a SQL DATETIME datatype. Obviously. Makes sense.

Except that the user interface to that system had no way of specifying the time component, or for that matter the time zone, of the birth date in mention, and so would simply record whatever was the current time and time zone for the user entering the data (and also for any system pushing data into it). Hence, if your birth date was April 1, 1990, and the person entering that into the system was on the West Coast of the United States at 4:45 p.m., then your birth time would be entered in that timestamp as 4:45PM PST (or PDT depending on the time of year, oh joy). And guess what? Anyone then viewing that date from, say, across the international date line? They will always see your birthday as April 2, 1990. "What?" I hear you shout. "*No one* thinks like that!" But that CRM system did!

That is then to say when comparing things like birth *dates* (not times), look just at the date part, huh? Hmmm..."date part"...where have I heard that one before? We don't have date of birth in our sample data, but we can check it out with SQL variables:

```
DECLARE @CustomerDOB DATETIME = '1990-04-01T12:53:49.000'
DECLARE @IncomingDOB DATE =      '1990-04-01'
SELECT
    CASE
        WHEN DATEPART(yyyy, @CustomerDOB) = DATEPART(yyyy, @IncomingDOB)
         AND DATEPART(mm,   @CustomerDOB) = DATEPART(mm,   @IncomingDOB)
         AND DATEPART(dd,   @CustomerDOB) = DATEPART(dd,   @IncomingDOB)
            THEN 'Match!'
        ELSE 'No Match!'
    END [Do They Match?];
```

Do They Match?

Match!

Or, more concisely, since we just want the year, month, and day:

```
DECLARE @CustomerDOB DATETIME = '1990-04-01T12:53:49.000'
DECLARE @IncomingDOB DATE =      '1990-04-01'
SELECT
    CASE
        WHEN YEAR(@CustomerDOB)  = YEAR(@IncomingDOB)
         AND MONTH(@CustomerDOB) = MONTH(@IncomingDOB)
         AND DAY(@CustomerDOB)   =  DAY(@IncomingDOB)
            THEN 'Match!'
        ELSE 'No Match!'
    END [Do They Match?];
```

Do They Match?

Match!

Or how about using just one logical comparison? Can we pull that off? Yes, we can!

```
DECLARE @CustomerDOB DATETIME = '1990-04-01T12:53:49.000'
DECLARE @IncomingDOB DATE =      '1990-04-01'
SELECT
    CASE
        /*
            Style #23 is ISO 8601 format YYYY-MM-DD
        */
        WHEN CONVERT(VARCHAR(50), @CustomerDOB, 23) =
             CONVERT(VARCHAR(50), @IncomingDOB, 23)
            THEN 'Match!'
```

```
        ELSE 'No Match!'
    END [Do They Match?];
```

Do They Match?
Match!

Or, if you are on a modern enough SQL Server to enjoy the DATE and TIME datatypes as opposed to being stuck with just DATETIME, then we can just "truncate" any messy timestamp and thus not have to look up what the SQL Server format number for ISO 8601 YYYY-MM-DD is in the CONVERT function. Like this:

```
DECLARE @CustomerDOB DATETIME = '1990-04-01T12:53:49.000'
DECLARE @IncomingDOB DATE =     '1990-04-01'
SELECT
    CASE
        WHEN CAST(@CustomerDOB AS DATE) = @IncomingDOB
            THEN 'Match!'
        ELSE 'No Match!'
    END [Do They Match?];
```

Do They Match?
Match!

Enough about getting two valid dates to match. How do we know if they are both valid? Presumably your customer data is in a proper database with a proper DATE or DATETIME style datatype. But the incoming data could be in any format. We've seen that SQL assignments, CAST and CONVERT, can handle a lot of different input formats such as numbers, words, and abbreviations:

```
DECLARE @CustomerDOB DATETIME = '1990-04-01T12:53:49.000'
DECLARE @IncomingDOB DATE =     'April 1, 1990'
SELECT
    CASE
        WHEN CAST(@CustomerDOB AS DATE) = CAST(@IncomingDOB AS DATE)
            THEN 'Match!'
        ELSE 'No Match!'
    END [Do They Match?];
```

Do They Match?
Match!

But remember there is also ISDATE, which can weed errors from SQL when you try to CAST it. Without it, the following code will fail with "Conversion failed when converting date and/or time from character string":

```
DECLARE @CustomerDOB DATETIME =     '1990-04-01T12:53:49.000'
DECLARE @IncomingDOB VARCHAR(50) = 'Aprool 1, 1990'     /* Misspelled */
```

```
SELECT
    CASE
        WHEN CAST(@CustomerDOB AS DATE) = CAST(@IncomingDOB AS DATE)
            THEN 'Match!'
        ELSE 'No Match!'
    END [Do They Match?];
```

So instead you can protect yourself like this:

```
DECLARE @CustomerDOB DATETIME = '1990-04-01T12:53:49.000'
DECLARE @IncomingDOB VARCHAR(50) = 'Aprool 1, 1990'
SELECT
    CASE
        WHEN ISDATE(@IncomingDOB) = 1
            AND CAST(@CustomerDOB AS DATE) = CAST(@IncomingDOB AS DATE)
            THEN 'Match!'
        ELSE 'No Match!'
    END [Do They Match?];
```

Do They Match?
No Match!

While on the subject of invalid dates, there are also cases where a date is perfectly valid as a date but invalid "semantically" in the system. My favorite example of "birth dates in the future" comes to mind. You may or may not want to check for such things, but ultimately they will be wrong on one side or the other, and hence a match won't occur. Bad data happens; sometimes it is just part of the process and why we will be scoring our matches at the end of the book. But just to show how to check for such things, here are a couple of "semantic" date checks that sometimes come in handy. We have three errors represented by different SQL variables:

@FutureDOB

Probably a data entry error, where "1990-04-01" got entered as "2990-04-01."

@TooYoungDOB

If you do not want to or can't legally do business with minors (because they can't sign a contract), it is good to have a "too young" check. In our case, it is less than 18 years old.

@HesDeadJim

Similarly, anyone over some arbitrary limit—I use 110 years old—is probably not a valid, or at least "active," customer.

```
DECLARE @FutureDOB     DATETIME = '2990-04-01' /* Oops, data entry error */
DECLARE @TooYoungDOB   DATETIME = '2020-01-20' /* Here, too              */
DECLARE @HesDeadJimDOB DATETIME = '1890-04-01' /* Probably not alive     */
```

```
/*
    Two result sets in this example: First, the various outputs of DATEDIFF.
*/
SELECT
    DATEDIFF(dd,   GETDATE(), @FutureDOB)     [DOB # Days in Future],
    DATEDIFF(yyyy, GETDATE(), @TooYoungDOB)   [DOB # Years Into Past],
    DATEDIFF(yyyy, GETDATE(), @HesDeadJimDOB) [DOB # Years Into Past];
```

DOB # Days in Future	DOB # Years Into Past	DOB # Years Into Past
353073	-3	-133

You can then use such information in various data quality checks:

```
DECLARE @FutureDOB     DATETIME = '2990-04-01'
DECLARE @TooYoungDOB   DATETIME = '2020-01-20'
DECLARE @HesDeadJimDOB DATETIME = '1890-04-01'
/*
    Then how to use those as validity checks.
*/
SELECT
    CASE
        /*
            Any positive # is in the future.
        */
        WHEN DATEDIFF(dd, GETDATE(),  @FutureDOB) > 0 THEN 'Not Born Yet!'
        ELSE 'Valid.'
    END [Is Birthday Valid?],
    CASE
        /*
            Pick an age with whom you may not legally do business - 18?
        */
        WHEN DATEDIFF(yyyy, GETDATE(), @TooYoungDOB) > -18
        THEN 'Too Young to Sign Contract!'
        ELSE 'Valid.'
    END [Is Customer Old Enough?],
    CASE
        /*
            110 years old s.b. celebrated - but are they doing biz with you?
        */
        WHEN DATEDIFF(yyyy, GETDATE(), @HesDeadJimDOB) <= -110
        THEN 'He''s Dead, Jim'
        ELSE 'Alive'
    END [Past Best By Date?];
```

Is Birthday Valid?	Is Customer Old Enough?	Past Best By Date?
Not Born Yet!	Too Young to Sign Contract!	He's Dead, Jim

Got two-year dates coming in? Be aware of SQL Server's windowing on DATEs: currently the cutoff is 2049 (years less than "49" are presumed in the 21st century while any "50" or over represent the 20th century), as demonstrated in the following example. (This cutoff can be changed using sp_configure; for details, see the SQL Server documentation: *https://oreil.ly/8LD46*.)

```
SELECT
    YEAR('04-01-00') [04-01-00],
    YEAR('04-01-20') [04-01-20],
    YEAR('04-01-40') [04-01-40],
    YEAR('04-01-49') [04-01-49],
    YEAR('04-01-50') [04-01-50],
    YEAR('04-01-60') [04-01-60],
    YEAR('04-01-80') [04-01-80];
```

04-01-00	04-01-20	04-01-40	04-01-49	04-01-50	04-01-60	04-01-80
2000	2020	2040	2049	1950	1960	1980

Need a different "window" and don't want to (or can't) override SQL Server's settings? Let's say we're bringing in mortgage maturity dates and we know in advance they are all in this century:

```
DECLARE @MortgageMaturity DATE = '04-01-80'
SELECT
    @MortgageMaturity [As Imported],
    CASE
        WHEN YEAR(@MortgageMaturity) < 2000
            THEN DATEADD(yyyy, 100, @MortgageMaturity)
        ELSE @MortgageMaturity
    END [Actual Maturity Date];
```

As Imported	Actual Maturity Date
1980-04-01	2080-04-01

Final Thoughts on Dates

Human beings sure are fond of dates and times, despite both being imaginary constructs, and business and science like to collect a lot of them. Moreover, even taking relativistic effects out of the equation (ahem), dates and times are subject to a variety of distortions, including in their syntactic expressions, even within the same culture. Consider that the average adult in a business setting in the United States can successfully parse or puzzle out all of the following as the same date:

- 4/1/2023
- 04/01/2023
- 04-01-2023

- 04/01/23
- 2023-04-01
- 2023-04-01T00:00:00Z
- 20230401
- April 1, 2023
- April First, Two Thousand Twenty Three
- Best by APR 01 23
- April Fool's!

SQL conversions can help with some of those, but not all of them. Then there is always invalid data. Does your user interface catch the month and day swapped? Do the systems integrations into your system catch that in CSVs and other representations where the date is just a string? Internationalization makes this hard problem even harder! Can you tell the difference when someone used to European date formats entered "1/4/2023" instead of "4/1/2023"? Note that *both* are valid dates in *either* representation, so how can you tell?

Checking for "impossible data" on dates often yields results. I recommend doing so, especially if the reason you are doing the matching is for a systems migration. The new system may have stricter standards on things like dates than your current system, so it is good to get that data cleaned up as soon as possible.

Sometimes, like with names, it may not be worth a data quality effort; they are what they are. With something hard like addresses, there are companies that sell address cleansing and normalization software and services; if you can afford it, use one of them (just don't trust their latitude and longitude results!). But with dates often just some simple "sanity checks" will expose the easiest problems. You can "surface" those types of tests in a weekly report so the data stays clean on an ongoing basis even beyond the work you are doing for the matching at hand. A double win!

It is easy for a human to look at "J1m L3#m3R" and know that's not a valid name—yet. Maybe some hacker somewhere named their kid something like that for fun. But it is much, much harder for either a human or a system to look at a perfectly formatted date and know whether it is "semantically valid" for the given application. Birth dates in the future are rarely valid for most systems (I am sure there are exceptions). But sometimes the errors can be more subtle.

Take a loan billing date. Many systems default or require those dates to always be at the first of the month for ease of interest calculations, mass mailings, and so on. So, "4/1/2023" is a perfectly fine date for that attribute in that system, but "4/2/2023," while a valid date, is not. Do you know the various business limits placed on your date fields? What if another system is importing data into your system and their business restrictions are different? How do you handle that?

Finally, we learned early in this chapter that time as a data component to match against is rarely helpful and usually gets in the way. This is another example of not necessarily wanting all the data you can get your hands on. Sometimes it is better to truncate or round dates, too. Is it necessary to match on "Customer since 4/1/2023," or is "Customer since 2023" good enough?

This is even more true when trying to match something like log files between two systems for forensics. Even with a uniform synchronized time source that both systems use, there can be "clock drift" between the two. Plus there is the network and processing latency of two systems communicating across a rack backplane or across the planet on the internet to consider, and that varies from event to event (some transactions take longer than others). Even in something as seemingly "precise" as matching events across the logs of two systems, you need to get "fuzzy!"

One approach is to find an average latency for an event to complete between the two systems and then look for matches within something like *2x* of that length to be safe. For example, you can check using DATEDIFF and a date part parameter of milli second (or synonyms ms as here) to look for events within one second of each other, which would be a good safe window if your average latency for events between the two systems was something like 500ms:

```
DECLARE @Sys1Event1Time DATETIME = '2023-04-01T00:00:01.123Z'
DECLARE @Sys2Event1Time DATETIME = '2023-04-01T00:00:02.004Z'
DECLARE @Sys1Event2Time DATETIME = '2023-04-01T00:00:03.734Z'
DECLARE @Sys2Event2Time DATETIME = '2023-04-01T00:00:05.898Z'
SELECT
  DATEDIFF(ms, @Sys1Event1Time, @Sys2Event1Time) [Event 1 Time Δ in ms],
  CASE
    WHEN  DATEDIFF(ms, @Sys1Event1Time, @Sys2Event1Time) <= 1000 THEN 'Maybe?'
    ELSE 'Not the Same Event!'
  END [Sys1 and Sys2 Events #1 Correlated?],
  DATEDIFF(ms, @Sys1Event2Time, @Sys2Event2Time) [Event 2 Time Δ in ms],
  CASE
    WHEN  DATEDIFF(ms, @Sys1Event2Time, @Sys2Event2Time) <= 1000 THEN 'Maybe?'
    ELSE 'Not the Same Event!'
  END [Sys1 and Sys2 Events #2 Correlated?];
```

Event 1 Time Δ in ms	Sys1 and Sys2 Events #1 Correlated?	Event 2 Time Δ in ms	Sys1 and Sys2 Events #2 Correlated?
880	Maybe?	2163	Not the Same Event!

Note the question mark in the result. That's to remind us that being outside that latency window may prove it is *not* the same event, but being inside it does not prove it *is*! Loosen up! Remind yourself to be "fuzzy" once in a while!

## CHAPTER 6

Email

Everyone hates email, but now that use of Social Security numbers for data matching is (rightly) becoming scarce, I lean on email addresses fairly heavily. Why? While everyone hates email, everyone tends to have at least one email address, and with few exceptions they tend to be unique (I have an aunt and uncle who share an email address, and that happens, but it is rare). Along with mobile phone numbers, if you have a match on email, your likelihood of a false positive is small.

What Makes a Valid Email Address?

One thing that can throw off matching on email addresses is that Gmail allows optional periods on the recipient side, but their presence or absence makes no difference to Google! Hence, to Gmail, but not to most software:

mortimer.snedley@gmail.com = mortimersnedley@gmail.com

How do you handle this? Remove the periods, of course:

```
SELECT
    COUNT(*) [Exact Email Matches]
FROM crm.NormalizedCustomer C
INNER JOIN dbo.PotentialMatches P ON
    REPLACE(C.Email, '.', '') = REPLACE(P.email, '.', '');
```

Exact Email Matches
39

If you read all the requests for comments (RFCs) on email addresses (and there are a lot of them), you will come to the conclusion that most attempts to validate email addresses on data entry are misguided. Email addresses can contain almost any character, and any format you think they require is probably mistaken. However, valid email addresses do need to contain two specific characters: an @ to separate the delivery address from the domain and at least one . to separate the top-level domain (TLD) from the rest of the domain name (the domain name can have subdomains separated by multiple periods, but there has to be at least one period).

You would think you may want to add this check (if you do add it, do so before you normalize out all the punctuation):

```
SELECT
    email [Invalid Address]
FROM dbo.PotentialMatches
WHERE
    0 IN (CHARINDEX('@', email), CHARINDEX('.', email));
```

Invalid Address
dkines@examplecom

It can be useful to cleanse the dataset before the import. Note that in the following example we drop a row from the prior matches by eliminating the invalid ID. However, for our purposes, was that the right thing to do? Only you can decide.

```
SELECT
    COUNT(*) [Exact Email Matches]
FROM crm.NormalizedCustomer C
INNER JOIN dbo.PotentialMatches P ON
    REPLACE(C.Email, '.', '') = REPLACE(P.email, '.', '')
WHERE
    /*
        This presumes your customer data is clean and only
        looks at the import.
    */
    0 NOT IN (CHARINDEX('@', P.email), CHARINDEX('.', P.email));
```

Exact Email Matches
38

Ultimately, normalize the two and just hope for the best! Speaking of normalizing, email addresses can have a lot of other punctuation in them; you may want to replace all of the following characters:

```
SELECT
    COUNT(*) [Exact Email Matches]
FROM crm.NormalizedCustomer C
INNER JOIN dbo.PotentialMatches P ON
    REPLACE
    (
        TRANSLATE(C.Email, '@."<>,', '        '), ' ', ''
    ) = REPLACE(TRANSLATE(P.email, '@."<>,', '        '), ' ', '')
```

```
WHERE
    0 NOT IN (CHARINDEX('@', P.email), CHARINDEX('.', P.email));
```

Exact Email Matches

38

You may have multiple email address fields on a customer record in your data. My advice is to match against all of them, because as with phone numbers, people have multiple email addresses and often enter them in the wrong box (putting their home email in the work email address field, or their mobile number in their "home" number because who has land lines anymore?). We have only one email address in our test dataset, so I will demonstrate it here with SQL variables:

```
DECLARE @HomeEmail     VARCHAR(50) = 'mortimer.snedley@example.com'
DECLARE @WorkEmail     VARCHAR(50) = 'mortimer.snedley.jr@snedley.test'
DECLARE @IncomingEmail VARCHAR(50) = 'mortimer.snedley.jr@snedley.test'
SELECT
    CASE
        /*
            Test incoming against both home and work email columns.
        */
        WHEN @IncomingEmail IN (@HomeEmail, @WorkEmail) THEN 'Match!'
        ELSE 'No Match!'
    END [Did The Incoming Email Match?];
```

Did The Incoming Email Match?

Match!

Final Thoughts on Email

I find that validation—that is, checking that an email address is syntactically correct—is a black hole and not worth the time, at least not for fuzzy data matching. If you are a data steward for customer demographic data, your view may be different.

Getting a match on an email address is usually a Good Thing. However, the converse of *not* getting a match doesn't mean it's *not* the same person! Consider the following:

- Gmail allows adding a + and then additional text to the right side of your email address to use to help filter replies (and figure out who sold your name to a marketing list). For example, *mortimer.snedley+amazon@gmail.com* is a fine Gmail address. It is a fairly rare practice, so do you care? Do you even want to test for such things? I don't, but I bring it up, because normalizing that email address will leave "mortimersnedleyamazongmailcom," which is not going to match your customer (unless you're Amazon). If you are going to cleanse such things, you would want to remove everything from the plus sign to the right, but only in Gmail addresses.

- Gmail also allows adding any number of arbitrary dots (or removing all of them). *mortimersnedley@gmail.com*, *mortimer.snedley@gmail.com*, and *mort.imer.sned .ley@gmail.com* are all valid and point to the same address. Some people again use that to keep track of who has what email address, and again, I don't check for it (and normalizing the email address will make it moot, anyway).

- There are temporary email address services that create "throwaway" email inboxes precisely for such things as product registrations, etc. You may have a completely valid email address that the customer used once to obfuscate against your knowing more about them (after all, they just wanted to enter that drawing for a game console!).

- There *are* people who share an email address. It's rare, but it does occur, especially in households where because of age, tech-savvy, language skills, or whatever, one person is "taking care of business" for both and using the same email address for both. We will see that this can also occur with mobile phone numbers. These can cause "duplicate matches." We will see how to handle those later.

- You may have their home email address and they gave their work address, or vice versa. Or someone simply entered the wrong one in the wrong field. It happens.

In the end, email is a good field for fuzzy matching if you have it, but it is not a panacea. It is just one more attribute adding to our certainty.

## CHAPTER 7

Phone Numbers

With the death of using tax IDs for most data matching (we will talk a bit about them at the end of this chapter), phone numbers, especially mobile phone numbers, are about as close to being a publicly available unique identifier as we'll ever be able to access. Yes, like email addresses, some people share phone numbers, but the percentage is small and, with the ongoing expansion of mobile phone use, dwindling.

We will look at various issues with phone numbers, including formatting (of course), lack of information (area code, country code), too much information (notes tacked on the end of the number), and the fact that there sure are a lot of them. Does anyone still have a pager? Should you check against it? Let's talk about all of that!

What Makes a "Phone Number"?

By this point you should recognize the drill. If you think about a field or fields you're trying to match on for more than a few seconds, you can immediately start to think of things that will get in the way of that. Phone numbers are no exception. Consider the following:

- (800) 555-1234
- +1 (800) 555-1234
- 800-555-1234
- 1-800-555-1234
- 8005551234
- 18005551234
- (800) 555-1234 Ext. 67 (How does your data handle extensions? How does the incoming data represent it?)

- 8005551234,,67 (Many modern mobile phones and phone systems still understand and can dial old-style modem "AT commands," in this case to pause a few seconds after connecting to (800) 555-1234 and then dial 67.)

- 555-555-1234 Aunt Judy's # (Phone fields in many systems are freeform text, so things like this will start creeping into your data. This is common when there is a simple fixed set of fields or a drop-down list for "phone number type" to denote home, mobile, work, etc. The problem is that your users don't categorize their thoughts about their data in the same way you do. So it would be typical to see something like this with a phone number type selected of "Other." They had to capture that extra info somehow!)

Note that doesn't even delve into whether there are valid country codes, area codes, exchanges, and the like in any of these examples!

Mostly we can just normalize a phone number as usual. We have some new characters we may have to remove (that +, for one), but you know how to do that. If anything, that "Ext. 67" should give you pause, as should the country code on the front of some (but not all!) of the numbers. Those country codes (leading "1" or "+1" in this case) keep us from just using a brute-force "take the first 10 characters using LEFT after normalizing and be done" approach. If you are *sure* your data doesn't have it, the "take the first 10 characters using LEFT after normalizing and be done" approach is what you want to do. Let's use a SQL variable to see how to normalize a phone number that is not necessarily pathological (I see stuff like this in phone fields all the time). I have broken out each function so each is easier to read "from the inside out":

```
/*
    Lots of non-numeric junk in this one.
*/
DECLARE @PhoneNumber VARCHAR(50) = '(800) 555-1234 Ext. 67'
SELECT
    /*
        Take the LEFTmost 10
    */
    LEFT
    (
        /*
            After REPLACE-ing all spaces with empty strings
        */
        REPLACE
        (
            /*
                After TRANSLATE-ing "impossible" characters to spaces.
            */
            TRANSLATE
            (
                @PhoneNumber,
                '() -.,+#ABCDEFGHIJKLMNOPQRSTUVWXYZ',  /* From these */
```

```
                            '              '   /* to spaces */
            ),
            ' ', ''
        ),
        10
    ) [Normalized Phone #];
```

```
Normalized Phone #
```
8005551234

Note that if you find keeping track of all those spaces in the TRANSLATE hard, you can use another character—something improbable, like the caret (^):

```
DECLARE @PhoneNumber VARCHAR(50) = '(800) 555-1234 Ext. 67'
SELECT
    LEFT
    (
        REPLACE
        (
            TRANSLATE
            (
                @PhoneNumber,
                '() -.,+#ABCDEFGHIJKLMNOPQRSTUVWXYZ',  /* From these */
                '^^^^^^^^^^^^^^^^^^^^^^^^^^^^^^^^^^^'   /* to carets  */
            ),
            '^', ''                                    /* Use ^ here */
        ),
        10
    ) [Normalized Phone #];
```

```
Normalized Phone #
```
8005551234

But what about those pesky country codes? If it's just 1s for the United States and Canada, you have it pretty easy:

```
DECLARE @NormalizedPhone VARCHAR(50) = '18005551234'
SELECT
    CASE
        WHEN LEFT(@NormalizedPhone, 1) = '1' AND LEN(@NormalizedPhone) > 9
            /* Take just 10 digits, which will drop off extensions, too. */
            THEN SUBSTRING(@NormalizedPhone, 2, 10)
        ELSE @NormalizedPhone
    END [Leading 1 Removed];
```

```
Leading 1 Removed
```
8005551234

"But wait!" you splutter. "I live in England" (that's why you can splutter in English, and for that matter splutter at all), "and my country code is 44." Ah, indeed—a problem. Once we get to where we aren't looking for a leading "1," it gets tricky. How do you know whether you are looking at a one-, two-, or three-digit country code? (There are longer ones, but they all start with "1.")

Well, how good is the data? After normalizing it, can you trust the length to only be the phone number and possibly a country code? Then you could just do a RIGHT and take off what you need. But now you have another problem—different countries have different phone number lengths, so how do you know how much you need? You may end up with a gigantic CASE to try to handle it all.

Yet don't forget our previous example. Instead of a toll-free number, maybe we have a San Diego phone number. And it also has an extension. Hmmm....

```
DECLARE @PhoneNumber VARCHAR(50) = '(442) 555-1234 Ext. 67'
SELECT
    /*
       After replacing all carets with empty strings
    */
    REPLACE
    (
        TRANSLATE
        (
            @PhoneNumber,
            '() -.,+#ABCDEFGHIJKLMNOPQRSTUVWXYZ',
            '^^^^^^^^^^^^^^^^^^^^^^^^^^^^^^^^^^^'
        ), '^', ''
    ) [Normalized Phone #];
```

Normalized Phone #
442555123467

Pray, how can thee tell that this number is a San Diego number, and not something with a 44 country code for England? Bwa-hahahaha! You cannot! So what to do? I don't know; it depends on your data. If the situation is only a few records out of hundreds, thousands, or millions, then handle them manually or have end users clean up the data (harder than it sounds). If it is a much larger problem, you may have to get creative. That *Country* field I dismissed in "Country" on page 88 may come in handy after all!

Another thing: like with physical addresses (home, mailing, billing) and email addresses (home and work), you are likely to have multiple phone numbers for your customers. My recommendation is to match the incoming phone number to all of them (yes, including fax and pager if you have the fields in your customer data and there's any data in those columns!). And if the incoming data has multiple phone fields, I still recommend doing an *m:n* match between them all. You will almost

always find more hits that way, trust me. *No one* enters phone numbers correctly! The
following is not that uncommon of a scenario:

```
SELECT
    (SELECT
        COUNT(*)
     FROM crm.NormalizedCustomer C
     INNER JOIN dbo.PotentialMatches P ON
         REPLACE(TRANSLATE(C.HomePhone, '() -.,+#', '^^^^^^^^'), '^', '') =
         REPLACE(TRANSLATE(P.phone1, '() -.,+#', '^^^^^^^^'), '^', '')
    ) [Home Phone = phone1],
    (SELECT
        COUNT(*)
     FROM crm.NormalizedCustomer C
     INNER JOIN dbo.PotentialMatches P ON
         REPLACE(TRANSLATE(C.HomePhone, '() -.,+#', '^^^^^^^^'), '^', '') =
         REPLACE(TRANSLATE(P.phone2, '() -.,+#', '^^^^^^^^'), '^', '')
    ) [Home Phone = phone2],
    (SELECT
        COUNT(*)
     FROM crm.NormalizedCustomer C
     INNER JOIN dbo.PotentialMatches P ON
         REPLACE(TRANSLATE(C.MobilePhone, '() -.,+#', '^^^^^^^^'), '^', '') =
         REPLACE(TRANSLATE(P.phone1, '() -.,+#', '^^^^^^^^'), '^', '')
    ) [Mobile Phone = phone1],
    (SELECT
        COUNT(*)
     FROM crm.NormalizedCustomer C
     INNER JOIN dbo.PotentialMatches P ON
         REPLACE(TRANSLATE(C.MobilePhone, '() -.,+#', '^^^^^^^^'), '^', '') =
         REPLACE(TRANSLATE(P.phone2, '() -.,+#', '^^^^^^^^'), '^', '')
    ) [Mobile Phone = phone2];
```

Home Phone = phone1	Home Phone = phone2	Mobile Phone = phone1	Mobile Phone = phone2
24	67	40	32

How to tell at the end how many distinct matches you may have? (For example,
sometimes people enter their mobile number in both the home number and mobile
number fields.)

```
SELECT
    COUNT(*) [# Customers Matched By Phone]
FROM
(
    SELECT
        C.LastName [Last Name],
        C.FirstName [First Name],
        C.HomePhone [Matched Phone #]
    FROM crm.NormalizedCustomer C
    INNER JOIN dbo.PotentialMatches P ON
        REPLACE(TRANSLATE(C.HomePhone, '() -.,+#', '^^^^^^^^'), '^', '') =
```

```
        REPLACE(TRANSLATE(P.phone1, '() -.,+#', '^^^^^^^^'), '^', '')
    UNION       /* UNIONs drop dups without the "ALL" */
    SELECT
        C.LastName [Last Name],
        C.FirstName [First Name],
        C.HomePhone [Matched Phone #]
    FROM crm.NormalizedCustomer C
    INNER JOIN dbo.PotentialMatches P ON
        REPLACE(TRANSLATE(C.HomePhone, '() -.,+#', '^^^^^^^^'), '^', '') =
        REPLACE(TRANSLATE(P.phone2, '() -.,+#', '^^^^^^^^'), '^', '')
    UNION
    SELECT
        C.LastName [Last Name],
        C.FirstName [First Name],
        C.HomePhone [Matched Phone #]
    FROM crm.NormalizedCustomer C
    INNER JOIN dbo.PotentialMatches P ON
        REPLACE(TRANSLATE(C.MobilePhone, '() -.,+#', '^^^^^^^^'), '^', '') =
        REPLACE(TRANSLATE(P.phone1, '() -.,+#', '^^^^^^^^'), '^', '')
    UNION
    SELECT
        C.LastName [Last Name],
        C.FirstName [First Name],
        C.HomePhone [Matched Phone #]
    FROM crm.NormalizedCustomer C
    INNER JOIN dbo.PotentialMatches P ON
        REPLACE(TRANSLATE(C.MobilePhone, '() -.,+#', '^^^^^^^^'), '^', '') =
        REPLACE(TRANSLATE(P.phone2, '() -.,+#', '^^^^^^^^'), '^', '')
) A;
```

Customers Matched By Phone
26

Note that result is different than any of the four counts we got individually (and is typical in my experience).

What about extensions? If they are in the phone number itself, I usually just ignore them using LEFT. You may have well-formed data schemas, and *Extension* may be its own field in your customer data. Personally, I have never found extensions useful for matching, so I usually truncate them away. Your needs may vary. If you do need to parse extensions out, check out the section on getting suffixes out of surname fields (see page 63).

One Final Note on Tax IDs

Social Security numbers are getting rarer and rarer in datasets and for good reason. However, if you do end up having tax IDs in your data on both sides of the attempted match, then many of the same issues covered by phone numbers apply. For example, are your SSNs formatted "555-55-5555" or "555555555"? You know what to do there. But what about obfuscation, also known as *masking*, where one side or the other has something like "***-**-5555"? In that case you can simply do something like the following, which uses SQL variables to emulate columns between the two datasets:

```
DECLARE @CustomerSSN VARCHAR(50) = '555-55-5555'
DECLARE @InputSSN    VARCHAR(50) = '***-**-5555'
SELECT
    CASE
        WHEN RIGHT(@CustomerSSN, 4) = RIGHT(@InputSSN, 4) THEN 'Match!'
        ELSE 'No Match!'
    END [Do They Match?];
```

Do They Match?
Match!

 You will get many more false positives on this given that there will be only 10,000 unique possibilities within four digits. I rarely see tax IDs come in on an external list to match against anymore, so it just isn't that much of an issue, but if you have to use an obfuscated ID, keep it in mind.

When Identifiers Don't Identify

There are some religious groups in the United States that are exempted from the Social Security Act due to their beliefs. If they do business with you and your customer system requires entering a Social Security number, you may find that your users are entering "999999999." And also "111111111." And also "123456789." How will you know? I look for such things explicitly in the data, usually with something similar to this:

```
SELECT * FROM Customer
-- Unlikely tax id numbers.
WHERE ssn IN ('000000000', '111111111', '222222222',
              '333333333', '444444444', '555555555',
              '666666666', '777777777', '888888888',
              '999999999', '123456789', '111223333');
```

If your company has conventions around such things, like "Always use '999999999,'" that's great. But I wouldn't trust it and would still look for the others. At the end of the day it isn't necessarily worth filtering those out ahead of time—the lack of a match will be enough.

There is a Social Security Administration algorithm for detecting valid SSNs, but it's easier to go for the obvious ones and move on.

Final Thoughts on Phone Numbers (and Tax IDs)

The "one-trick pony" of this whole book continues to be normalization, and the same is true here (there will be some new tricks in the later chapters of the book, I promise). Phone numbers are a great thing to have, and if you match on them, you can almost (almost!) throw all the other attributes away. Good luck with that.

If your production data is coming from a CRM system, then likely the phone numbers may be very "loose" and you will have some data quality issues even on the production side. You will need to clean that up. This doesn't have to be in the CRM system itself (data owners can get touchy about such things), but it can be in the extracted copy of the data you are working with.

Phone numbers and tax IDs have valid, well-known lengths, and it is worth checking them before even attempting to match. Tax IDs are especially susceptible to the "dropped leading 0s" problem you can see when importing data feeds from CSVs and the like. Be careful about that. Review the example on padding with RIGHT in Chapter 2.

Tax IDs may be obfuscated, increasing the number of false positives if you try to match on them. Similarly, phone numbers can be incomplete. Unless you're a very small business in a very small locale with only a single area code (rare, anymore!), you will want more than "555-1234" scribbled on that contest entry form. You will want more, but that may be all you get. This problem is similar to the obfuscated tax ID one in that you can still attempt some matching on the shortened value (e.g., by ignoring all area codes, at least when one side or the other is missing it). Of course, that then increases the risk of false positive matches. You can decide if that is necessary when you get to scoring. See Chapter 10. Many of the nuances in this work end up being business decisions, not technology ones.

Finally, both phone numbers and tax IDs may have "unreal data" in them. Consider the tax ID example for handling people without one. Similarly, many systems require a phone number to be entered. It is rare, but there are still people out there who don't have a phone. How is your system handling that? Do you know what your users are entering? A few "sniff" tests often bring up some surprises.

But then, without surprises there would be no need for fuzziness.

## CHAPTER 8

Bad Characters

How often do you think about letters? Numbers? Punctuation? Whitespace? Character encoding? Character sets? Collation sequences? The differences between CHAR and VARCHAR and NVARCHAR and TEXT? If you are used to working with textual data, then maybe a lot. However, many people, even those working every day with SQL or other programming languages, don't think about such things until forced to. Let's force ourselves to, a little, because it matters to fuzzy data matching, especially the incoming data.

Data Representations

There are many ways you can receive the incoming data, but typically if it is from an external entity, it is probably going to end up coming in as follows:

A "flat file"
> A comma-separated values (CSV) file or other simple delimited format like tab or | delimiters (all very common, but CSV is by far the most common)

Excel
> Not as frequent

XML
> Especially from vendors

JSON
> Ditto

Proprietary or standardized formats
> HL7 for health, M13 for crop insurance, and so on

If you're lucky, you will get a schema or doc describing the fields, their formats, the acceptable data ranges, etc. Often you just have to crack open the file and look at the column names and the data. For our purposes we'll presume we are receiving a CSV file.

How that CSV file gets into your database server so you can compare it against your customer data is another story. Are you responsible for doing it, or is it someone else with the appropriate privileges? If the latter, it is important because import choices may get made that will affect you, the downstream consumer of that data. Consider the Azure Data Studio import wizard screen shown in Figure 8-1.

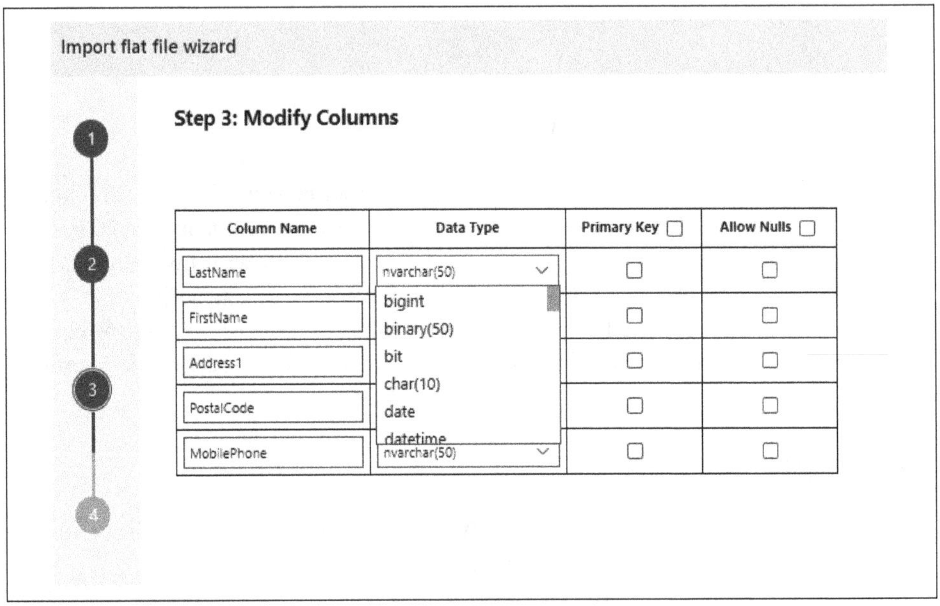

Figure 8-1. Azure Data Studio import wizard screen

SQL Server Management Studio offers similar functionality, as do many other tools (see Figure 8-2).

In our example, both tools sample the incoming data and try to make some intelligent choices about it. First it detects the column names from the header row in the import data (if any), as shown in *Column Name* in the ADS import wizard and *Destination* in SSMS. These column names can be overridden to local standards as you want. The next choices present some problems.

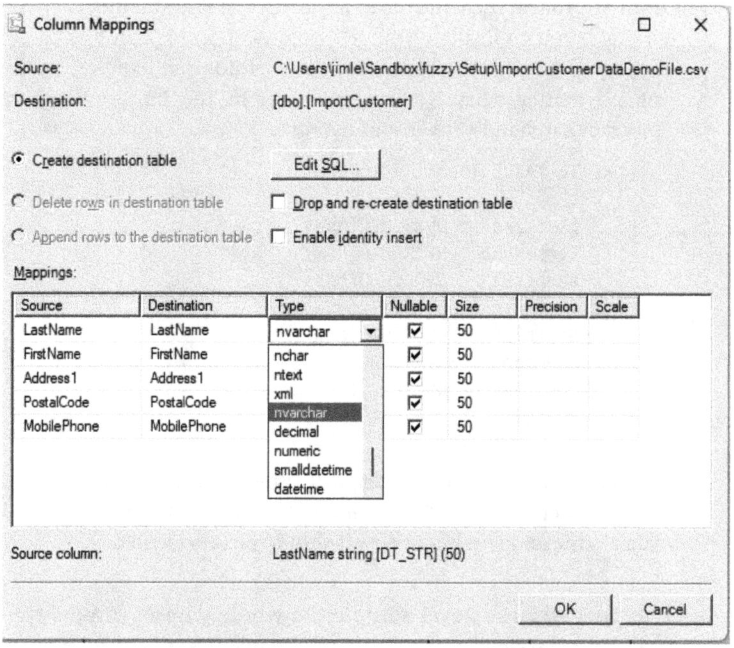

Figure 8-2. SSMS import wizard screen

Data Type (*Type* in the SSMS example) is a prime example of choices that are made, first by the tool and then perhaps by the person using the tool, that can have material impact on how easy or hard it is to work with the imported data downstream. In most cases, the default is something like NVARCHAR(50). This is usually safe enough. But in some cases the data may be padded on the right with spaces, or the person picks the CHAR datatype, and now you will have to be doing RTRIM or TRIM on everything to get it in sync with your presumably VARCHAR or NVARCHAR customer data (if you have the CHAR datatype in the customer data, you're already used to working with it).

Note, too, that sometimes the import wizard will intuit something from the data that isn't true. While not in our data, we know from prior discussions the tool may want to make something like *zip* or *taxid* an INT because it correctly detects the column contains all numeric values. As we have seen, we then have to work around that, and it is almost certainly not what you want. But that doesn't stop systems from doing it anyway. ZIP codes, tax IDs, phone numbers—I've seen them all represented as numeric datatypes! For all such things that may come in represented as "simple numbers" but actually are strings with positional components that can't be dropped, you want to make sure you override the datatype to something like NVARCHAR(50) to match the others.

It is hard to test the data ahead of time while it is still in a CSV file, so it is better to insulate yourself from it upon import. I often call setting up an import table as follows a "plutonium handler," meaning no matter what is thrown at you in the import data, the importer can handle it without dying:

```
CREATE TABLE ImportCustomer
(
      LastName    NVARCHAR(MAX),
      FirstName   NVARCHAR(MAX),
      Address     NVARCHAR(MAX),
      City        NVARCHAR(MAX),
      State       NVARCHAR(MAX),
      ZIPCode     NVARCHAR(MAX),
      MobilePhone NVARCHAR(MAX),
      Email       NVARCHAR(MAX)
)
```

You can then ETL out of *ImportCustomer* into a more rational schema after you have done some EDA and convinced yourself the data is sane and you know how it should be represented.

Also note, these import wizards never sample the whole dataset (unless the dataset is smaller than their sample size—typically 1,000 rows). You could have a column defined as NVARCHAR(50) where later data causes the import to fail because the data for that field is longer than the column definition. For a simple one-off import, the fix is simple: increase the number or do something like VARCHAR(MAX) and retry. But if you have set up a table already and are doing periodic imports into it, the first may work, but a later file days or months later may fail, and you have an ALTER TABLE in your future. This is why if you can get a schema for the import file from the beginning and make sure the target import table is defined to accommodate its data, you will be happier.

You can check the file's character encoding with various tools, but the safest bet is to choose NVARCHAR (SQL's Unicode VARCHAR datatype) to allow the most flexibility in receiving and correctly interpreting the incoming data.

As for the *Primary Key* column, I usually never mark anything as the primary key, even if assured by the vendor. For one, I may be bringing in data from multiple sources, and there could be collisions violating uniqueness. I also almost always turn on *Allow Nulls* for all columns, even if the source of the data and my own visual check says there won't be any in a given column. I would rather the import be successful and deal with anomalies in the data via SQL than have to deal with data cleanup at the file level. You may feel differently.

Invisible Whitespace

Say what? I mean, "whitespace" is already invisible, right? But guess what? The TRIM family of functions has a different view of what whitespace is than perhaps you think coming from another programming language. The SQL Server documentation (*https://oreil.ly/gXEhi*) for LTRIM says:

> Removes space character char(32) or other specified characters from the start of a string.

Catch that? If you are used to TRIM in another language removing tabs and other whitespace characters, the default behavior of SQL's TRIM will surprise you! Let's say the data import file was poorly formed and a tab character snuck into one of the data fields, maybe as an extra delimiter (it happens). We will fake it with a SQL variable here:

```
/*
    CHAR(9) is the ASCII code for a TAB character
*/
DECLARE @FirstName VARCHAR(50) = CHAR(9) + CHAR(9) + 'Mortimer'
/*
    Show that there is whitespace even after TRIM
*/
SELECT
    '''' + @FirstName + ''''          [Before TRIM],
    '''' + TRIM(@FirstName) + '''' [After TRIM (Wha?)];
```

Before TRIM	After TRIM (Wha?)
' Mortimer'	' Mortimer'

So, to get rid of something like that leading tab, we need to specify what we want trimmed. However, the behavior to do that is new with SQL Server 2022, so you will probably not be allowed to use TRIM. That's a bummer. We could use our friend TRANSLATE to get everything we don't like into a space character and then do a TRIM on that:

```
DECLARE @FirstName VARCHAR(50) = CHAR(9) + CHAR(9) + 'Mortimer'
SELECT
    '''' + @FirstName + '''' [Before TRIM],
    /*
        Translate any TAB (CHAR(9)) characters to spaces, then TRIM.
    */
    '''' + TRIM(TRANSLATE(@FirstName, CHAR(9), ' ')) + '''' [After TRIM];
```

Before TRIM	After TRIM
' Mortimer'	'Mortimer'

That's better, but it doesn't really scale, because Unicode comprises 149,186 characters and 25 of those are considered whitespace (*https://oreil.ly/PXrK1*), with another six considered similar characters (e.g., a "zero-width space" is not considered whitespace, but I have encountered it in data as a word separator!). Switching to an "em" space, for example, we would have to use `CHAR(8195)` instead (the decimal representing the character for the "em" space):

```
/*
    Now with a leading em space to show we're outside of ASCII range
*/
DECLARE @FirstName NVARCHAR(50) = NCHAR(8195) + 'Mortimer'
SELECT
    '''' + @FirstName + ''''                                    [Before TRIM],
    '''' + TRIM(TRANSLATE(@FirstName, NCHAR(8195), N' ')) + '''' [After TRIM];
```

Before TRIM	After TRIM
' Mortimer'	'Mortimer'

So, your `TRANSLATE` and `TRIM` would have to look something like this to be complete:

```
DECLARE @FirstName NVARCHAR(50) = NCHAR(8195) + 'Mortimer'
SELECT
    '''' + @FirstName + '''' [Before TRIM],
    '''' + TRIM(TRANSLATE(@FirstName,
            /*
                31 "space-like" characters
            */
            NCHAR(9)   +  /* HT    */
            NCHAR(10)  +  /* LF    */
            NCHAR(11)  +  /* VT    */
            NCHAR(12)  +  /* FF    */
            NCHAR(13)  +  /* CR    */
            NCHAR(32)  +  /* Space */
            NCHAR(133) +  /* NEL   */
            /*
                See Unicode ref for rest
            */
            NCHAR(160)  +
            NCHAR(5760) +
            NCHAR(6158) +
            NCHAR(8192) +
            NCHAR(8193) +
            NCHAR(8194) +
            NCHAR(8195) +
            NCHAR(8196) +
            NCHAR(8197) +
            NCHAR(8198) +
            NCHAR(8199) +
            NCHAR(8200) +
            NCHAR(8201) +
```

```
NCHAR(8202)  +
NCHAR(8203)  +
NCHAR(8204)  +
NCHAR(8205)  +
NCHAR(8232)  +
NCHAR(8233)  +
NCHAR(8239)  +
NCHAR(8287)  +
NCHAR(8288)  +
NCHAR(12288) +
NCHAR(65279),
/*
    31 UNICODE spaces to translate to (note "N").
*/
N'                              ')) +
'''' [After TRIM (Unicode!)];
```

Before TRIM	After TRIM (Unicode!)
' Mortimer'	'Mortimer'

Given I don't often deal with internationalized data, I don't bother with all that, but you have to understand your data needs and know such techniques exist. Also note that the previous example translates *embedded* space-like characters into spaces, which the REPLACE will then remove. However, I find that approach generally satisfactory, because often such characters are a leftover of the wonky source of the import data, like a table in a Word document or HTML page copied into an Excel spreadsheet and then imported into SQL Server. You're lucky it works at all!

Later, when you're wanting to normalize that data and get rid of those embedded spaces, you'll be happy they are all spaces.

COLLATE

SQL supports a lot of collations (sort orders, used for not just ORDER BY but determining < and > and <>, too). They are language, locale, and character set aware and can specify case sensitivity as well. Let's look, using SQL Server's built-in fn_help collations function:

```
SELECT COUNT(*) [How Many Collations?] FROM fn_helpcollations();
```

How Many Collations?
5508

Let's look at a few:

```
SELECT TOP 10
    name [Collation Name],
```

```
        description [Collation Description]
    FROM fn_helpcollations();
```

	Collation Name	Collation Description
0	Albanian_BIN	Albanian, binary sort
1	Albanian_BIN2	Albanian, binary code point comparison sort
2	Albanian_CI_AI	Albanian, case-insensitive, accent-insensitive, kanatype-insensitive, width-insensitive
3	Albanian_CI_AI_WS	Albanian, case-insensitive, accent-insensitive, kanatype-insensitive, width-sensitive
4	Albanian_CI_AI_KS	Albanian, case-insensitive, accent-insensitive, kanatype-sensitive, width-insensitive
5	Albanian_CI_AI_KS_WS	Albanian, case-insensitive, accent-insensitive, kanatype-sensitive, width-sensitive
6	Albanian_CI_AS	Albanian, case-insensitive, accent-sensitive, kanatype-insensitive, width-insensitive
7	Albanian_CI_AS_WS	Albanian, case-insensitive, accent-sensitive, kanatype-insensitive, width-sensitive
8	Albanian_CI_AS_KS	Albanian, case-insensitive, accent-sensitive, kanatype-sensitive, width-insensitive
9	Albanian_CI_AS_KS_WS	Albanian, case-insensitive, accent-sensitive, kanatype-sensitive, width-sensitive

So there are a lot of collations, and some are pretty obscure, e.g., `Albanian_CI_AI_KS_WS` being "Albanian, case-insensitive, accent-insensitive, kanatype-sensitive, width-sensitive." Well, OK, then! That's clear!

Here's the deal: you usually don't care...except when you do. The SQL Server default collation tends to be reasonable, so anything you import into a new table should be handled "OK." On my system the default collation is `SQL_Latin1_General_CP1_CI_AS`, which we can see is as follows:

```
SELECT
    description [Default SQL Server Collation]
FROM fn_helpcollations()
WHERE name = 'SQL_Latin1_General_CP1_CI_AS';
```

Default SQL Server Collation
Latin1-General, case-insensitive, accent-sensitive, kanatype-insensitive, width-insensitive for Unicode Data, SQL Server Sort Order 52 on Code Page 1252 for non-Unicode Data

"Latin1-General, case-insensitive, accent-sensitive, kanatype-insensitive, width-insensitive for Unicode Data, SQL Server Sort Order 52 on Code Page 1252 for non-Unicode Data." That's a mouthful! But basically the things we care about are that it is the *Latin1* character set, that it is case-insensitive (we almost always want that), and if we have to get into the weeds, we see what code page is being used for "non-Unicode data."

Why do I bring this up? Because I worked for a long time on a popular CRM system whose default collation was persistently different than the default for that instance of SQL Server. Like this:

```
/*
    Create and populate our "customer" table. Note the collation.
*/
SELECT * INTO staging.CustomerTable
FROM
(
    SELECT
        'Snedley'  COLLATE Latin1_General_100_CS_AI_SC_UTF8 [LastName],
        'Mortimer' COLLATE Latin1_General_100_CS_AI_SC_UTF8 [FirstName]
) A;

/*
    Create and populate our "import" table - values are the same, yes?
    But note the different collation!
*/
SELECT * INTO staging.ImportTable
FROM
(
    SELECT
        'Snedley'  COLLATE SQL_Latin1_General_CP1_CI_AS [LastName],
        'Mortimer' COLLATE SQL_Latin1_General_CP1_CI_AS [FirstName]
) A;
```

Let's look at what we just set up. First, the customer table:

```
SELECT * FROM staging.CustomerTable;
```

LastName	FirstName
Snedley	Mortimer

Then, the import table:

```
SELECT * FROM staging.ImportTable;
```

LastName	FirstName
Snedley	Mortimer

Ah, they look the same, yes? Beautiful. We can match to our heart's content—let's try!

```
SELECT
    COUNT(*) [Number of Matches]
FROM staging.CustomerTable C
INNER JOIN staging.ImportTable I ON
    C.LastName = I.LastName
    AND C.FirstName = I.FirstName;

*  mssql+pyodbc://{os.environ["DEMO_UID"]}:***@TestDB
        (pyodbc.ProgrammingError) ('42000', '[42000] [Microsoft][ODBC SQL
Server Driver][SQL Server]Cannot resolve the collation conflict between
"SQL_Latin1_General_CP1_CI_AS" and "Latin1_General_100_CS_AI_SC_UTF8" in the
equal to operation. (468) (SQLExecDirectW)')
        . . .
```

We don't get our expected result set; instead, we get a `Cannot resolve the collation conflict` error. What a pain. To fix it, every time you have a comparison, in a `JOIN`, `WHERE` clause, `IIF`, or whatever, you have to specify which collation you want to use on one side or the other (or both):

```
SELECT
    COUNT(*) [Number of Matches]
FROM staging.CustomerTable C
INNER JOIN staging.ImportTable I ON
        /*
            Specifying the import table's collation on the customer table
            columns.
        */
        C.LastName  COLLATE SQL_Latin1_General_CP1_CI_AS = I.LastName
    AND C.FirstName COLLATE SQL_Latin1_General_CP1_CI_AS = I.FirstName;
```

Number of Matches
1

Note the addition of `COLLATE SQL_Latin1_General_CP1_CI_AS` to the two comparisons in the `INNER JOIN`. This is overriding the *CustomerTable*'s default collation of `Latin1_General_100_CS_AI_SC_UTF8` with the *ImportTable*'s collation instead. You could just as easily swap them, like this:

```
SELECT
    COUNT(*) [Number of Matches]
FROM staging.CustomerTable C
INNER JOIN staging.ImportTable I ON
        /*
            Specifying the customer table's collation on the import table
            columns.
        */
        C.LastName = I.LastName  COLLATE Latin1_General_100_CS_AI_SC_UTF8
    AND C.FirstName = I.FirstName COLLATE Latin1_General_100_CS_AI_SC_UTF8;
```

Number of Matches
1

At the end of the day, specifying `COLLATE` all over the place is not fun, so it is better to import everything and then ETL it over into a collation of your choosing, typically one that matches your CRM or other production data.

Cleaning Up the Input Data

We'll cover more on data quality in Chapter 11, but these are the general steps I take toward achieving data quality:

1. Import everything into some form of VARCHAR or NVARCHAR column to make sure the import works.

2. Check for data quality issues such as bad dates, NULLs where there shouldn't be any, etc.

3. Correct those with one or more ETLs into new tables.

4. Move on toward normalization and data matching.

As to step 2, because of our liberal "accept everything" policy on imports, you have a likelihood of having bad data, e.g., of having a date value in a birth date column that isn't valid. It could be from a problem in the source system, a problem in the encoding of the import file, a misunderstanding of the schema, or maybe even data corruption in transit.

The following shows common tests and transformations to run, depending on the datatype and your expectations:

```
/*
   Maybe the incoming date isn't WRONG - it just
   isn't using your locale!
*/
DECLARE @SpanishDOB VARCHAR(50) = '1 de abril de 1990'
/*
    The incoming data turns out to be in hex,
    but you think it's numeric. Common with keys.
*/
DECLARE @CustomerId VARCHAR(50) = '0x123ABC'
/*
    Middle name is often missing.
*/
DECLARE @MiddleName VARCHAR(50)
SELECT
    ISDATE(@SpanishDOB)        [Valid Date?],
    ISNUMERIC(@CustomerId)     [Valid Numeric Id?],
    /*
       Users don't like seeing NULLs, so typically
       COALESCE them out.
    */
    COALESCE(@MiddleName, '') [Middle Name];
```

Valid Date?	Valid Numeric Id?	Middle Name
0	0	

We can then use that type of logic to create additional filters in a WHERE clause or additional columns with "flag" values to weed out invalid or impossible values.

This is where our friends ISDATE, ISNUMERIC, ISNULL, and COALESCE come in handy (with the caveats we discussed in Chapter 2). If you have the ability to create a view, then you will want to wrap all this type of logic up in some sort of "normalized input view" and then consume only that. Otherwise, you can use a CTE at the top of every one of your queries to do the same thing. What the heck am I talking about? Let's say we have the following import table with some questionable values. Eyeballing the data, we can see we will need to "guard" against some of the inputs:

```
/*
    Our "import" table.
*/
CREATE TABLE staging.ImportTable
(
    CustomerId VARCHAR(50) NULL,
    LastName VARCHAR(50) NULL,
    FirstName VARCHAR(50) NULL,
    MiddleName VARCHAR(50) NULL,
    DOB VARCHAR(50) NULL
);

/*
    Populate a problem record. Note leaving out MiddleName, so it will get NULL.
*/
INSERT INTO staging.ImportTable (CustomerId, LastName, FirstName, DOB)
    VALUES('0x123ABG', 'Snedley', 'Mortimer', '1 de abril de 1990')
/*
    Now populate a good record.
*/
INSERT INTO staging.ImportTable (CustomerId, LastName, FirstName,
                                 MiddleName, DOB)
    VALUES('0x123ABC', 'Snedley', 'Mortimer', 'J', 'April 1, 1990');

SELECT * FROM staging.ImportTable;
```

	CustomerId	LastName	FirstName	MiddleName	DOB
0	0x123ABG	Snedley	Mortimer	NULL	1 de abril de 1990
1	0x123ABC	Snedley	Mortimer	J	April 1, 1990

Anticipating the problems we already see and not wanting to code around them at every query, pretend the following CTE is a "view" we can always reference to have "clean(er)" data. In the SQL query, I aligned the result set column names to the right so you can more clearly see each column getting its own treatment:

```
/*
    NormalizedCustomer represents an approach we could use to
    make a view with the same logic as this CTE to guard against
    bad incoming data.
*/
WITH NormalizedCustomer
AS
(
    SELECT
```

```
    /*
        Assume if the id doesn't come in as a valid number it
        must be a hex constant. Otherwise force to 0.
    */
    CASE
        WHEN ISNUMERIC(CustomerId) = 1 THEN CAST(CustomerId AS INT)
        ELSE COALESCE(CAST(TRY_CONVERT(VARBINARY(50), CustomerId, 1)
                        AS INT), 0)
    END                                         [Customer Id],
    LastName                                    [Last Name],
    LEFT(FirstName, 1)                          [First Initial],
    /*
        Users hate NULLs.
    */
    LEFT(COALESCE(MiddleName, ''), 1)           [Middle Name],
    CASE
        WHEN ISDATE(DOB) = 1 THEN CAST(DOB AS DATE)
        ELSE '' END                             [DOB],
    CASE
        WHEN ISDATE(DOB) = 1 THEN CAST(1 AS BIT)
        ELSE CAST(0 AS BIT)
    END                                         [Valid DOB?]
    FROM staging.ImportTable
)
SELECT
    *
FROM NormalizedCustomer;
```

	Customer Id	Last Name	First Initial	Middle Name	DOB	Valid DOB?
0	0	Snedley	M		1900-01-01	False
1	1194684	Snedley	M	J	1990-04-01	True

But wait, why is there "1900-01-01" for the first row, when we explicitly said if there is a bad date string to make it an empty string? It's because SQL had to pick a datatype for the result column and it chose DATE from the explicit CAST in the CASE. Because that column is not considered nullable, SQL chose the default value for a DATE, which is January 1, 1900.

There will be more on these topics in Chapter 11.

Final Thoughts on Bad Characters

The biggest place I see things like Unicode whitespace or other unexpected control characters is typically in imports coming from CSVs and Excel files, or sometimes even copy-and-pasted out of Word or an email. Anyone who has had Word's autocorrect change single and double quotes (' and ") to their "smart" equivalents (e.g., "smart quotes") knows what I am talking about. Hilarity ensues. I have also read where some organizations use invisible whitespace (especially zero-width spaces) in varying combinations throughout a document or file to uniquely watermark each copy. Whatever the reason, the characters you are expecting and the ones you receive may not align.

As with almost every chapter so far, this is often a data quality issue. There will be more about that in Chapter 11. Remember again that there will be columns you need and have to clean up, but if the data is particularly noisy and the column is of marginal value, maybe you don't need to expend the effort to "save" that attribute. Remember the discussion on locations in Chapter 4. If something like *city* is giving you pain because of these types of problems, if you aren't ultimately going to use it in the final comparisons, just drop it from your analysis (not your data!) and move on. Less is often more.

When it comes to dealing with two datasets with different collation sequences, my advice is to ETL one or the other into another table that has the same collation as the other dataset. Then you are not overriding with COLLATE on every comparison and not making SQL do it "under the covers" (which still has a cost).

I end with this thought—note that "liberal" and "fuzzy" are synonyms when thinking about data:

> Be conservative in what you send, be liberal in what you accept.
>
> —Postel's Law (*https://oreil.ly/V2KMm*)

## CHAPTER 9

Orthogonal Data

"orthogonal" (adjective)

1. of or involving right angles; at right angles

2. statistically independent

Or, as some people say, orthogonal data is like trying to cram 10 pounds (or kilos) of "stuff" in a 5-pound (or kilo) bag. We will look at what I mean by that, because there are multiple variations on the theme.

The approaches described in this chapter are for dealing with a set of problems that often arise in legacy applications such as on mainframes or some vended applications. It is popular to disparage the design of such systems and the techniques used, but it should be remembered that the constraint for these applications was often the lack of ability to make changes in the data schemas in a timely or cost-effective manner (or at all). The solutions often provided "escape hatches," that is, data fields in the schema with looseness or complete freedom as to their contents. These could then be used by "the business" to store whatever it needs in the system at the correct level: customer, loan, experiment, whatever.

This obviously becomes an instant data governance issue! "Obviously," that is, to us now. At the time such patterns were common because the pain point was strong enough to warrant them, despite the dangers. They were architectural decisions made to solve specific problems in a very "elegant" manner, when viewed from optimizing *a limited ability to make systemic changes.* Many years and in some cases decades later, the constraints faced by modern architects are different. In fact, you could argue instead of too little "change velocity" in systems, now there may be too much!

Every generation optimizes for its own problems. That's why you are here reading this: to learn to deal with the last generation's problems while you create the ones for the next generation. Don't get haughty, OK?

A Common Problem, A Common Solution, A New Common Problem

There will be times where you might be called upon to try to join or uncover similarities between fields that hold freeform data. Typically this is text, but this can also be true of "free-range" numeric and date fields, often called *user fields* or *custom fields* or *extension fields*. The idea is that many systems have been built with an escape hatch where a company or a group of users can decide to use a given field for their own purposes. Often, they are used to add a "join key"—a customer ID, say—to an external system, so when data from that system comes back in, it can be joined back up to our customer data easily. It's a very common pattern.

Let's say you work for Foo Corp, who has a third-party vendor, BarCo, that provides some sort of services to Foo Corp. There is systems integration between the two companies, in that some data extracts are sent between the two to facilitate the process.

In the following example, BarCo gives us an integration field, *CustomField1*, to use how we want. Typically in such approaches whenever we send data to the vendor we put a join key into a custom field, such as our internal CRM customer ID value. Then, when the vendor sends us back the customer data later, they include the same field and value for the same customer, and we can use that to map back to our internal data. In our case, we will assume *CustomField1* holds our customer key.

In the following example, two SQL table variables represent our customer and import tables:

```
/*
    Our customer table.
*/
CREATE TABLE staging.CustomerTable
(
    CustomerId INT NOT NULL,
    LastName VARCHAR(50) NULL,
    FirstName VARCHAR(50) NULL,
    MiddleName VARCHAR(50) NULL,
    DOB DATE NULL
);

/*
    Populate a customer record.
*/
INSERT INTO staging.CustomerTable (CustomerId, LastName, FirstName, DOB)
    VALUES(123, 'Snedley', 'Mortimer', '1990-04-01');

/*
    The table of data we get back from the vendor.
*/
```

```
CREATE TABLE staging.ImportTable
(
    LastName VARCHAR(50) NULL,
    FirstName VARCHAR(50) NULL,
    /*
        The total our customer bought from the partner.
    */
    TotalPurchased MONEY NULL,
    /*
        The partner sends us back our customer id here.
    */
    CustomField1 VARCHAR(50) NULL
);

/*
    Here is the record we received from the vendor.
*/
INSERT INTO staging.ImportTable
    (LastName, FirstName, TotalPurchased, CustomField1)
    VALUES('Snedley', 'Mortimer', '$3459.00', '123');

/*
    Test the incoming data to see if we have any matches on key.
*/
SELECT
    C.CustomerId [Customer Id],
    C.LastName [Last Name],
    C.FirstName [First Name],
    I.TotalPurchased [Total Purchased],
    CASE WHEN I.CustomField1 IS NOT NULL THEN 'Yes'
        ELSE 'No' END [Did We Match on Key?]
FROM staging.CustomerTable C
LEFT JOIN staging.ImportTable I ON
    /*
        Using CustomField1 as join key. Quite common pattern.
    */
    C.CustomerId = I.CustomField1;
```

Customer Id	Last Name	First Name	Total Purchased	Did We Match on Key?
123	Snedley	Mortimer	3459.0000	Yes

Note that SQL Server takes care of converting the VARCHAR *CustomField1* to a numeric datatype for comparison with the *CustomerId* field.

This approach of custom fields passed back and forth is common, and not a bad one. You have to protect against the quality of the data coming back, and you have to have agreement within your own company on how you're using it, but that's simple data governance, right? Right?

The problem comes when there are:

- A limited number of such custom fields available
- Multiple groups of users interested in using them
- Competing user needs, even within a given group

Let's say you're given *CustomField1*, *CustomField2*, and *CustomField3* by your vendor. Upon original integration, you decide on the following:

CustomField1
    Holds the customer key

CustomField2
    Holds the customer date of birth (maybe for an age check by the vendor)

CustomField3
    Is held in reserve

All is good. Data is sent back and forth, and the system works for some time (data governance at work—huzzah!):

LastName	FirstName	TotalPurchased	CustomField1	CustomField2	CustomField3
Abdallah	Johnetta	$100.00	4	5/20/1991	NULL

Then another department comes and wants to interface with the system. They discover the limited schema for passing data back and forth doesn't meet their needs, and after a meeting between the groups ("Data governance! Yes!"), it is decided the new department can use *CustomField3* for passing customer nicknames (the vendor wants to offer your customers a very personalized experience):

CustomField1
    Holds the customer key

CustomField2
    Holds the customer date of birth (maybe for an age check by the vendor)

CustomField3
    Nickname

Fine. All is still good. Time passes, and more data is built up in the databases on both sides:

LastName	FirstName	TotalPurchased	CustomField1	CustomField2	CustomField3
Abdallah	Johnetta	$100.00	4	5/20/1991	NULL
Acey	Geoffrey	$250.00	5	12/26/1989	Jeff

You know what's coming, don't you? Yes, you do. Don't run!

Either a third group or one of the original groups (probably Marketing) decides they now have a *fourth* data element to pass back and forth. It is absolutely required, and we can't get around it. The vendor is adamant they won't add another custom field. Besides, the integrations are built and tested, so why touch those? So, after another meeting ("Governance?"), one of two decisions will be made.

The first approach is based on the fact not all customers have the same need, so we can "wedge" an orthogonal value (there's that term!) into the field in such a way there is never any clash. In other words, if date of birth is going back and forth but the new need is to pass something that Marketing pinky-swear guarantees will never apply to any but corporate customers ("who have no birth dates!" This is the brilliant idea in the meeting), then maybe we can just use *CustomField2* to hold that new data, right? If you're lucky, it may also be a date, say, incorporation date. Or, given the VARCHAR nature of these types of fields, it may be something else such as a company purchasing agent name. Who knows? The point is, this decision is easy to make, looks like it was given due consideration ("We had a meeting about it!"), and happens *all the time*:

LastName	FirstName	TotalPurchased	CustomField1	CustomField2	CustomField3
Abdallah	Johnetta	$100.00	4	5/20/1991	NULL
Acey	Geoffrey	$250.00	5	12/26/1989	Jeff
Acme Corp	NULL	$1,245.00	1	8/19/1901	NULL

Reusing the *LastName* field for the company name isn't necessarily a bad decision here, since we have the join key (customer ID) in *CustomField1*.

The second approach comes when the first decision can't be made. And while just as understandable as the first, this one is pure evil. Something new needs to be tracked (email, so the vendor can send your mutual customer a bill). A customer may or may not have an email address: some humans don't, but many corporations do (*info@example.com*). What to do? What to do?

Another meeting is held ("Governance!" [sigh]), and the decision is made to reuse one of the existing fields by adding the new data to it. Looking around, it seems obvious that *CustomField1* is being used for the key, and that's probably not a good idea to touch. *CustomField2* is (so far) holding only dates, and (for now) we want to keep it that way because we have some data quality checks around those now in the integration, so..."it was decided" (nice and passive voice, like "Mistakes were made") to add the new data to *CustomField3*. But don't despair! There will be "standards":

1. If there is already nickname data being passed back and forth in *CustomField3*, any new email address information will be added after a comma (not a space, or you can't have nicknames like "Billy Bob"), e.g., "Billy Bob,*bb@example.com*".

2. If there is not already a nickname, then the email address will be sent going forward in *CustomField3*.

3. If, at a future date, a nickname is added, *CustomField3* will be modified to have the nickname first followed by a comma and the email address, to keep with the "standard" in #1.

4. Otherwise, *CustomField3* will remain empty if there is no nickname or email value already there.

Hence:

CustomField1
    Holds the customer key

CustomField2
    Holds the customer date of birth or incorporation date if company

CustomField3
    Nickname (optional), email (optional)

And:

LastName	FirstName	TotalPurchased	CustomField1	CustomField2	CustomField3
Abdallah	Johnetta	$100.00	4	5/20/1991	johnetta_abdallah@example.com
Acey	Geoffrey	$250.00	5	12/26/1989	Jeff,geoffrey@example.com
Acme Corp	NULL	$1,245.00	1	8/19/1901	NULL

If that "standard" is promulgated by some sort of system integration, you might have a chance of it staying standard. However, if the end users using the vendor system can "monkey with" the custom fields—in fact, if they are responsible for maintaining them by hand—then hilarity ensues. Given enough time, it will not be uncommon to see values like this in *CustomField3*:

```
Mort
Mort,mortimer.snedley@example.com
mortimer.snedley@example.com
mortimer.snedley@example.com,Mort
```

In fact, if the end users are keeping all those custom fields up by hand (probably *not* the customer ID, but I have seen it happen), then over an even longer time there will be nicknames and email addresses in *CustomField2* and dates in *CustomField3*, unless the vendor is "smart" and gives datatypes for each custom field, e.g., *CustomInt1*, *CustomDate2*, and *CustomString3* in our example. But not in this case!

Now you are given a task after the most recent changes have run a while. Maybe regulations changed and now it is against the law in some jurisdictions to give an outside vendor your customer's email address without prior permission. You need to send an update to the vendor. One brute-force approach is to overwrite just the nicknames in *CustomField3*, overwriting anything else that might have been there. That is fine...as long as the customer has a nickname. But there are records at the vendor with just email addresses. OK, so you can find those with CHARINDEX('@', CustomField3) > 0 and clear them out; most people don't have "@" in their nicknames. We've solved it easily with something like this:

```
SELECT
    CASE
        WHEN CustomField3 IS NULL THEN NULL
        /*
            If users always got it right and email
            is always after the comma.
        */
        WHEN CHARINDEX(',', CustomField3) > 0
            THEN LEFT(CustomField3, CHARINDEX(',' CustomField3) - 1)
        /*
            Or they messed up and put email first.
        */
        WHEN CHARINDEX(',', CustomField3) > 0
            AND CHARINDEX('@', CustomField3) > 0
            AND CHARINDEX(',', CustomField3) > CHARINDEX('@', CustomField3)
            THEN RIGHT(CustomField3, CHARINDEX(',', CustomField3) + 1)
        /*
            Should be just a nickname otherwise.
        */
        ELSE CustomField3
    END [Transformed CustomField3]
FROM ImportData;
```

But what if there had been three orthogonal pieces of data in *CustomField3*? It happens. We'll say spouse's name. By this point, most pretense at governance is gone, or it is so convoluted and special cased that no one remembers it all ("Governance? Ha! Lemme tell you about governance..."). And the order of the pieces of data in the field are any which way. If you can convince your business to allow rebuilding all the values in a certain order, maybe all is well. Extract them from the customer data, build a new synthetic *CustomField3* value from it, and overwrite the old value. Do a cleanup at the end looking for CHARINDEX('@', CustomField3) > 1 to catch any stragglers. If "the business" wants to keep the values in the field in the same order they were, whatever order it was, and only elide the date of birth, it gets much more difficult.

It gets more difficult still if you are then given that vendor data as some sort of extract. Perhaps your company bought another company and this is how they encoded things. And you are tasked with...matching email addresses out of *CustomField3*! It's a silly example, but I've seen worse. Anyway, given these assumptions:

- There are zero, one, two, or three values in *CustomField3*.

- The values are separated from one another by commas. There are no "embedded commas" in any of the three custom fields (no commas in nicknames).

How can you go about seeing if you can get that email address out of something where it may be any of the following:

```
NULL
Mort
Mort,mortimer.snedley@example.com
mortimer.snedley@example.com
mortimer.snedley@example.com,Mort
Mort,Blanche
Mort,mortimer.snedley@example.com,Blanche
mortimer.snedley@example.com,Blanche
mortimer.snedley@example.com,Blanche,Mort
```

...and on and on? Think this example is contrived? You bet! Think something like it doesn't happen every day on "legacy systems"? Think again!

 One of my tech reviewers protested all this certainly isn't best practice and something like JSON should be used for all this instead. Indeed! Except in the legacy systems over which I and the people I work for have no control but deal with every day, often end users are expected to maintain these custom fields by hand via a user interface, perhaps in a "green screen" mainframe terminal emulator or perhaps in a modern web-based UI that still is just a wrapper on top of a mainframe system. Expecting such users to get the data correctly entered and maintained with something as simple as commas is hard enough, as shown. Expecting them to type in JSON correctly would be impossible.

Make no mistake: the whole point of this chapter is not creating systems as they should be, but dealing with real-world systems as they are. In dealing with data you will often have no control over what you are given. That is the point of this entire book: how to be given a festering pile of "data" and not be victimized by it, but be able to extract value from it no matter its "quality."

Anyway, let's finish this contrived-yet-real-enough example:

```
CREATE TABLE staging.CustomFields
(
```

```
    CustomField3 VARCHAR(50) NULL
);

INSERT INTO staging.CustomFields VALUES(NULL)
INSERT INTO staging.CustomFields VALUES('Mort')
INSERT INTO staging.CustomFields VALUES('Mort,mortimer.snedley@example.com')
INSERT INTO staging.CustomFields VALUES('mortimer.snedley@example.com')
INSERT INTO staging.CustomFields VALUES('mortimer.snedley@example.com,Mort')
INSERT INTO staging.CustomFields VALUES('Mort,Blanche')
INSERT INTO staging.CustomFields
    VALUES('Mort,mortimer.snedley@example.com,Blanche')
INSERT INTO staging.CustomFields VALUES('mortimer.snedley@example.com,Blanche')
INSERT INTO staging.CustomFields
    VALUES('mortimer.snedley@example.com,Blanche,Mort');

SELECT
  CustomField3,
  CASE
    /*
        If NULL no worries.
    */
    WHEN CustomField3 IS NULL THEN 'No Email Found'
    /*
        If no @ in string, no email address found.
    */
    WHEN CHARINDEX('@', CustomField3) = 0 THEN 'No Email Found'
    /*
        If @ and no comma, then only email address in string.
    */
    WHEN CHARINDEX('@', CustomField3) > 0
      AND CHARINDEX(',', CustomField3) = 0
      THEN CustomField3
    /*
        If the email is first on the left, grab it.
    */
    WHEN CHARINDEX('@', CustomField3) > 0
      AND CHARINDEX(',', CustomField3) > CHARINDEX('@', CustomField3)
      THEN LEFT(CustomField3, CHARINDEX(',', CustomField3) - 1)
    /*
        If email is in the middle, then hold on!
    */
    WHEN CHARINDEX(',', CustomField3) > 0
      AND CHARINDEX('@', RIGHT(CustomField3, LEN(CustomField3) -
                  CHARINDEX(',', CustomField3))) >
        CHARINDEX(',', CustomField3)
      AND CHARINDEX('@', RIGHT(CustomField3, LEN(CustomField3) -
                  CHARINDEX(',', CustomField3))) <
        CHARINDEX(',', RIGHT(CustomField3, LEN(CustomField3) -
                  CHARINDEX(',', CustomField3)))
      THEN SUBSTRING(CustomField3,
              CHARINDEX(',', CustomField3) + 1,
              CHARINDEX(',',  RIGHT(CustomField3,
                      LEN(CustomField3) -
```

```
                  CHARINDEX(',', CustomField3))) - 1)
    /*
       If the email is last on the right, grab it.
    */
    WHEN CHARINDEX(',', CustomField3) > 0
      AND CHARINDEX('@', CustomField3) > CHARINDEX(',', CustomField3)
      THEN RIGHT(CustomField3, LEN (CustomField3) - CHARINDEX(',', CustomField3))
    ELSE 'No Email Found'
  END [Email?]
FROM staging.CustomFields;
```

	CustomField3	Email?
0	NULL	No Email Found
1	Mort	No Email Found
2	Mort,mortimer.snedley@example.com	mortimer.snedley@example.com
3	mortimer.snedley@example.com	mortimer.snedley@example.com
4	mortimer.snedley@example.com,Mort	mortimer.snedley@example.com
5	Mort,Blanche	No Email Found
6	Mort,mortimer.snedley@example.com,Blanche	mortimer.snedley@example.com
7	mortimer.snedley@example.com,Blanche	mortimer.snedley@example.com
8	mortimer.snedley@example.com,Blanche,Mort	mortimer.snedley@example.com

You can carry that SUBSTRING technique to ridiculous lengths (see, e.g., the following
example), and I have in the past. You can also use TRANSLATE or REPLACE to get certain characters changed to make parsing different parts out easier.

```
/*
    The following only works well with precisely two commas.
*/
DECLARE @ThreeThings VARCHAR(50) = 'First,Second,Third'
SELECT
    LEFT(@ThreeThings, CHARINDEX(',', @ThreeThings) -1)          [1st],
    SUBSTRING
    (
        @ThreeThings,
        CHARINDEX(',', @ThreeThings) + 1,
        LEN(@ThreeThings) -
            CHARINDEX(',', @ThreeThings) -
            CHARINDEX(',', REVERSE(@ThreeThings))
    )                                                            [2nd],
    RIGHT(@ThreeThings, CHARINDEX(',', REVERSE(@ThreeThings)) - 1) [3rd];
```

1st	2nd	3rd
First	Second	Third

I am not saying do something like that yourself, mind you. I am just saying I have. You can solve the same problem multiple ways, and sometimes I find it a challenge to use different approaches. That is not to say I was bored that day, but consider the following real-world problem where I used this trick recently—parse the file type (suffix) out of the following file paths. Be sure to note the different suffix lengths:

```
C:\Users\lehmer\Sandbox\FooCorp.SampleSolution\Foo.MyApp.config
C:\Users\lehmer\Sandbox\FooCorp.SampleSolution\Foo.MyApp.cs
C:\Users\lehmer\Sandbox\FooCorp.SampleSolution\Foo.MyApp.csproj
C:\Users\lehmer\Sandbox\FooCorp.SampleSolution\Foo.MyApp.dtsx
C:\Users\lehmer\Sandbox\FooCorp.SampleSolution\Foo.MyApp.sln
C:\Users\lehmer\Sandbox\FooCorp.SampleSolution\Foo.MyApp.sql
```

Or for us Linux folk:

```
/home/lehmer/Sandbox/FooCorp.SampleSolution/Foo.MyApp.config
/home/lehmer/Sandbox/FooCorp.SampleSolution/Foo.MyApp.cs
/home/lehmer/Sandbox/FooCorp.SampleSolution/Foo.MyApp.csproj
/home/lehmer/Sandbox/FooCorp.SampleSolution/Foo.MyApp.dtsx
/home/lehmer/Sandbox/FooCorp.SampleSolution/Foo.MyApp.sln
/home/lehmer/Sandbox/FooCorp.SampleSolution/Foo.MyApp.sql
```

Using *exactly* the previous technique with REVERSE, it is easy to quickly figure out what the length parameter to the RIGHT function should be and not have to parse left-to-right one period (full stop) at a time.

Many SQL dialects have a split_part function that does exactly what we need. It is sad to me that Transact-SQL doesn't have that or something similar. If you have split_part, use it!

Lather, Rinse, Repeat

Orthogonal data isn't bad; it just is. "Stuff happens." People need to get their jobs done and will shove the proverbial 10 bushels of $#!+ into any convenient 5-liter (dry volume) container if it helps them accomplish what they need to do. You just have to be aware of it and know how to deal with it. At some point SQL is not the correct tool for doing that. Something that supports regular expressions could come in handy, even though:

> some people, when confronted with a problem, think "I know, I'll use regular expressions." Now they have two problems.
>
> —Jamie Zawinski (*https://oreil.ly/6VSUO*)

Some dialects of SQL allow for regular expressions. Alas, my beloved Transact-SQL does not.

I once worked on a systems integration project where a 20-byte "Short description" field (this was on a mainframe) upon analysis had eight orthogonal values being held in that field, with various delimiters, ordering of the data, formats, and abbreviations! Getting that data out was "fun." Recently I encountered another example, like this:

```
1234 9876 06 A
```

That contains four values in a single 16-character "user-defined" text field (and they aren't even using two characters; we could expand!). The first two represent two IDs or cross-reference keys—one to an issuing bank, one to a servicing bank, and the next two are typical mainframe (one and two character) data codes representing information about that specific loan that needed to be visible on the other system in which this field is surfaced, mostly for regulatory reporting reasons. Again, this is a common "real-world" pattern! If you are dealing with a system on either "side" of your matching that is more than a decade old, I would be surprised if there isn't something going on somewhere within the data just like this.

Finally, the previous example with *CustomField3* was contrived. How about a more real-world one? What if you were given a dataset with a field in it called *address* that had exactly that in it: the complete address, street, city, state, and ZIP? It is a fun exercise to task yourself with figuring out how to pull those four fields out for matching *using pure SQL*. To make it easy to play with, let's assume the format is as follows:

```
street_address,city,state,zip
123 Main,Pleasantville,IL,62366
```

We have everything we need to do this already in this chapter or prior ones. Let's have some fun:

```
DECLARE @FullAddress VARCHAR(50) = '4 Kohler Memorial Dr, Brooklyn, NY 11230'
SELECT
    /*
        Street is easy.
    */
    LEFT
    (
        @FullAddress,
        PATINDEX('%, %', @FullAddress) - 1
    )                                                       [Street Address],
    /*
        City is hardest - grab the string between the
        the first comma we found above and the next.
        This is the hardest thing to understand in the book.
        You've seen this before, though. Don't be afraid.
    */
    LEFT
    (
        /*
            The remainder after grabbing street address.
        */
```

```
RIGHT
(
    @FullAddress, LEN(@FullAddress) - PATINDEX('%, %', @FullAddress) - 1
),
/*
    How much of it comprises city (the land between the two commas).
    Take the function calls apart "from the inside out." You got this.
*/
LEN
(
    RIGHT
    (
        @FullAddress,
        LEN(@FullAddress) -
        PATINDEX('%, %', @FullAddress) - 1
    )
) -
PATINDEX
(
    '%, %',
    RIGHT
    (
        @FullAddress,
        LEN(@FullAddress) -
        PATINDEX('%, %', @FullAddress)
    )
)
)                                              [City],
/*
    State is somewhat easy - it is the first
    two characters of the rightmost eight -
    ZIP code and the intervening space take
    up the other six characters at the end.
*/
LEFT(RIGHT(@FullAddress, 8), 2)                [State],
/*
    ZIP is easiest.
*/
RIGHT(@FullAddress, 5)                          [ZIP Code];
```

Street Address	City	State	ZIP Code
4 Kohler Memorial Dr	Brooklyn	NY	11230

As you can see, the technique extracting the city can be expanded indefinitely, working left to right and pulling off the "next" thing you are interested in, but it quickly gets convoluted because you have to keep including the prior functions as part of the positioning for the next "clause" to extract. Maybe a code generator can do it, but it gets really complicated for a human to understand quickly (at least for this human typing this). Instead, we can "ETL" our way along (see the chapter on data quality). We can emulate that approach here, using staging tables to gather our results as we go:

```sql
SELECT '4 Kohler Memorial Dr, Brooklyn, NY 11230' FullAddress
INTO staging.FullAddress;

SELECT
    LEFT(FullAddress, PATINDEX('%, %', FullAddress) - 1) [Street Address],
    RIGHT
    (
        FullAddress,
        LEN(FullAddress) - PATINDEX('%, %', FullAddress) - 1
    ) Remainder
INTO staging.GetStreetAddress
FROM staging.FullAddress;

SELECT
    [Street Address],
    LEFT(Remainder, PATINDEX('%, %', Remainder) - 1) City,
    RIGHT
    (
        Remainder,
        LEN(Remainder) - PATINDEX('%, %', Remainder) - 1
    ) Remainder
INTO staging.GetCity
FROM staging.GetStreetAddress;

SELECT
    [Street Address],
    City,
    LEFT(Remainder, CHARINDEX(' ', Remainder) - 1) State,
    RIGHT
    (
        Remainder,
        LEN(Remainder) - CHARINDEX(' ', Remainder)
    ) ZIP
INTO staging.GetTheRest
FROM staging.GetCity;

SELECT
    [Street Address],
    City,
    State,
    ZIP
FROM staging.GetTheRest;
```

Street Address	City	State	ZIP
4 Kohler Memorial Dr	Brooklyn	NY	11230

This approach is not as performant, but you can see it is much easier to understand what is going on by doing each chunk as its own ETL and always working left-to-right and just pulling off the next leftmost chunk we are interested in based on the delimiters.

Of course, these approaches are fragile and are sensitive to the formatting of the delimiters (a comma without a following space in the data would throw it all off). However, for a lot of the types of one-off data matching exercises I am involved in, you would be surprised how often something fuzzy like the preceding is "good enough"!

Final Thoughts on Orthogonal Data

I have been around long enough to help commit some of the "sins" described in this chapter. I've certainly designed "loose" interfaces for coupling unrelated systems that end up having data quality issues at a future time. Guilty. "It seemed like a good idea at the time" is my only defense.

That said, the problems being solved were real, and for better or worse the systems you have to import data from (or worse, push data to!) may have all the issues described in this chapter. It doesn't help to complain, unless you know Marty McFly or Doc Brown and can go back in time and fix it at its source (and if you do, please don't shout at me when you see me—we were doing our best!).

Instead, it helps to recognize common patterns:

There is no pattern.
> The data is all over the place. There are things that look like drop-down values, amounts, dates—everything—all in one field. In this case use GROUP BY (or get fancy and use pivot tables) to summarize everything in categories. If you can filter all the dates together, all the numbers together, all the text together, and see their distributions in the data, with links to detail records if needed, it often helps "the business" to see the "shape" of the data better.

Wow, eight items at once!
> We've covered parsing apart fields in depth, including names and addresses. If you've read this far in the book, you now well understand why. It is a problem that will recur throughout your data career, so get good at handling it.

Well, NOW what?
> Often I am tasked to deal with this type of data when moving to a new system and getting the legacy data into shape for the impending export and import. It is quite common to realize somewhat late in a project that these user-defined fields

need to "explode" into multiple new drop-down lists in the new system, with well-worded entries instead of just obscure codes. That will improve data quality, for sure, and is a great goal. But beware: the *business analysis* required for all that may be much more costly than the technical implementation. Often understanding the nuances of legacy systems requires the most expert (and valuable, and over-scheduled) subject matter experts you have. You already know that attention from these people is commonly a bottleneck.

Now's not the time for emotions.

This data got this way day after day, decade after decade. Analyzing it, including all the hooks into your applications, integrations, reports, and the like, takes a lot of time, effort, and money (thank you for your support!). Cleaning, correcting, and documenting it all are often necessary and costly. Implementing better solutions may require whole new projects, sponsorship, and budgets and divert from other initiatives. At times like these, people can get a bit testy about it all! Put on your data face and just remind everyone, "It took a long time to get here, many in this meeting may have helped make decisions that they rue today, and the best we can do is analyze it, ruthlessly cut, prioritize what's left, and re-implement it." Simple, right? Ha! But blame games on top of all that don't help, and this is somewhere I believe people in a "data" role can truly help, by adopting a facilitative persona that is "Just the facts, ma'am."

In some ways, this chapter is all about the human factor, in data entry, in data governance, in data analysis. This is the topic that brings all that humanity out! Especially when an executive realizes that an already overdue project is going to be more so because the user-defined field analysis shows there are 59 new fields to add to Salesforce! And then all the integrations to get them into the data warehouse! So that then all the Power BI and other reports can be changed! "Where are we going to find the time, people, and money to do all that?" they shout.

This is why sometimes you will end up "moving old garbage into the new house," because this effort was underestimated and the project ran out of time. Don't say I didn't warn you. If there is plenty of warning a new system is coming—and there always is, with requests for proposals (RFPs), vendor visits and demos, bids, contract negotiations, training, change management, etc.—then you have time to start doing all this analysis *in advance*. Get business users weaned off adding new values to the existing user-defined fields. Maybe get those 59 fields created and moved to Salesforce and all the other work from that finished before the migration analysis for the new system begins, instead of because of it.

In other words, sometimes as a keen, analytical data person, you may have to be "fuzzy" in a human way and help keep people grounded and focused on solutions, no matter how imposing or far off it all seems. Good luck with that!

## PART III

Bringing It Together

## CHAPTER 10

The Big Score

So far we've talked about matching data and all its challenges, including making sure it's the same type of data or compatible, that the representations of the data are the same (is it "IA" or "Iowa"?), and so on. But now what do we *do* with it all? How do we decide whether our "fuzzy" match is actually pretty damned precise?

We build something called a *score*. Now, "scoring" sounds all fancy and is the subject of doctoral-level theses in all kinds of industries, but for our purposes it is a simple thing. From the Glossary:

> *Score*
> A simple number that implies the strength of a given match based on the sum of the matching attributes (columns).

That's it.

The rest of this chapter will show you how to make that simple sentence a reality, including which columns to choose and which to ignore, how to tell what a "good" score (match) is, and how to tune the scoring process and (usually) make it simpler. I am a simple guy. Simpler is better.

What Will We Want?

For each dataset there will be a different number of attributes you will match upon, and more importantly, there will be a fairly *small* set—usually around five, typically not more than ten—that can comfortably be used to confidently call a match with some acceptable measure of accuracy, that are "material" to the results, in other words.

You then tune that score and run filtering queries where the results are either above a given x (probable matches) or below it (probable nonmatches). Note the x. You have to start by basically guessing a cutoff, or one will be obvious in the results. Note the "probables." In many cases you can be sure. If you have two datasets of US citizens and find matches on all of the following in your customer data for a given import row, then you can be sure you have the same person (and a great import dataset):

- Last name
- First initial
- First 10 characters of street address
- Five-digit ZIP code
- DOB
- Email address
- Mobile phone
- Gender

Even our couple, Don and Donna, would end up disambiguating around their birthdays *and* genders *and* email addresses *and* mobile phone...unless there are two Pats married somewhere who are a same-sex couple born on the same day and share the same phone and email address. And with eight billion people on the planet there probably are, but they're also probably *not* in our data!

So, that's the "big idea." You have read through this book to get to this simple idea: for each dataset you have to match against, you will pick a set of attributes to match upon and then add 1 (or more) for each match and see what the results are. The distribution of the scores will almost automatically show what is a good "cutoff score." It will also allow you to play around with adding and subtracting attributes to that score to see if they make a material difference. You will often find matching on more attributes doesn't mean a better match! If you match on the first 10 characters of street address (which will include the number and at least a few characters of the street) and the ZIP code, do you *need* to also match on PO box, city, and state? Probably not, so leave them out. If you build attribute matches and find they aren't adding value, *remove them!* Your queries will run faster and be easier to maintain.

What about that previous comment about adding "1 (or more)"? Well, "some matches are more equal than others," to misuse Orwell, and we will end up considering whether it makes a difference if we count mobile phone or email as having a higher value on matches than ZIP codes or first initials. The tendency is to try to get fancy, but often the simplest scores are Good Enough™. Many times you are working against limited time, limited budget, or limited data quality and pragmatism is key.

Let's look! For the purposes of our play time, we will use the attributes previously described to build a score and then play around with the resulting matches. For the purposes of this chapter, we will treat all data on both sides as already normalized and with errors (bad email, etc.) filtered out. The data will already be in its "best shape for success" (see Chapter 11 for more):

```
/*
    Remember this view? Here are our customers.
*/
SELECT TOP 10
    LastName,
    FirstName,
    Address1,
    PostalCode,
    MobilePhone
    -- ...and so on...
FROM crm.NormalizedCustomer
ORDER BY LastName, FirstName;
```

	LastName	FirstName	Address1	PostalCode	MobilePhone
0	NULL	NULL	443 Arroyo Rd	87740	NULL
1	NULL	NULL	457 Prairie View St	80301	NULL
2	NULL	NULL	123 Snell Ave	65101	NULL
3	Abdallah	Johnetta	1088 Pinehurst St	27514	9195559345
4	Acey	Geoffrey	7 West Ave #1	60067	8475551734
5	Acuff	Weldon	73 W Barstow Ave	60004	8475552156
6	Adkin	Barbra	4 Kohler Memorial Dr	11230	7185553751
7	Agramonte	Fausto	5 Harrison Rd	10038	2125551783
8	Ahle	Delmy	65895 S 16th St	02909	4015552547
9	Albares	Cammy	56 E Morehead St	78045	9565556195

So, let's just quickly look at what I am talking about. If we match a dataset back with itself, attribute by attribute, the matches must be perfect, yes? Here *crm.Normalized Customer* represents both our customer data (alias "C") and our import data (alias "I"). This is why we can get away with looking for perfect equality matches here, when most of the book is about anything but:

```
SELECT
(
    SELECT
        COUNT(*)
    FROM crm.NormalizedCustomer
) [Total Customers],
(
    SELECT
        COUNT(*)
```

```
          FROM crm.NormalizedCustomer C
          INNER JOIN crm.NormalizedCustomer I ON
                  COALESCE(C.LastName, '')    = COALESCE(I.LastName, '')
              AND COALESCE(C.FirstName, '')   = COALESCE(I.FirstName, '')
              AND COALESCE(C.Company, '')     = COALESCE(I.Company, '')
              AND COALESCE(C.Address1, '')    = COALESCE(I.Address1, '')
              AND COALESCE(C.City, '')        = COALESCE(I.City, '')
              AND COALESCE(C.County, '')      = COALESCE(I.County, '')
              AND COALESCE(C.State, '')       = COALESCE(I.State, '')
              AND COALESCE(C.PostalCode, '')  = COALESCE(I.PostalCode, '')
              AND COALESCE(C.country, '')     = COALESCE(I.country, '')
              AND COALESCE(C.MobilePhone, '') = COALESCE(I.MobilePhone, '')
              AND COALESCE(C.HomePhone, '')   = COALESCE(I.HomePhone, '')
              AND COALESCE(C.Email, '')       = COALESCE(I.Email, '')
              AND COALESCE(C.Web, '')         = COALESCE(I.Web, '')
      ) [# Matches];
```

Total Customers	# Matches
508	508

This means if we were scoring on each match, at the end the score for each must be the highest possible. In the following examples, we are going to use just five attributes to match on:

- *LastName*
- *FirstName*
- *Address1*
- *PostalCode*
- *MobilePhone*

If you think about it, this is not an unreasonable starting list. If you hit all five of these attributes, you are really unlikely to have the wrong person. In fact, for most people, if you hit mobile phone, you probably have the right person. We will look at that in a bit. First the naive case, though, and again, matching *crm.NormalizedCustomer* back with itself for convenience. Note that in the following examples each attribute (column) is checked individually, and each match will get its own row in the result set, with a column called *Attribute* telling us what column matched. The results of all the tests are then UNIONed together.

In the following, instead of CTEs, I will be creating and dropping various views. This will allow me to condense the examples down from their eye-watering original length and to point out only what changes in each example. Here are the three views that I will be using:

AttemptToMatch
This is where we will specify and refine our match logic.

ScoreMatches
This view will tell us how good we did.

ScoredCustomers
This is the resulting list of scored matches.

First, we create our naive *AttemptToMatch* view:

```
DROP VIEW IF EXISTS AttemptToMatch;

/*
    Attempt to join our customer data to our "import" data.
    We are using straight equality checks here for this
    example, even though we're going to get more fuzzy later.
*/
CREATE VIEW AttemptToMatch
AS
(
    SELECT
        C.LastName     [CustomerLastName],
        C.FirstName    [CustomerFirstName],
        C.Address1     [CustomerAddress1],
        C.PostalCode   [CustomerPostalCode],
        C.MobilePhone  [CustomerMobilePhone],
        I.LastName     [ImportLastName],
        I.FirstName    [ImportFirstName],
        I.Address1     [ImportAddress1],
        I.PostalCode   [ImportPostalCode],
        I.MobilePhone  [ImportMobilePhone]
    FROM   crm.NormalizedCustomer C
    LEFT OUTER JOIN crm.NormalizedCustomer I ON
            C.LastName     = I.LastName
        AND C.FirstName    = I.FirstName
        AND C.Address1     = I.Address1
        AND C.PostalCode   = I.PostalCode
        AND C.MobilePhone  = I.MobilePhone
);
```

Then, with the following code, we score our matches with the *ScoreMatches* view. For each attribute we find that matches, we return a row with a "1" for that attribute.

You may think instead of all these UNIONs you could do it all in a single SELECT with a CASE statement. You would be wrong.

```
DROP VIEW IF EXISTS ScoreMatches;

/*
    For every customer row, see if there is an import row that
    matches and if so, score one (1) attribute that matches.
    Then do it again for all the other attributes, UNIONing
    the results together.
*/
CREATE VIEW ScoreMatches
AS
(
    SELECT
        CustomerLastName,
        CustomerFirstName,
        CustomerAddress1,
        CustomerPostalCode,
        CustomerMobilePhone,
        'LastName' Attribute,
        IIF(ImportLastName IS NOT NULL, 1, 0) Score
    FROM  AttemptToMatch
    UNION
    SELECT
        CustomerLastName,
        CustomerFirstName,
        CustomerAddress1,
        CustomerPostalCode,
        CustomerMobilePhone,
        'FirstName' Attribute,
        IIF(ImportFirstName IS NOT NULL, 1, 0) Score
    FROM  AttemptToMatch
    UNION
    SELECT
        CustomerLastName,
        CustomerFirstName,
        CustomerAddress1,
        CustomerPostalCode,
        CustomerMobilePhone,
        'Address1' Attribute,
        IIF(ImportAddress1 IS NOT NULL, 1, 0) Score
    FROM  AttemptToMatch
    UNION
    SELECT
        CustomerLastName,
        CustomerFirstName,
        CustomerAddress1,
        CustomerPostalCode,
        CustomerMobilePhone,
```

```
        'PostalCode' Attribute,
        IIF(ImportPostalCode IS NOT NULL, 1, 0) Score
    FROM  AttemptToMatch
    UNION
    SELECT
        CustomerLastName,
        CustomerFirstName,
        CustomerAddress1,
        CustomerPostalCode,
        CustomerMobilePhone,
        'MobilePhone' Attribute,
        IIF(ImportMobilePhone IS NOT NULL, 1, 0) Score
    FROM  AttemptToMatch
);
```

How did we do?

```
SELECT TOP 10
    CustomerLastName,
    CustomerFirstName,
    CustomerAddress1,
    CustomerPostalCode,
    CustomerMobilePhone,
    /*
        BEHOLD! The secret to the whole chapter, if not the book!
    */
    SUM(Score) Score
FROM ScoreMatches
GROUP BY CustomerLastName, CustomerFirstName, CustomerAddress1,
        CustomerPostalCode, CustomerMobilePhone
ORDER BY SUM(Score) DESC, CustomerLastName, CustomerFirstName;
```

	Customer LastName	Customer FirstName	CustomerAddress1	Customer PostalCode	Customer MobilePhone	Score
0	Abdallah	Johnetta	1088 Pinehurst St	27514	9195559345	5
1	Acey	Geoffrey	7 West Ave #1	60067	8475551734	5
2	Acuff	Weldon	73 W Barstow Ave	60004	8475552156	5
3	Adkin	Barbra	4 Kohler Memorial Dr	11230	7185553751	5
4	Agramonte	Fausto	5 Harrison Rd	10038	2125551783	5
5	Ahle	Delmy	65895 S 16th St	02909	4015552547	5
6	Albares	Cammy	56 E Morehead St	78045	9565556195	5
7	Amigon	Minna	2371 Jerrold Ave	19443	2155551229	5
8	Amyot	Jutta	49 N Mays St	70518	3375551438	5
9	Andreason	Tasia	4 Cowesett Ave	07032	2015559002	5

We would expect no surprises. Since we are matching the dataset to itself, all five attributes matching on a row should yield a perfect score of "5." It's just that easy!

While we're still playing with a dataset that we know will match perfectly, we notice one other trick in our toolkit here. In this case we're only going to do a LEFT OUTER JOIN on *LastName*, since we don't want to do a full Cartesian join across all possible rows only to eliminate all the ones with zero matches at all. *LastName* seems like the best candidate.

Now we add the *ScoredCustomers* view, which is really just the final SELECT from earlier:

```
DROP VIEW IF EXISTS ScoredCustomers;

/*
    Score each customer by the number of attributes matched.
*/
CREATE VIEW ScoredCustomers
AS
(
    SELECT TOP 10
        CustomerLastName,
        CustomerFirstName,
        CustomerAddress1,
        CustomerPostalCode,
        CustomerMobilePhone,
        SUM(Score) Score
    FROM ScoreMatches
    GROUP BY CustomerLastName, CustomerFirstName, CustomerAddress1,
            CustomerPostalCode, CustomerMobilePhone
);
```

Using the *ScoredCustomers* view, we can now tell, in English, what we found matches on:

```
/*
    Here is the new part - using the STRING_AGG function to take all
    the match reasons (attributes) and concatenate one string of
    reasons for each match.
*/
SELECT
    C.CustomerLastName          [Last Name],
    LEFT(C.CustomerFirstName, 1) [First Initial],
    C.Score                     [Score],
    STRING_AGG(S.Attribute, ',') [Match Reasons]
FROM ScoredCustomers C
LEFT OUTER JOIN ScoreMatches S ON
        C.CustomerLastName    = S.CustomerLastName
    AND C.CustomerFirstName   = S.CustomerFirstName
    AND C.CustomerAddress1    = S.CustomerAddress1
    AND C.CustomerPostalCode  = S.CustomerPostalCode
    AND C.CustomerMobilePhone = S.CustomerMobilePhone
WHERE
    C.Score = 5
```

```
GROUP BY C.CustomerLastName, C.CustomerFirstName, C.CustomerAddress1,
         C.CustomerPostalCode, C.CustomerMobilePhone, C.Score;
```

	Last Name	First Initial	Score	Match Reasons
0	Abdallah	J	5	Address1,FirstName,LastName,MobilePhone,PostalCode
1	Acey	G	5	Address1,FirstName,LastName,MobilePhone,PostalCode
2	Acuff	W	5	Address1,FirstName,LastName,MobilePhone,PostalCode
3	Adkin	B	5	Address1,FirstName,LastName,MobilePhone,PostalCode
4	Agramonte	F	5	Address1,FirstName,LastName,MobilePhone,PostalCode
5	Ahle	D	5	Address1,FirstName,LastName,MobilePhone,PostalCode
6	Albares	C	5	Address1,FirstName,LastName,MobilePhone,PostalCode

See how each row has a list of reasons why it was matched? This can be useful to tune the score and to help end users to interpret the results. The same technique can be used when collecting errors on something like editing a customer entity. Then a list of all the errors can be presented to the user as a link to go fix them all.

Now that we've seen the general technique, we can now get a more "real-world" import dataset and look at how scoring changes.

We are going to refine our *AttemptToMatch* and *ScoreMatches* views to be able to handle real-world data, not just perfect datasets. Pay attention to the comments in the queries for what is going on:

```
DROP VIEW IF EXISTS AttemptToMatch;

CREATE VIEW AttemptToMatch
AS
(
    SELECT
        C.LastName    [CustomerLastName],
        C.FirstName   [CustomerFirstName],
        C.Address1    [CustomerAddress1],
        C.PostalCode  [CustomerPostalCode],
        C.MobilePhone [CustomerMobilePhone],
        I.LastName    [ImportLastName],
        I.FirstName   [ImportFirstName],
        I.Address1    [ImportAddress1],
        I.PostalCode  [ImportPostalCode],
        I.MobilePhone [ImportMobilePhone]
    FROM  crm.NormalizedCustomer C
    LEFT OUTER JOIN staging.ImportCustomer I ON
        /*
            Note the ORs, not ANDs. We want to OR all the
            attributes we are trying to match on, so that
            we even get false positives (last name = last
            name and nothing else).
            We are also starting to apply our matching "rules."
        */
```

```
            COALESCE(C.LastName, '') =
            COALESCE(I.LastName, '')
    OR COALESCE(LEFT(C.FirstName, 1), '') =
            COALESCE(LEFT(I.FirstName, 1), '')
    OR COALESCE(LEFT(C.Address1, 10), '') =
            COALESCE(LEFT(I.Address1, 10), '')
    OR COALESCE(LEFT(C.PostalCode, 5), '') =
            COALESCE(LEFT(I.PostalCode, 5), '')
    OR COALESCE(REPLACE(C.MobilePhone, '-', ''), '') =
            COALESCE(REPLACE(I.MobilePhone, '-', ''), '')
);
```

Now we change *ScoreMatches* to handle NULL comparisons correctly:

```
DROP VIEW IF EXISTS ScoreMatches;

CREATE VIEW ScoreMatches
AS
(
    SELECT
        CustomerLastName,
        CustomerFirstName,
        CustomerAddress1,
        CustomerPostalCode,
        CustomerMobilePhone,
        'LastName' Attribute,
        IIF(CustomerLastName IS NOT NULL
            AND ImportLastName IS NOT NULL
            AND CustomerLastName = ImportLastName, 1, 0) Score
    FROM AttemptToMatch
    UNION
    SELECT
        CustomerLastName,
        CustomerFirstName,
        CustomerAddress1,
        CustomerPostalCode,
        CustomerMobilePhone,
        'FirstName' Attribute,
        IIF(CustomerFirstName IS NOT NULL
            AND ImportFirstName IS NOT NULL
            AND LEFT(CustomerFirstName, 1) =
                LEFT(ImportFirstName, 1), 1, 0) Score
    FROM AttemptToMatch
    UNION
    SELECT
        CustomerLastName,
        CustomerFirstName,
        CustomerAddress1,
        CustomerPostalCode,
        CustomerMobilePhone,
        'Address1' Attribute,
        IIF(CustomerAddress1 IS NOT NULL
            AND ImportAddress1 IS NOT NULL
```

```
                    AND LEFT(CustomerAddress1, 10) =
                        LEFT(ImportAddress1, 10), 1, 0) Score
        FROM AttemptToMatch
        UNION
        SELECT
            CustomerLastName,
            CustomerFirstName,
            CustomerAddress1,
            CustomerPostalCode,
            CustomerMobilePhone,
            'PostalCode' Attribute,
            IIF(CustomerPostalCode IS NOT NULL
                AND ImportPostalCode IS NOT NULL
                AND LEFT(CustomerPostalCode, 5) =
                    LEFT(ImportPostalCode, 5), 1, 0) Score
        FROM AttemptToMatch
        UNION
        SELECT
            CustomerLastName,
            CustomerFirstName,
            CustomerAddress1,
            CustomerPostalCode,
            CustomerMobilePhone,
            'MobilePhone' Attribute,
            IIF(CustomerMobilePhone IS NOT NULL
                AND ImportMobilePhone IS NOT NULL
                AND REPLACE(CustomerMobilePhone, '-', '') =
                    REPLACE(ImportMobilePhone, '-', ''), 1, 0) Score
        FROM AttemptToMatch
    );
```

Let's re-create *ScoredCustomers*, too, to show the highest scores first:

```
DROP VIEW IF EXISTS ScoredCustomers;

CREATE VIEW ScoredCustomers
AS
(
    SELECT TOP 100 PERCENT
        CustomerLastName,
        CustomerFirstName,
        CustomerAddress1,
        CustomerPostalCode,
        CustomerMobilePhone,
        SUM(Score) Score
    FROM ScoreMatches
    GROUP BY CustomerLastName, CustomerFirstName, CustomerAddress1,
        CustomerPostalCode, CustomerMobilePhone
    ORDER BY SUM(Score) DESC, CustomerLastName, CustomerFirstName
);
```

How did we do?

```
SELECT TOP 35  -- There is a LONG tail of 1's, I'm only going to show you once.
    C.CustomerLastName    [Last Name],
    C.CustomerFirstName   [First Name],
    C.CustomerAddress1    [Address],
    C.CustomerPostalCode  [Postal Code],
    C.CustomerMobilePhone [Mobile Phone],
    C.Score,
    STRING_AGG(S.Attribute, ', ')
        WITHIN GROUP (ORDER BY S.Attribute) [Match Reasons]
FROM ScoredCustomers C
LEFT OUTER JOIN ScoreMatches S ON
        COALESCE(C.CustomerLastName, '') =
        COALESCE(S.CustomerLastName, '')
    AND COALESCE(LEFT(C.CustomerFirstName, 1), '') =
        COALESCE(LEFT(S.CustomerFirstName, 1), '')
    AND COALESCE(LEFT(C.CustomerAddress1, 10), '') =
        COALESCE(LEFT(S.CustomerAddress1, 10), '')
    AND COALESCE(LEFT(C.CustomerPostalCode, 5), '') =
        COALESCE(LEFT(S.CustomerPostalCode, 5), '')
    AND COALESCE(REPLACE(C.CustomerMobilePhone, '-', ''), '') =
        COALESCE(REPLACE(S.CustomerMobilePhone, '-', ''), '')
WHERE
    /*
        Only looking at customers where we get at least a partial hit.
    */
    C.Score > 0
    AND S.Score > 0
GROUP BY C.CustomerLastName, C.CustomerFirstName, C.CustomerAddress1,
        C.CustomerPostalCode, C.CustomerMobilePhone, C.Score
ORDER BY C.Score DESC;
```

	Last Name	First Name	Address	Postal Code	Mobile Phone	Score	Match Reasons
0	Bayless	Merilyn	195 13n N	95054	4085555015	5	Address1, FirstName, LastName, MobilePhone, PostalCode
1	Brideau	Junita	6 S Broadway St	07009	9735553423	5	Address1, FirstName, LastName, MobilePhone, PostalCode
2	Chavous	Roslyn	63517 Dupont St	39211	6015559632	5	Address1, FirstName, LastName, MobilePhone, PostalCode
3	Galam	Britt	2500 Pringle Rd Se #508	19440	2155553304	5	Address1, FirstName, LastName, MobilePhone, PostalCode
4	Garcia Lopez	Janey	40 Cambridge Ave	53715	6085557194	5	Address1, FirstName, LastName, MobilePhone, PostalCode

	Last Name	First Name	Address	Postal Code	Mobile Phone	Score	Match Reasons
5	Kines	Donte	3 Aspen St	01602	5085558576	5	Address1, FirstName, LastName, MobilePhone, PostalCode
6	Layous	Ma	78112 Morris Ave	06473	2035553388	5	Address1, FirstName, LastName, MobilePhone, PostalCode
7	Maisto	Reena	9648 S Main	21801	4105551863	5	Address1, FirstName, LastName, MobilePhone, PostalCode
8	Mirafuentes	Becky	30553 Washington Rd	07062	9085558409	5	Address1, FirstName, LastName, MobilePhone, PostalCode
9	Nunlee	Gary	2 W Mount Royal Ave	46040	3175556023	5	Address1, FirstName, LastName, MobilePhone, PostalCode
10	O'Connor	Kaitlyn	2 S Biscayne Blvd	21230	4105554903	5	Address1, FirstName, LastName, MobilePhone, PostalCode
11	Perin	Lavera	678 3rd Ave	33196	3055557291	5	Address1, FirstName, LastName, MobilePhone, PostalCode
12	Rochin	Xuan	2 Monroe St	94403	6505555072	5	Address1, FirstName, LastName, MobilePhone, PostalCode
13	Schmierer	Pamella	5161 Dorsett Rd	33030	3055558970	5	Address1, FirstName, LastName, MobilePhone, PostalCode
14	Snedley	Blanche	443 Arroyo Rd	87740	5755550956	5	Address1, FirstName, LastName, MobilePhone, PostalCode
15	Snedley	Mortimer	443 Arroyo Rd	87740	5755550956	5	Address1, FirstName, LastName, MobilePhone, PostalCode
16	Snedley, Jr.	Mortimer	443 Arroyo Rd	87740	5755550957	5	Address1, FirstName, LastName, MobilePhone, PostalCode
17	Staback	Martina	7 W Wabansia Ave #227	32822	4075556908	5	Address1, FirstName, LastName, MobilePhone, PostalCode
18	Timenez	Loreta	47857 Coney Island Ave	20735	3015556420	5	Address1, FirstName, LastName, MobilePhone, PostalCode

	Last Name	First Name	Address	Postal Code	Mobile Phone	Score	Match Reasons
19	Zurcher	Jerry	77 Massillon Rd #822	32937	3215555938	5	Address1, FirstName, LastName, MobilePhone, PostalCode
20	Degroot	Novella	303 N Radcliffe St	96720	8085554775	4	Address1, FirstName, MobilePhone, PostalCode
21	Eroman	Ilene	2853 S Central Expy	21061	4105559018	4	Address1, FirstName, LastName, MobilePhone
22	Hamilton	Charlene	985 E 6th Ave	95407	7075551771	4	Address1, FirstName, LastName, PostalCode
23	Husser	Selma	9 State Highway 57 #22	07306	2015558369	4	Address1, FirstName, LastName, MobilePhone
24	Waycott	Kanisha	5 Tomahawk Dr	90006	3235552780	3	Address1, FirstName, LastName
25	NULL	NULL	123 Snell Ave	65101	NULL	2	Address1, PostalCode
26	NULL	NULL	443 Arroyo Rd	87740	NULL	2	Address1, PostalCode
27	NULL	NULL	457 Prairie View St	80301	NULL	2	Address1, PostalCode
28	Treston	Lucy	57254 Brickell Ave #372	01602	5085555250	2	FirstName, PostalCode
29	Abdallah	Johnetta	1088 Pinehurst St	27514	9195559345	1	FirstName
30	Acey	Geoffrey	7 West Ave #1	60067	8475551734	1	FirstName
31	Adkin	Barbra	4 Kohler Memorial Dr	11230	7185553751	1	FirstName
32	Ahle	Delmy	65895 S 16th St	02909	4015552547	1	FirstName
33	Albares	Cammy	56 E Morehead St	78045	9565556195	1	FirstName
34	Amigon	Minna	2371 Jerrold Ave	19443	2155551229	1	FirstName

Now this gets interesting! We limited it to SELECT TOP 35 because of the long tail of "1" scores (hundreds). But we have 20 full matches on "Address1, FirstName, Last-Name, MobilePhone, PostalCode." These are pretty much guaranteed, or as good as we are going to get. Then we get some "4" scores on various permutations, then a single three, a couple of "2"s (matching on address and postal code can be interesting, but first name and postal code not so much), and then a long, long sequence of "1" scores matching on "FirstName" (which is actually first initial, so completely unsurprising).

We can now see that somewhere above "2" is our probable score cutoff. Is "3" good enough? "4"? Do you want to require only "5"s? Another thing to consider with partial matches (scores in this case less than five). Are some scores of 3 better than other scores? Perhaps. A score of 3 matching on last name, first name, and mobile phone is probably better than one matching on first name, address, and postal code. On the other hand, the latter might be considered a strong enough match itself. These are going to end up being business decisions, and this is where the tuning begins.

Check this out. Don't want to have that long string here? Want to have a reference table somewhere that has all the possible reason permutations and then just have a key to that here in this result set? Easy. Look for the comments in the following example:

```
SELECT TOP 10
    C.CustomerLastName    [Last Name],
    C.CustomerFirstName   [First Name],
    C.CustomerAddress1    [Address],
    C.CustomerPostalCode  [Postal Code],
    C.CustomerMobilePhone [Mobile Phone],
    C.Score,
    /*
        We are doing the same STRING_AGG to get the ordered reason list
        as before, but then we are hashing those with the MD5 algorithm
        (cute, yes?), and then casting that to a BIGINT, et voila! There
        is your artificial key for your "Reasons" join table. Don't say
        I never taught you anything.
    */
    CAST
    (
        HASHBYTES
        (
            'MD5',
            STRING_AGG(S.Attribute, ', ')
            WITHIN GROUP (ORDER BY S.Attribute)
        )
        AS BIGINT
    ) [Match Reasons]
FROM ScoredCustomers C
LEFT OUTER JOIN ScoreMatches S ON
        COALESCE(C.CustomerLastName, '') =
        COALESCE(S.CustomerLastName, '')
    AND COALESCE(LEFT(C.CustomerFirstName, 1), '') =
        COALESCE(LEFT(S.CustomerFirstName, 1), '')
    AND COALESCE(LEFT(C.CustomerAddress1, 10), '') =
        COALESCE(LEFT(S.CustomerAddress1, 10), '')
    AND COALESCE(LEFT(C.CustomerPostalCode, 5), '') =
        COALESCE(LEFT(S.CustomerPostalCode, 5), '')
    AND COALESCE(REPLACE(C.CustomerMobilePhone, '-', ''), '') =
        COALESCE(REPLACE(S.CustomerMobilePhone, '-', ''), '')
WHERE
        C.Score > 0
    AND S.Score > 0
GROUP BY C.CustomerLastName, C.CustomerFirstName, C.CustomerAddress1,
        C.CustomerPostalCode, C.CustomerMobilePhone, C.Score
ORDER BY C.Score DESC;
```

	Last Name	First Name	Address	Postal Code	Mobile Phone	Score	Match Reasons
0	Bayless	Merilyn	195 13n N	95054	4085555015	5	857095584674320384
1	Brideau	Junita	6 S Broadway St	07009	9735553423	5	857095584674320384

	Last Name	First Name	Address	Postal Code	Mobile Phone	Score	Match Reasons
2	Chavous	Roslyn	63517 Dupont St	39211	6015559632	5	857095584674320384
3	Galam	Britt	2500 Pringle Rd Se #508	19440	2155553304	5	857095584674320384
4	Garcia Lopez	Janey	40 Cambridge Ave	53715	6085557194	5	857095584674320384
5	Kines	Donte	3 Aspen St	01602	5085558576	5	857095584674320384
6	Layous	Ma	78112 Morris Ave	06473	2035553388	5	857095584674320384
7	Maisto	Reena	9648 S Main	21801	4105551863	5	857095584674320384
8	Mirafuentes	Becky	30553 Washington Rd	07062	9085558409	5	857095584674320384
9	Nunlee	Gary	2 W Mount Royal Ave	46040	3175556023	5	857095584674320384

We've had the big reveal: if you count the number of attributes on which two items fuzzily "match," you can use that sum as a simple "score" to detect how good you're doing. And it works! But it can be better.

Tuning Scores

We've talked about how "Some matches are more equal than others" (to misquote Orwell), and the first idea to make things clearer is to raise the score given to certain matches. Let's try. As mentioned, mobile phone is an excellent match; if we find it, do we even need the others? Let's give finding a mobile phone match a score of "5" and see what happens. We will change the *ScoreMatches* view accordingly:

```
DROP VIEW IF EXISTS ScoreMatches;

CREATE VIEW ScoreMatches
AS
(
    SELECT
        CustomerLastName,
        CustomerFirstName,
        CustomerAddress1,
        CustomerPostalCode,
        CustomerMobilePhone,
        'LastName' Attribute,
        IIF(CustomerLastName IS NOT NULL
            AND ImportLastName IS NOT NULL
            AND CustomerLastName = ImportLastName, 1, 0) Score
    FROM AttemptToMatch
    UNION
    SELECT
        CustomerLastName,
        CustomerFirstName,
        CustomerAddress1,
        CustomerPostalCode,
        CustomerMobilePhone,
        'FirstName' Attribute,
        IIF(CustomerFirstName IS NOT NULL
```

```
            AND ImportFirstName IS NOT NULL
            AND LEFT(CustomerFirstName, 1) =
                LEFT(ImportFirstName, 1), 1, 0) Score
    FROM AttemptToMatch
    UNION
    SELECT
        CustomerLastName,
        CustomerFirstName,
        CustomerAddress1,
        CustomerPostalCode,
        CustomerMobilePhone,
        'Address1' Attribute,
        IIF(CustomerAddress1 IS NOT NULL
            AND ImportAddress1 IS NOT NULL
            AND LEFT(CustomerAddress1, 10) =
                LEFT(ImportAddress1, 10), 1, 0) Score
    FROM AttemptToMatch
    UNION
    SELECT
        CustomerLastName,
        CustomerFirstName,
        CustomerAddress1,
        CustomerPostalCode,
        CustomerMobilePhone,
        'PostalCode' Attribute,
        IIF(CustomerPostalCode IS NOT NULL
            AND ImportPostalCode IS NOT NULL
            AND LEFT(CustomerPostalCode, 5) =
                LEFT(ImportPostalCode, 5), 1, 0) Score
    FROM AttemptToMatch
    UNION
    SELECT
        CustomerLastName,
        CustomerFirstName,
        CustomerAddress1,
        CustomerPostalCode,
        CustomerMobilePhone,
        'MobilePhone' Attribute,
        IIF(CustomerMobilePhone IS NOT NULL
            AND ImportMobilePhone IS NOT NULL
            /*
                Making the score for this hit 5.
            */
            AND REPLACE(CustomerMobilePhone, '-', '') =
                REPLACE(ImportMobilePhone, '-', ''), 5, 0) Score
    FROM AttemptToMatch
);
```

We're going to pull 35 again so we can see a longer tail and see what changed:

```
SELECT TOP 35
    C.CustomerLastName    [Last Name],
    C.CustomerFirstName   [First Name],
```

```
        C.CustomerAddress1     [Address],
        C.CustomerPostalCode   [Postal Code],
        C.CustomerMobilePhone  [Mobile Phone],
        C.Score,
        STRING_AGG(S.Attribute, ', ')
            WITHIN GROUP (ORDER BY S.Attribute) [Match Reasons]
FROM ScoredCustomers C
LEFT OUTER JOIN ScoreMatches S ON
            COALESCE(C.CustomerLastName, '') =
            COALESCE(S.CustomerLastName, '')
        AND COALESCE(LEFT(C.CustomerFirstName, 1), '') =
            COALESCE(LEFT(S.CustomerFirstName, 1), '')
        AND COALESCE(LEFT(C.CustomerAddress1, 10), '') =
            COALESCE(LEFT(S.CustomerAddress1, 10), '')
        AND COALESCE(LEFT(C.CustomerPostalCode, 5), '') =
            COALESCE(LEFT(S.CustomerPostalCode, 5), '')
        AND COALESCE(REPLACE(C.CustomerMobilePhone, '-', ''), '') =
            COALESCE(REPLACE(S.CustomerMobilePhone, '-', ''), '')
WHERE
        C.Score > 0
    AND S.Score > 0
GROUP BY C.CustomerLastName, C.CustomerFirstName, C.CustomerAddress1,
        C.CustomerPostalCode, C.CustomerMobilePhone, C.Score
ORDER BY C.Score DESC;
```

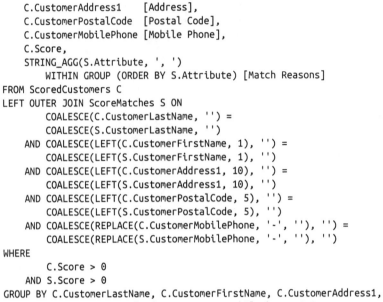

	Last Name	First Name	Address	Postal Code	Mobile Phone	Score	Match Reasons
0	Bayless	Merilyn	195 13n N	95054	4085555015	9	Address1, FirstName, LastName, MobilePhone, PostalCode
1	Brideau	Junita	6 S Broadway St	07009	9735553423	9	Address1, FirstName, LastName, MobilePhone, PostalCode
2	Chavous	Roslyn	63517 Dupont St	39211	6015559632	9	Address1, FirstName, LastName, MobilePhone, PostalCode
3	Galam	Britt	2500 Pringle Rd Se #508	19440	2155553304	9	Address1, FirstName, LastName, MobilePhone, PostalCode
4	Garcia Lopez	Janey	40 Cambridge Ave	53715	6085557194	9	Address1, FirstName, LastName, MobilePhone, PostalCode
5	Kines	Donte	3 Aspen St	01602	5085558576	9	Address1, FirstName, LastName, MobilePhone, PostalCode
6	Layous	Ma	78112 Morris Ave	06473	2035553388	9	Address1, FirstName, LastName, MobilePhone, PostalCode

	Last Name	First Name	Address	Postal Code	Mobile Phone	Score	Match Reasons
7	Maisto	Reena	9648 S Main	21801	4105551863	9	Address1, FirstName, LastName, MobilePhone, PostalCode
8	Mirafuentes	Becky	30553 Washington Rd	07062	9085558409	9	Address1, FirstName, LastName, MobilePhone, PostalCode
9	Nunlee	Gary	2 W Mount Royal Ave	46040	3175556023	9	Address1, FirstName, LastName, MobilePhone, PostalCode
10	O'Connor	Kaitlyn	2 S Biscayne Blvd	21230	4105554903	9	Address1, FirstName, LastName, MobilePhone, PostalCode
11	Perin	Lavera	678 3rd Ave	33196	3055557291	9	Address1, FirstName, LastName, MobilePhone, PostalCode
12	Rochin	Xuan	2 Monroe St	94403	6505555072	9	Address1, FirstName, LastName, MobilePhone, PostalCode
13	Schmierer	Pamella	5161 Dorsett Rd	33030	3055558970	9	Address1, FirstName, LastName, MobilePhone, PostalCode
14	Snedley	Blanche	443 Arroyo Rd	87740	5755550956	9	Address1, FirstName, LastName, MobilePhone, PostalCode
15	Snedley	Mortimer	443 Arroyo Rd	87740	5755550956	9	Address1, FirstName, LastName, MobilePhone, PostalCode
16	Snedley, Jr.	Mortimer	443 Arroyo Rd	87740	5755550957	9	Address1, FirstName, LastName, MobilePhone, PostalCode
17	Staback	Martina	7 W Wabansia Ave #227	32822	4075556908	9	Address1, FirstName, LastName, MobilePhone, PostalCode
18	Timenez	Loreta	47857 Coney Island Ave	20735	3015556420	9	Address1, FirstName, LastName, MobilePhone, PostalCode
19	Zurcher	Jerry	77 Massillon Rd #822	32937	3215555938	9	Address1, FirstName, LastName, MobilePhone, PostalCode
20	Degroot	Novella	303 N Radcliffe St	96720	8085554775	8	Address1, FirstName, MobilePhone, PostalCode
21	Eroman	Ilene	2853 S Central Expy	21061	4105559018	8	Address1, FirstName, LastName, MobilePhone

	Last Name	First Name	Address	Postal Code	Mobile Phone	Score	Match Reasons
22	Husser	Selma	9 State Highway 57 #22	07306	2015558369	8	Address1, FirstName, LastName, MobilePhone
23	Hamilton	Charlene	985 E 6th Ave	95407	7075551771	4	Address1, FirstName, LastName, PostalCode
24	Waycott	Kanisha	5 Tomahawk Dr	90006	3235552780	3	Address1, FirstName, LastName
25	NULL	NULL	123 Snell Ave	65101	NULL	2	Address1, PostalCode
26	NULL	NULL	443 Arroyo Rd	87740	NULL	2	Address1, PostalCode
27	NULL	NULL	457 Prairie View St	80301	NULL	2	Address1, PostalCode
28	Treston	Lucy	57254 Brickell Ave #372	01602	5085555250	2	FirstName, PostalCode
29	Abdallah	Johnetta	1088 Pinehurst St	27514	9195559345	1	FirstName
30	Acey	Geoffrey	7 West Ave #1	60067	8475551734	1	FirstName
31	Adkin	Barbra	4 Kohler Memorial Dr	11230	7185553751	1	FirstName
32	Ahle	Delmy	65895 S 16th St	02909	4015552547	1	FirstName
33	Albares	Cammy	56 E Morehead St	78045	9565556195	1	FirstName
34	Amigon	Minna	2371 Jerrold Ave	19443	2155551229	1	FirstName

Hmmm...the top 20 remain the top 20 because five matches on five attributes is as good as it gets. The "shape" of the curve is basically the same; there is a bit of a change where there are some "8" scores, and then it immediately drops to "4." Maybe that helps you see your cutoff point easier.

But in general I find applying a higher score to some fields over others is not as useful an idea as you would think. If last name and ZIP code are more "valid" than suffix or city, why can't we give them a "5" and the latter two a "1" and still keep all the checks and add everything up? Because it rarely actually helps and can make tuning the cutoff more complicated. If you do want to go this way, then my advice is to start with a "1" score for every attribute match and then slowly and carefully change the scoring one attribute at a time and see if it materially affects the results or just "shifts everything upwards" by the new score.

Perhaps the more important thing to ask is, "Do we even need anything other than mobile phone?" Good question, let's see. We will change the *AttemptToMatch* and *ScoreMatches* views to consider only the *MobilePhone* attribute:

```
DROP VIEW IF EXISTS AttemptToMatch;

CREATE VIEW AttemptToMatch
AS
(
    SELECT
        C.LastName      [CustomerLastName],
        C.FirstName     [CustomerFirstName],
```

```
            C.Address1    [CustomerAddress1],
            C.PostalCode  [CustomerPostalCode],
            C.MobilePhone [CustomerMobilePhone],
            I.LastName    [ImportLastName],
            I.FirstName   [ImportFirstName],
            I.Address1    [ImportAddress1],
            I.PostalCode  [ImportPostalCode],
            I.MobilePhone [ImportMobilePhone]
        FROM  crm.NormalizedCustomer C
        LEFT OUTER JOIN staging.ImportCustomer I ON
            COALESCE(REPLACE(C.MobilePhone, '-', ''), '') =
            COALESCE(REPLACE(I.MobilePhone, '-', ''), '')
)

DROP VIEW IF EXISTS ScoreMatches;

CREATE VIEW ScoreMatches
AS
(
    SELECT
        CustomerLastName,
        CustomerFirstName,
        CustomerAddress1,
        CustomerPostalCode,
        CustomerMobilePhone,
        'MobilePhone' Attribute,
        IIF(CustomerMobilePhone IS NOT NULL
            AND ImportMobilePhone IS NOT NULL
            /*
                Changed it back to 1.
            */
            AND REPLACE(CustomerMobilePhone, '-', '') =
                REPLACE(ImportMobilePhone, '-', ''), 1, 0) Score
    FROM AttemptToMatch
);
```

How did that do? Did that change anything? Let's see how many matches we get:

```
SELECT
    C.CustomerLastName    [Last Name],
    C.CustomerFirstName   [First Name],
    C.CustomerAddress1    [Address],
    C.CustomerPostalCode  [Postal Code],
    C.CustomerMobilePhone [Mobile Phone],
    C.Score
FROM ScoredCustomers C
LEFT OUTER JOIN ScoreMatches S ON
    COALESCE(REPLACE(C.CustomerMobilePhone, '-', ''), '') =
    COALESCE(REPLACE(S.CustomerMobilePhone, '-', ''), '')
WHERE
    /*
        Only looking at customers where we get at least a partial hit.
    */
```

```
        C.Score > 0
    AND S.Score > 0
GROUP BY C.CustomerLastName, C.CustomerFirstName, C.CustomerAddress1,
        C.CustomerPostalCode, C.CustomerMobilePhone, C.Score
ORDER BY C.Score DESC;
```

	Last Name	First Name	Address	Postal Code	Mobile Phone	Score
0	Snedley	Mortimer	443 Arroyo Rd	87740	5755550956	12
1	Snedley	Blanche	443 Arroyo Rd	87740	5755550956	4
2	Snedley, Jr.	Mortimer	443 Arroyo Rd	87740	5755550957	3
3	O'Connor	Kaitlyn	2 S Biscayne Blvd	21230	4105554903	2
4	Perin	Lavera	678 3rd Ave	33196	3055557291	1
5	Rochin	Xuan	2 Monroe St	94403	6505555072	1
6	Schmierer	Pamella	5161 Dorsett Rd	33030	3055558970	1
7	Staback	Martina	7 W Wabansia Ave #227	32822	4075556908	1
8	Timenez	Loreta	47857 Coney Island Ave	20735	3015556420	1
9	Zurcher	Jerry	77 Massillon Rd #822	32937	3215555938	1
10	Bayless	Merilyn	195 13n N	95054	4085555015	1
11	Brideau	Junita	6 S Broadway St	07009	9735553423	1
12	Chavous	Roslyn	63517 Dupont St	39211	6015559632	1
13	Degroot	Novella	303 N Radcliffe St	96720	8085554775	1
14	Eroman	Ilene	2853 S Central Expy	21061	4105559018	1
15	Galam	Britt	2500 Pringle Rd Se #508	19440	2155553304	1
16	Garcia Lopez	Janey	40 Cambridge Ave	53715	6085557194	1
17	Husser	Selma	9 State Highway 57 #22	07306	2015558369	1
18	Kines	Donte	3 Aspen St	01602	5085558576	1
19	Layous	Ma	78112 Morris Ave	06473	2035553388	1
20	Maisto	Reena	9648 S Main	21801	4105551863	1
21	Mirafuentes	Becky	30553 Washington Rd	07062	9085558409	1
22	Nunlee	Gary	2 W Mount Royal Ave	46040	3175556023	1

We had 20 perfect matches before; now we have 23 (all matching on just phone number this time). That could be a "good enough" (that phrase again) cut for your business, and you're done! Only you can decide.

What about those scores above "1"? That means we've found matches on duplicate mobile phones in our data. That could be OK; we've talked about partners (rarely) sharing a mobile phone or (more commonly) an email address. But "12" seems "high." We will be digging into why later.

Eliminating Duplicates

Duplicates happen. Or more precisely, near duplicates or apparent duplicates happen. And sometimes the rare true duplicate:

> Data steward: "Oh, that was a duplicate record in the CRM; we merged it with the original after you pointed it out. Thanks!"

We are going to look at how duplicates happen—in the customer data, in the source data—because of our own processing. Then we will look at how (and when) to minimize them, using techniques such as DISTINCT, GROUP BY, MAX(ModifiedOn), hashes, and ye olde SOUNDEX.

Duplicate Data

Poor John Smith. Which one? All of them, in some sense. How many are there in the world? Millions? How many are in your customer data? Tens? Hundreds?

That's the easiest "duplicate data" to understand and explain to a businessperson. It isn't exactly duplicate data; it just appears that way on first examination because we aren't looking at enough "attributes" (data points about Mr. Smith). To "deduplicate" these apparent duplicates, let's look at all the columns available:

```
SELECT
/*
    Let's look at all columns to decide what else we can match against.
*/
    *
FROM crm.NormalizedCustomer
WHERE
    LastName LIKE 'Snedley%'        /* Ignoring suffixes for now */
    AND LEFT(FirstName, 1) = 'M'    /* Looking at first initial  */
ORDER BY LastName, FirstName, Company;
```

Oh, my. In Table 10-1, we see both the father and son (presumably, because they share a lot of demographic info, like address) plus a couple of those pesky "person-like entities" I prattle on about (when not ranting or preaching I am often prattling...ask my friends). We want to keep using that first initial because of prior discussions ("Jim" versus "James" versus "Jimmy"). So we need to add some more attributes (columns) to our filter (WHERE clause):

```
SELECT
    *
FROM crm.NormalizedCustomer
WHERE
    LastName LIKE 'Snedley%'
    AND LEFT(FirstName, 1) = 'M'
    AND Company IS NULL   /* Get rid of those pesky person-like entities */
ORDER BY LastName, FirstName, Company;
```

Table 10-1. Match candidates

	LastName	FirstName	Company	Address1	City	County	State	PostalCode	Country	MobilePhone	HomePhone	Email	Web
0	Snedley	Mortimer	NULL	443 Arroyo Rd	Raton	Colfax	NM	87740	US	5755550956	5755550956	mortimer.snedley@example.com	NULL
1	Snedley	Mortimer	Mortimer Snedley Estate	443 Arroyo Rd	Raton	Colfax	NM	87740	U.S.	5755550956	5755550956	mortimer.snedley@example.com	NULL
2	Snedley	Mortimer	Mortimer Snedley Trust	443 Arroyo Rd	Raton	Colfax	NM	87740	United States	5755550956	5755550956	NULL	NULL
3	Snedley, Jr.	Mortimer	NULL	443 Arroyo Rd	Raton	Colfax	NM	87740	USA	5755550957	5755550956	mortimer.snedley@example.com	NULL

Table 10-2. Get rid of person-like entities

	LastName	FirstName	Company	Address1	City	County	State	PostalCode	Country	MobilePhone	HomePhone	Email	Web
0	Snedley	Mortimer	NULL	443 Arroyo Rd	Raton	Colfax	NM	87740	US	5755550956	5755550956	mortimer.snedley@example.com	NULL
1	Snedley, Jr.	Mortimer	NULL	443 Arroyo Rd	Raton	Colfax	NM	87740	USA	5755550957	5755550956	mortimer.snedley@example.com	NULL

In Table 10-2, we can see address is a problem (common with families, especially rural families that live close together and all have P.O. boxes for addresses), so let's look at mobile phone, which is typically a good match. If we follow my advice of checking phone numbers against all available customer phone attributes (mobile, work, home, fax, pager, etc.), then that doesn't buy us anything because Mort has the same number for both his home and mobile phone, which is then shared as a home phone with Junior. Perhaps the house has no landline (more and more common) and the dad gave his mobile number for both. Then maybe the son said he didn't really have a home phone at all and gave his dad's mobile number as his emergency contact number and the representative shoved it in the home phone field to have it "somewhere." It happens.

Anyway:

```
SELECT
    *
FROM crm.NormalizedCustomer
WHERE
    LastName LIKE 'Snedley%'
    AND LEFT(FirstName, 1) = 'M'
    AND Company IS NULL
    AND '5755550956' IN (MobilePhone, HomePhone) -- Check both
ORDER BY LastName, FirstName, Company;
```

Yup, that didn't help (see Table 10-3). In the end, with this very limited dataset, the best we can do is un-wildcard the last name and be explicit. This will drop off "Snedley, Jr.," though, which isn't what we want if we were actually looking for the son, who sometimes doesn't like going by "Junior":

```
SELECT
    *
FROM crm.NormalizedCustomer
WHERE
    LastName = 'Snedley'   -- No longer a wildcard but an exact search
    AND LEFT(FirstName, 1) = 'M'
    AND Company IS NULL
    AND '5755550956' IN (MobilePhone, HomePhone)
ORDER BY LastName, FirstName, Company;
```

We have gotten rid of the "duplicate" (see Table 10-4), but is it what we want? I don't think so. I usually leave both when the matches (score) are high, because it may be up to a business person reading a dashboard or report to understand the context and choose the appropriate person, or perhaps they actually want both the father and the son!

Table 10-3. *Still possible duplicates*

	LastName	FirstName	Company	Address1	City	County	State	PostalCode	Country	MobilePhone	HomePhone	Email	Web
0	Snedley	Mortimer	NULL	443 Arroyo Rd	Raton	Colfax	NM	87740	US	5755550956	5755550956	mortimer.snedley@example.com	NULL
1	Snedley, Jr.	Mortimer	NULL	443 Arroyo Rd	Raton	Colfax	NM	87740	USA	5755550957	5755550956	mortimer.snedley@example.com	NULL

Table 10-4. *No dups but not what we want*

	LastName	FirstName	Company	Address1	City	County	State	PostalCode	Country	MobilePhone	HomePhone	Email	Web
0	Snedley	Mortimer	NULL	443 Arroyo Rd	Raton	Colfax	NM	87740	US	5755550956	5755550956	mortimer.snedley@example.com	NULL

All this to hammer home you must know the data as well as you can, and you must be in communication with "the business" throughout this process to help make such decisions and understand the nuances of your employer's or client's data.

Finally, sometimes real duplicate data exists. Perhaps it is a symptom of an import error and restart. Perhaps a customer service representative entered a new customer record without looking to see if the customer on the phone already existed (it happens; they have time metrics they must hit). When you find these duplicates, it is almost always the correct answer to get them merged on the production side (usually not your job, but most mature CRM systems have an ability to merge, and even detect and automerge if you are brave enough, duplicate records). The algorithms used are usually customizable and—surprise!—are a series of attributes to match on to decide if something is a true duplicate.

On the import side, you can simply drop pesky dups out of the dataset with an ETL, dealing with it with something like this:

```
SELECT COUNT(*) [Original Customer Count] FROM dbo.PotentialMatches;
```

Original Customer Count
0 34

Let's see if there are any apparent duplicates in our customer data when we consider just these attributes:

```
SELECT DISTINCT   /* Drop dups */
    last_name,
    first_name,
    company_name,
    address,
    city,
    state,
    zip,
    phone1,
    email
INTO staging.Dedup
FROM dbo.PotentialMatches;

SELECT COUNT(*) [Deduped Customer Count] FROM staging.DeDup;
```

Deduped Customer Count
0 33

Want to see who was dropped and maybe examine a few more source attributes first before deciding it was "duplicate enough"?

```
SELECT TOP 10
    COUNT(*) Total,
```

```
        last_name,
        first_name,
        company_name,
        address,
        city,
        state,
        zip,
        phone1,
        email
    FROM dbo.PotentialMatches
    GROUP BY last_name, first_name, company_name, address, city, state,
             zip, phone1, email
    HAVING COUNT(*) > 1
    ORDER BY COUNT(*) DESC, last_name, first_name, company_name
```

	Total	last _name	first _name	company _name	address	city	state	zip	phone1	email
0	2	O'Connor	Kaitlyn	NULL	2 S Biscayne Blvd	Baltimore	MD	21230-4903	410-555-4903	kaitlyn.ogg @example .com

We see that Kaitlyn O'Connor with a *Total* of "2" is our duplicate. After checking that the import record is a true duplicate, you can use the *staging.Dedup* table as the new source for your downstream processing, safely knowing there is only one Ms. O'Connor in there. Or if you are feeling particularly brave, you can delete one of the duplicate rows out of the original data.

Beware Automated Processes!

Sometimes, for whatever reason—errors in the import process, duplicates in the source data, human error—you get 1:*n* matches when you were expecting 1:1, and they actually appear to be true duplicates. If additional data is available, you may want to consider adding *CreatedOn* or *ModifiedOn* and then deciding which to use and whether the latest date is truly the greatest. For example, are you sure your *Modified On* dates are the last true human touch and not some trivial automated process that updates records each night? Perhaps a job doing geolocation tagging like latitude and longitude? Or updates from nightly processing on the mainframe core?

And watch out for those automated processes! They can change things for the better: ZIP+4 is generally better than not having it, making the USPS happy with your mailings; latitude and longitude *may* be better depending on your address quality; these are all good reasons for having a process for cleaning up and normalizing addresses. But just make sure you are aware of how it all works so you don't write matching code that has results that shift under your feet. "Hey! We had 100 matches yesterday, and yet none today on the same import data! What gives?" Maybe something changed all your customer data, hmmm?

Duplicated Data

The previous example dealt with "duplicate" or "apparently duplicate" data where there were actually multiple rows in either the customer or import dataset that were similar enough across multiple attributes to, well, *appear* duplicated.

I use the term *duplicated data* here to denote data that wasn't duplicated when we started our processing—ETLs, data cleansing, scoring—but somehow those processes added duplicates (or apparent duplicates) into a downstream dataset.

Sometimes this is wanted. There will be lots of apparent duplicates in the upstream source for scoring (every row gets a "1" for just being in the result set, remember) on something like matching on first initial, but we want those—in that particular dataset! But we want further downstream processing to (at some point) aggregate and SUM those records on that score and get down to one per customer. We hope.

Let's look at a simple example with our favorite family, the Snedleys. As you will remember, there is Mortimer (nicknamed "Mort"), Blanche (aka "The Widow Snedley," but we haven't yet gotten to Chapter 11, on data quality), and Mortimer Snedley, Jr. ("Junior").

```
SELECT
    last_name,
    first_name,
    address,
    city,
    state,
    zip,
    phone1
FROM staging.Dedup
WHERE
    last_name LIKE 'Snedley%'
    AND company_name IS NULL   -- No pesky person-like entities for now
ORDER BY last_name, first_name;
```

	last_name	first_name	address	city	state	zip	phone1
0	Snedley	Blanche	443 Arroyo Road	Raton	NM	87740-0956	575-555-0956
1	Snedley	Mortimer	443 Arroyo Road	Raton	NM	87740-0956	575-555-0956
2	Snedley, Jr.	Mortimer	443 Arroyo	Raton	NM	87740-0957	575-555-0957
3	Snedley, Jr.	Mortimer	443 Arroyo Road	Raton	NM	87740-0957	575-555-0957

We already see one problem! We didn't really dedup *staging.Dedup*! Note one of Junior's addresses is not like the others. OK, let's go ahead and normalize it all on the way to ideally deduping correctly this time:

```
SELECT DISTINCT  /* Drop dups */
    last_name LastName,
    LEFT(first_name, 1) FirstName,
```

```
        TRANSLATE(company_name, '.,-()', '    ') Company,
        LEFT(address, 10) Address1,
        city City,
        state State,
        LEFT(RIGHT('00000' + CAST(zip AS VARCHAR(5)), 5), 5) PostalCode,
        REPLACE(TRANSLATE(phone1, '-()', '   '), ' ', '') MobilePhone,
        CASE
            WHEN email IS NULL THEN NULL
            WHEN CHARINDEX('@', email) = 0
                OR CHARINDEX('.', email) = 0 THEN NULL
            ELSE email
        END Email
    INTO staging.Dedup
    FROM dbo.PotentialMatches;

    SELECT COUNT(*) [Deduped Customer Count] FROM staging.DeDup;
```

Deduped Customer Count
0 33

Still 33! But then we remember, Junior has a different mobile phone, and we're not bringing over home phone. So we can still disambiguate him on both last name and mobile phone:

```
SELECT
    LastName,
    FirstName,
    Address1,
    City,
    State,
    PostalCode,
    MobilePhone
FROM staging.Dedup
WHERE
    LastName LIKE 'Snedley%'
    AND Company IS NULL
ORDER BY LastName, FirstName;
```

	LastName	FirstName	Address1	City	State	PostalCode	MobilePhone
0	Snedley	B	443 Arroyo	Raton	NM	87740	5755550956
1	Snedley	M	443 Arroyo	Raton	NM	87740	5755550956
2	Snedley, Jr.	M	443 Arroyo	Raton	NM	87740	5755550957
3	Snedley, Jr.	M	443 Arroyo	Raton	NM	87740	5755550957

Wait, what? We just somehow introduced what appear to be two real duplicates, from a table that we know (know) has no duplicates because of that SELECT DISTINCT into dedups. This, with a 33, told us we hadn't really changed anything—we still had the same deduped data as before. But now we have two dups. What gives? Simple. I left off an attribute:

```
SELECT
    LastName,
    FirstName,
    Address1,
    City,
    State,
    PostalCode,
    MobilePhone,
    Email
FROM staging.Dedup
WHERE
    LastName LIKE 'Snedley%'
    AND Company IS NULL
ORDER BY LastName, FirstName;
```

	LastName	FirstName	Address1	City	State	PostalCode	MobilePhone	Email
0	Snedley	B	443 Arroyo	Raton	NM	87740	5755550956	mortimer.snedley@example.com
1	Snedley	M	443 Arroyo	Raton	NM	87740	5755550956	mortimer.snedley@example.com
2	Snedley, Jr.	M	443 Arroyo	Raton	NM	87740	5755550957	mortimer.snedley.jr@example.com
3	Snedley, Jr.	M	443 Arroyo	Raton	NM	87740	5755550957	mortimer.snedley@example.com

And we see Junior has two email addresses, one that acknowledges his juniorness, perhaps for business or legal reasons, and one that doesn't give away he comes from a long line of proud Morts. It's all good—we all present different faces in different environments. Anyway, great! We understand where our "apparent duplicates" (see why I keep hammering on "apparent") came from. Often it is just that: simple human error on my part. Perhaps I really do want to drop off that email address (the fake regulatory change I mentioned in Chapter 9), so I just need to add a DISTINCT on the way down to fewer columns to dedup my newly duped data from the deduped source:

```
SELECT DISTINCT  /* Add this, but know why you are doing it */
    LastName,
    FirstName,
    Address1,
    City,
    State,
    PostalCode,
    MobilePhone
FROM staging.Dedup
WHERE
    LastName LIKE 'Snedley%'
```

```
        AND Company IS NULL
    ORDER BY LastName, FirstName;
```

	LastName	FirstName	Address1	City	State	PostalCode	MobilePhone
0	Snedley	B	443 Arroyo	Raton	NM	87740	5755550956
1	Snedley	M	443 Arroyo	Raton	NM	87740	5755550956
2	Snedley, Jr.	M	443 Arroyo	Raton	NM	87740	5755550957

There is so much more to say on this, but it depends on how you have done your processing up to the point you start getting apparent duplicates. The answer is often to start unrolling, step-by-step, how you got there, with the most recent steps first. This is why I like to do a lot of ETLs into staging tables along the way so that I can check each one for sanity and move on after I am comfortable with it and therefore should never have to retreat more than a step or two to figure out what I did wrong.

Final Thoughts on Scoring

Our toolchest is growing and getting useful, and with scoring we've learned another trick:

Normalizing data
> Removing punctuation and pesky issues like abbreviations. This helps solve a whole class of problems when matching data.

Parsing data
> Making new data out of "complex" strings. Removing data quality issues at the "raw representation" layer of characters and collations.

Scoring data
> Understanding how well two disparate datasets match. And doing so in a way that, combined with the preceding, makes all of our assumptions explicit, repeatable, and tunable.

What's not to like?

This scoring technique is so powerful, and yet it is so simple. And notice how well you can apply it to other areas. I've used similar techniques to score lists from Marketing into some spectrum of "qualified lead or opportunity." Interesting note about those contest entry forms I mock: they do have one "tell" in them for interested, or at least sincere, people. If a row is completely and accurately filled out, they may well be sincerely interested in a follow-up call, at least telling them they won that game console!

You can use scoring to fruitfully find matches across log files from disparate systems. Did we match within the time window? Did we match on user ID? Did we match on the first 10 characters of the error text? Did the "from" IP address in one match the "client" IP address in the other?

Sometimes the simplest score is just a "hit." If you find something in some text, add "1." Keep adding "1" with each new find. We will use that technique heavily when we discuss impact analysis in Chapter 13.

There are still a few cool tricks upcoming (for example, code-generating code to search code for code, also in Chapter 13), but with just these three techniques—normalizing, parsing, and scoring—you can do a lot with "fuzzy" matching!

## CHAPTER 11

Data Quality, or GIGO

GIGO

1. Garbage In, Garbage Out
Usually said in response to lusers who complain that a program didn't "do the right thing" when given imperfect input or otherwise mistreated in some way. Also commonly used to describe failures in human decision making due to faulty, incomplete, or imprecise data.

2. Garbage In, Gospel Out
This more recent expansion is a sardonic comment on the tendency human beings have to put excessive trust in "computerized" data.

—*The Jargon File (https://oreil.ly/p6DFZ)*

This chapter should have been first perhaps. But often our job is not to clean up data in production or the import datasets. You may only be a contractor with no authority, or there is no time. Often even if a data cleanup effort is put in place, it is a one-time shot, and then "entropic drift" begins to happen where the same mistakes keep getting made and the data quality (DQ) slowly degrades again. Without procedures and processes in place to keep the data clean, often such efforts happen around system migrations and then everything reverts back to "normal" (that is, no edit checks during or after data entry or import).

This chapter looks at various things we can do to deal with data quality—both guarding from the lack of it and making it better.

Sneaking Data Quality In

My favorite method of surfacing DQ issues to field staff who have the access and ability to clean it up in the source system is to put it on their pre-existing dashboard or queue. Many shops have some such system where people go to pull their work items for the day. If you can insert new DQ rows into their dashboard, they become just another work item to be picked up and worked. You want such items to be as follows:

Clear
> "The date of birth for customer Mortimer Snedley is in the future. Please correct." is good. "Bad birth date." is not as good. "Fix this customer!" is terrible.

Actionable
> Give a link directly to the screen where the correction can be made.

Necessary
> Birth dates are often important for tax purposes, so it is good to get them cleaned up. This isn't the place for Marketing to want to make sure users ask customers for their favorite color, for example.

If the edit checks can't be built into the UI (and often they can't, or you can't check for everything because it slows the UX down too much), then having items show up on a dashboard either semi-immediately or the next day through some DQ "tripwire" process can be enough. The user sees it—"Oh, no! I was in a hurry yesterday!"—and goes to correct it while it is still fresh in their minds (and thanks to the handy link you put in the dashboard or report for them to click to correct it). It is better to have small checks rather than group too many together. For example, it is better to have two checks like this:

- Birthday in the future
- Birthday more than 110 (or whatever) years ago

than combine both into a single logical test with an OR between them. "Bad birth date" may not indicate what is wrong immediately to a busy customer service representative, so you want to make sure your messages let them know quickly and exactly what needs to be fixed, or ultimately they may start ignoring the DQ items.

Impossible Data

This is my term for data that is valid in terms of the data schema, but semantically from a business point of view make no sense. Birth dates or anniversaries or dates of death in the future all come to mind ("Dates are hard"). But there are others. How about these?

Marital Status not NULL or "Unknown"
> On a customer record representing an entity (corporation, partnership, etc.). Note that sometimes for "person-like entities" this is an OK data point, or at least not as harmful (since the tax ID points back to a real person).

Gender not NULL *or "Unknown"*
On a customer record representing an entity.

Date of Birth, Date of Death, or Anniversary not NULL *or "Unknown"*
On a customer record representing an entity. You get the drift.

While we're on the topic, are you capturing "deceased" ("date of death" is better) on your customer record? That can be another useful filter.

Why are these examples important? If gender or marital status is used for scoring and you're not careful to filter out companies in your WHERE clauses, it could lead to not matching because one side of the data has the gender or marital status and the other doesn't, and hence perhaps the score falls below your threshold. And yes, you can use that WHERE clause—over and over and over again. Or if you have any power or sway, you can also try to get the data cleaned up at the source. If you do, it will have other benefits as well. Clean data is a must for high-quality system migrations, for example.

Simply Wrong

Of course, then there are things that are simply wrong. First and middle names are swapped. How would you even know? City and county are swapped: sometimes this can yield to some simple "EDA" in the form of just eyeballing the two columns together. "CSVs happen." They are, after all, simple text files, and the formatting if naively applied can often break on embedded commas within a field, for example. There are CSV encoding methods for this, but often you are getting a file produced by a junior programmer somewhere who took a simple approach and didn't look to see if any libraries were available to help, such as *Microsoft.VisualBasic.TextField Parser* (*https://oreil.ly/LYeGp*) (a .NET library—yes, you can reference it from C#).

Then there are misspellings and mistakes. Remember our discussion on many people entering "Ste. Genevieve" as "St. Genevieve"? Typos happen; people misspell. You will end up finding most of this when you are looking at the "long tail" of partial matches or those that didn't match at all and you are trying to figure out why. I often sit with a query results window open just scrolling through the data, looking for "disturbances in the Force."

Semantically Wrong

It is easy to talk about birthdays in the future or misspellings and understand impossible data. But then there is data that is impossible only to you—or your company anyway. For example, there are five allowable grades in the grading system: "A," "B," "C," "D," and "F." Yet, upon querying in your data, you find the following:

```
CREATE SCHEMA students;

CREATE TABLE students.Grades
(
```

```
        LastName VARCHAR(50),
        FirstName VARCHAR(50),
        Grade VARCHAR(50)
);

INSERT INTO students.Grades VALUES('Bachman', 'Jaclyn', 'B')
INSERT INTO students.Grades VALUES('Hellickson', 'Dottie', 'F')
INSERT INTO students.Grades VALUES('Herritt', 'Kirk', 'D')
INSERT INTO students.Grades VALUES('Koppinger', 'Nan', 'A')
INSERT INTO students.Grades VALUES('Lawler', 'Merlyn', 'H')
INSERT INTO students.Grades VALUES('Waycott', 'Kanisha', 'Dropped');

SELECT * FROM students.Grades
ORDER BY LastName, FirstName;
```

	LastName	FirstName	Grade
0	Bachman	Jaclyn	B
1	Hellickson	Dottie	F
2	Herritt	Kirk	D
3	Koppinger	Nan	A
4	Lawler	Merlyn	H
5	Waycott	Kanisha	Dropped

This is "obviously" wrong to a human expecting the letter grading system, but if the underlying field is VARCHAR(50) and the user interface doesn't put a drop-down list in front of the human to constrain their choices, then over time this is what you will get. You know how to handle this by now:

```
SELECT
    LastName [Last Name],
    FirstName [First Name],
    CASE
        WHEN Grade NOT IN ('A', 'B', 'C', 'D', 'F') THEN ''
        ELSE Grade END [Grade]
FROM students.Grades
ORDER BY LastName, FirstName;
```

	Last Name	First Name	Grade
0	Bachman	Jaclyn	B
1	Hellickson	Dottie	F
2	Herritt	Kirk	D
3	Koppinger	Nan	A
4	Lawler	Merlyn	
5	Waycott	Kanisha	

There are going to be all kinds of examples in your own data. Things that "should" have a drop-down in front of them but just offer the user a text field (and maybe some guidance in a tool tip). Beware number and date fields without constraints:

> Congratulations on being our customer since 989! We are celebrating the 40th year of our founding by giving every existing customer a 1% discount for every year they've been with us. You've earned a 1,034% discount!

The usual suspects. I am sure I bore you by now. And by now you know at least some approaches to handling them:

Tell an adult.
Let "the business" know about data quality issues and help them clean them up.

Filter records out.
Often "dropping records on the floor" can be the right thing to do, especially on garbage import datasets like that game console signup sheet.

Transform bad values.
Set them to NULL or some other "unknown" or "empty" value. If *not* NULL or empty string, make sure the value sorts to the top or bottom of the column and stands out easily, e.g., "_Unknown_."

ETL Your Way to Success

> All problems in computer science can be solved by another level of indirection.
> —Butler Lampson (*https://oreil.ly/amdvd*)

> All problems in data science can be solved by another level of ETL.
> —Jim Lehmer

If you don't have control over the data or can't create views in the database because of lack of access (contractor), you can often still use CTEs or better, temp tables, to extract, transform, and load your way through the datasets, gathering what you need in steps and depositing each step in a table representing the work up to that point.

The good news about this approach is it allows easy fallback. Let's say we set up a process where you do the following:

1. Import
Grab the data and stash it in import tables under your control (even if just temp session tables).

2. Clean
Use the import tables to do an initial DQ pass on both sides (customer and import), normalizing as you go, and stash those in new tables (maybe with a dq schema name).

3. Filter

Filter down to the working customer set you want (if not "all customers"). You could do this in the DQ step, but often the filter criteria change over time and it is easier to have this separate.

4. Score

Build the "match set" and score and put the results in their own tables.

This sounds all fancy and complicated. "Gee, you want me to use SQL Server Integration Service or Azure Data Factory or Mulesoft or something to get all this done?" No. It can all be done with simple SQL and in fact is one of my favorite statements. In this case, I am going to assume you have access to create tables in at least some schema in the database somewhere. Maybe you can create them in another database on the same server and then use three-part names to get access the customer data and get it into your database, such as *DataCleansing.dbo.ImportCustomer*. Or maybe you have control of a database not even on the same server; remember linked servers and four-part names, e.g., *DWServer.DataCleansing.dbo.ImportCustomer*.

Anyway, we're going to assume you've been given DDL (CREATE and DROP) access to a schema in the same database called *staging*. Check it out:

```
SELECT * INTO staging.Customers
FROM crm.NormalizedCustomer;

SELECT TOP 10
    LastName,
    FirstName
FROM staging.Customers
ORDER BY LastName, FirstName;
```

	LastName	FirstName
0	NULL	NULL
1	NULL	NULL
2	NULL	NULL
3	Abdallah	Johnetta
4	Acey	Geoffrey
5	Acuff	Weldon
6	Adkin	Barbra
7	Agramonte	Fausto
8	Ahle	Delmy
9	Albares	Cammy

SELECT * INTO <target> FROM <source> is so powerful. It creates a new "target" table with the same schema as the "source" table (or result set) and then populates it with data from the source table. You can filter what data comes over with a WHERE clause after the FROM clause, of course. Want to create an empty table with the same schema as the source?

```
SELECT * INTO staging.Customers
FROM crm.NormalizedCustomer WITH(NOLOCK)
/*
    Check out this cute trick in the WHERE clause.
*/
WHERE 0 = 1;
```

The connectivity this notebook uses won't let me show you just the column headers this way—bummer:

```
SELECT * FROM staging.Customers;
```

But I can prove the table was created with the correct columns:

```
/*
    This is pulling info from a set of SQL "catalog" tables,
    that is, metadata, that is kept in semi-standardized
    tables in the "sys" schema.
*/
SELECT
    C.name [Column Name]
FROM sys.columns C
INNER JOIN sys.tables T ON
    C.object_id = T.object_id
INNER JOIN sys.schemas S ON
    S.schema_id = T.schema_id
WHERE
    S.name = 'staging'
    AND T.name = 'Customers'
ORDER BY C.column_id
```

	Column Name
0	LastName
1	FirstName
2	Company
3	Address1
4	City
5	County
6	State
7	PostalCode
8	Country
9	MobilePhone
10	HomePhone
11	Email
12	Web

Cool, yes?

So, simply by using a series of SELECT * ... INTO ... queries we can build a simple "ETL" process where each step refines and filters our datasets, often into smaller (and quicker!) subsets to work with.

But note the most powerful part of this technique! We can confidently change our queries at the latest step, knowing we can always "fall back" (not the database term FALLBACK). An example will be helpful. We will work only with the customer side for now to keep it simple:

```
/*
    Import data into our own work area. This may not be practical
    without a WHERE clause to filter even at this step due to size.
    In this case we're going to emulate that with TOP 10.
*/
SELECT TOP 10 *
INTO staging.Customers
FROM crm.NormalizedCustomer
ORDER BY LastName;

/*
    Most of this data is already normalized by the NormalizedCustomer
    view we pulled from. In our case we will use this step to refine
    our column list.
*/
SELECT
    LastName,
    FirstName,
    Address1,
    PostalCode,
    MobilePhone
INTO staging.FilteredCustomers
FROM staging.Customers;

/*
    Start working with the customer data. Perhaps this is some EDA
    to understand matching to the import data.
*/
SELECT
    LastName,
    FirstName,
    Address1,
    PostalCode,
    MobilePhone
INTO staging.InterestingAreaCodes
FROM staging.FilteredCustomers
WHERE LEFT(MobilePhone, 3) IN ('847', '212', '401');

SELECT * FROM staging.InterestingAreaCodes;
```

	LastName	FirstName	Address1	PostalCode	MobilePhone
0	Acey	Geoffrey	7 West Ave #1	60067	8475551734
1	Acuff	Weldon	73 W Barstow Ave	60004	8475552156
2	Agramonte	Fausto	5 Harrison Rd	10038	2125551783
3	Ahle	Delmy	65895 S 16th St	02909	4015552547

We went through three steps with three resulting tables:

staging.Customers
  Raw dump or initial filter from production or data warehouse customer data.

staging.FilteredCustomers
  "Slicing and dicing" and transforming the data into a smaller working set with just the columns we need.

staging.InterestingAreaCodes
  Our current playground. The business is interested only in matching the import data against customers in these three area codes (for whatever reason).

Note that we can mangle and change the step for creating *staging.InterestingArea Codes,* or create a completely new table at this step, to our heart's content without having to go back and rerun the prior steps (sometimes expensive in terms of time or resources). Also, if while working downstream we realize we can refine our filter more, we only have to go back and rerun the step to re-create *staging.Filtered Customers* without having to go all the way back to re-creating *staging.Customers.* I will often have four or five steps of filtering and refinement, each allowing me to fall back to a prior step without a lot of rework and reruns. Of course, if the original source data changes, you may have to restart from the beginning. Having everything scripted helps, and there are projects where I have files named like these:

```
01-Import.sql
02-Normalize.sql
03-Clean.sql
04-Dedup.sql
05-Score.sql
99-Report.sql
```

Then I know I can repeat all the steps in the correct order, or just the later steps I need as I refine their logic. In a team environment this segregation into multiple components also allows handing off tasks to other people. It is not uncommon to have someone in charge of systems integrations and imports, someone else for making sure the data quality is up to standards, and finally someone doing the analysis for the business.

Using this approach you may have three steps filtering and massaging the customer data, and many more on the import data side, just because its schema, data, and encoding may all need transformations, and I often find it best to use different steps (and resulting tables) for each of those. But finally you will have both sides of the data in shape, and then you can begin the matching and scoring process. I almost always put the match and score data into a table, too, so that further reporting goes quickly.

 This technique can be used to create a quick and dirty backup of a single table, too. I often use this instead of a full database backup before a mass table change, because by the time a problem may be discovered, the database may have been changed enough that restoring from backup is infeasible. However, if you have a backup table laying around, you may be able to do an UPDATE to the production table using it as a source to recover some mangled information. Ask me how I know.

The following technique is described more in the section on code-generating code in Chapter 13. You can use something similar to generate a backup table name and then copy and run the result as its own SQL statement:

```
SELECT 'SELECT * INTO dbo.Foo' +
       FORMAT(GETDATE(), 'yyyyMMddHHmmss') +
       ' FROM dbo.Foo;';
```

```
SELECT * INTO dbo.Foo20230727100117 FROM dbo.Foo;
```

Final Thoughts on Data Quality

"Data" sounds so scientific to most people, but long-time data practitioners know it is often equivalent to "junk," to say it politely. But we don't get to say that in a way that means, "So I don't have to deal with it."

The first thing you can do, whether you're a full-time employee or a contractor working on a specific project, is report data quality issues when you find them. Often, just by finding the right person (the "data steward" in a shop with a formal, mature data practice), a lot of these matters can be resolved, at least on the production side.

On the incoming side, if you are receiving data from other organizations, you should treat it all like plutonium that will kill all your downstream processes dead. Handle it all with tongs. I don't trust *anything* on a typical import. Get it in as all VARCHAR(MAX) columns if you have to and then use ISDATE and similar functions to ensure each column contains the datatype you expect. Dealing with data exceptions at import time is by far the earliest and cleanest way to handle them. Remember Postel's law from

Chapter 8? Being liberal in what you accept isn't a law because it's a nice thing to do, like the Ten Commandments. It's a law because you have to do it anyway, like physics.

If you expect data quality problems, then you won't be grouchy when you encounter them. Nobody likes a whiner ("whinger" for you Commonwealth folk). Just use a series of ETLs to massage it into the shape you need and move on.

As we've already seen with dates, the hardest problem to solve in terms of data quality is data that is "schematically correct but semantically wrong." As a data scientist, it behooves you to understand your datasets and to understand each attribute's semantic limits as well as you can. Often doing some ETL and looking at the statistical outliers is a good start. Curiosity is your friend. "Hmmm...we track married, single, divorced, and unknown in *MaritalStatus*. I see we have 32,435 *M*s, 33,981 *S*s, 21,562 *D*s, 10,934 *U*s, and then 2 *X*s. What are those two?"

Often, if one column is "off," others may be as well. Remember our discussion of user-defined fields in Chapter 9? Often a series of such fields may all be exposed on a data entry screen as a group, with meaningful names like these:

```
User Field 1: _____
User Field 2: _____
User Field 3: _____
```

It is not uncommon for busy users, tabbing from field to field quickly to get the data entry completed, to land on the wrong field and enter the correct value for another field and not notice. This is a different kind of "off by one" error than most programmers think of. If all the fields are some form of VARCHAR, that kind of error can be challenging to find. You may even have to look across all three of the fields for a given value if the problem is prevalent enough (and it can be, if the system is still fronted by a "green screen").

Remember that "fuzzy" sometimes means we are matching just part of a string or looking for a pattern. It can mean using "windows" to allow for latency. It may include using fewer attributes than we have access to. And here, it can mean searching for something across multiple attributes at once, perhaps using all of these techniques together!

## CHAPTER 12

Tying It All Together

Now we're going to look at everything we've covered in one place. This chapter is going to take the datasets we've already been working with, and the examples from each chapter, and see what we can glean out of them to answer the following questions:

- How many existing customers are in the import data?
- Conversely, how many new prospects are in the import data?

Along the way we will have to do a lot of data cleanup and data normalization to answer those questions. You will re-meet the Snedleys, of course.

Approach

A lot of this could look something like functional programming. Remember this?

```
SELECT
  CustomField3,
  CASE
    /*
       If NULL no worries.
    */
    WHEN CustomField3 IS NULL THEN 'No Email Found'
    /*
       If no @ in string, no email address found.
    */
    WHEN CHARINDEX('@', CustomField3) = 0 THEN 'No Email Found'
    /*
       If @ and no comma, then only email address in string.
    */
```

```
    WHEN CHARINDEX('@', CustomField3) > 0
      AND CHARINDEX(',', CustomField3) = 0
      THEN CustomField3
    /*
        If the email is first on the left, grab it.
    */
    WHEN CHARINDEX('@', CustomField3) > 0
      AND CHARINDEX(',', CustomField3) > CHARINDEX('@', CustomField3)
      THEN LEFT(CustomField3, CHARINDEX(',', CustomField3) - 1)
    /*
      If email is in the middle, then hold on!
    */
    WHEN CHARINDEX(',', CustomField3) > 0
      AND CHARINDEX('@', RIGHT(CustomField3, LEN(CustomField3) -
                                CHARINDEX(',', CustomField3))) >
          CHARINDEX(',', CustomField3)
      AND CHARINDEX('@', RIGHT(CustomField3, LEN(CustomField3) -
                                CHARINDEX(',', CustomField3))) <
          CHARINDEX(',', RIGHT(CustomField3, LEN(CustomField3) -
                                CHARINDEX(',', CustomField3)))
      THEN SUBSTRING(CustomField3,
                    CHARINDEX(',', CustomField3) + 1,
                    CHARINDEX(',',  RIGHT(CustomField3,
                                    LEN(CustomField3) -
                                    CHARINDEX(',', CustomField3))) - 1)
    /*
        If the email is last on the right, grab it.
    */
    WHEN CHARINDEX(',', CustomField3) > 0
      AND CHARINDEX('@', CustomField3) > CHARINDEX(',', CustomField3)
      THEN RIGHT(CustomField3, LEN (CustomField3) - CHARINDEX(',', CustomField3))
    ELSE 'No Email Found'
  END [Email?]
FROM staging.CustomFields;
```

Think of that SELECT as an anonymous (lambda) function that takes no parameters and returns a transformed set of data from a known (to the caller and the function) dataset. Of course, with DDL (CREATE) access to the database we can create actual SQL functions and stored procedures that then can be called by name, passed parameters, etc.

However, we are going to use a series of simple ETL steps to massage our data along the way until it is all in the "shape" we want it, and then we can answer our questions at the end. If you come from a functional world, I have long maintained that this approach is analogous to the concept of "map-reduce":

```
SELECT transformed-columns /* All kinds of transformations can happen here. */
INTO target-table          /* ETL target table                              */
FROM source-table          /* ETL source table                              */
WHERE filter-conditions    /* All kinds of selection criteria here.         */
ORDER BY new-order         /* Great band! Hey, we can still have fun here.  */
```

It is similar in transforming datasets into new, summarized datasets, applying filtering and sorting along the way. It also lets the relational database engine do a lot of parallel processing and pipelining for you. Does that help? Observe another friend from a prior chapter:

```
/*
    Import data into our own work area. This may not be practical
    without a WHERE clause to filter even at this step due to size.
    In this case we're going to emulate that with TOP 10.
*/
SELECT TOP 10 *
INTO staging.Customers
FROM crm.NormalizedCustomer
ORDER BY LastName;
```

That's about as simple as it can get. Note that just like in functional programming, we are not usually changing the source data; we are transmuting it into something else and then working with that for our next step, and so on.

What's the Score?

For our purposes we have been given some import data from Marketing and have imported it using a tool like SQL Server Management Studio (SSMS) into *dbo .PotentialMatches*. The schema looks like this:

```
/*
    Aligned for discussion - I usually won't be this nice to you.
*/
CREATE TABLE dbo.PotentialMatches
(
        first_name    NVARCHAR(50) NULL,
        last_name     NVARCHAR(50) NULL,
        company_name  NVARCHAR(50) NULL,
        address       NVARCHAR(50) NULL,
        city          NVARCHAR(50) NULL,
        county        NVARCHAR(50) NULL,
        state         NVARCHAR(50) NULL,
        zip           NVARCHAR(50) NULL,
        country       NVARCHAR(50) NULL,
        phone1        NVARCHAR(50) NULL,
        phone2        NVARCHAR(50) NULL,
        email         NVARCHAR(50) NULL,
        web_address   NVARCHAR(50) NULL
)
```

It's a pretty typical schema for something imported by a tool. Just grab everything, stuff it into a VARCHAR type, and make sure they're all NULL-able because you don't trust the data source, even if they gave you a schema and pinky swore that required columns would always be non-NULL. Maybe, if you really end up pulling data from that vendor repeatedly and learn to trust them, you can change some of the datatypes to be more accurate (but beware importing ZIP codes as INT, for example!) and to have some of the columns be marked NOT NULL. But I would wait a while and see how their data quality is first.

Let's look at a few columns and rows by checking in on the Snedleys:

```
SELECT TOP 10
    first_name,
    last_name,
    company_name
FROM dbo.PotentialMatches
WHERE
    last_name LIKE '%Snedley%'
    OR company_name LIKE '%Snedley%'
ORDER BY last_name, first_name, company_name;
```

	first_name	last_name	company_name
0	NULL	NULL	Snedley & Sons, L.L.C.
1	Blanche	Snedley	NULL
2	Clive	Snedley	Pining Fjordlands Homeward, L.L.C.
3	Mortimer	Snedley	NULL
4	Mortimer	Snedley	Mortimer Snedley Estate
5	Mortimer	Snedley	Mortimer Snedley Trust
6	Mortimer	Snedley, Jr.	NULL
7	Mortimer	Snedley, Jr.	NULL
8	Mortimer	Snedley, Jr.	Snedley and Sons LLC

No real surprises, yet. We see that there are some rows with no first or last names, just company name, some with just first and last names and no company, and some with both.

Now we are at the point of the discussion where we must decide what we are going to score on. When we look at those input columns, we have apparent matching ones in our CRM system. Part of the "fuzzy" is guessing which columns map to which by name, but in our case the work has been done for us, and the column names all have mates in CRM. So out of those, which are the most useful to match on? Some we can immediately see aren't very helpful; multiple people can have the same website address, for example, if they work for the same company, and then a lot of our data (on both sides) has no website address at all. So, we automatically exclude it from further consideration (as always with the usual arm wave about "unless your business needs require it").

Conversely, from our internal domain knowledge we know *phone1* is the mobile phone number and *phone2* is the home or business phone number in our CRM system (this is memorialized in the *crm.NormalizedCustomer* view). We presume the same is true of the import data, but we're going to match both to both. Phones are pretty good disambiguators, as are emails, so they are automatically "in."

It may not have been conspicuous by its absence, but birth date is another "gold standard" for data matching. If you have a (semi-)complete name and date of birth, that is often all you need. Which is why you get asked those two data attributes to identify yourself whenever you are in a healthcare setting.

However, it is rare in terms of matching demographic data to have DOB on the incoming dataset. If it is there, your scoring may be very simple indeed, subject to the usual data quality scrubbing (birth dates in the future, etc.) But this book is about "fuzzy" data matching, when birthdays and tax IDs and other perfectly natural and artificial keys are not available to us for personally identifying information (PII) and privacy reasons or, if they are in the dataset, may be masked, raising the necessity to get "fuzzier"!

Out of 13 columns, we've decided on 4. We need to perhaps do a little EDA at this point: dig in the import file on the various columns, see what the distribution of values are, and see if there are enough values to even bother with. To give data to our intuitive decision about web addresses:

```
SELECT
    COUNT(*) [Total Rows],
    COUNT(web_address) [Non-NULL Values],
    COUNT(DISTINCT web_address) [Unique Web Domains]
FROM crm.Customer;
```

Total Rows	Non-NULL Values	Unique Web Domains
508	144	144

Given the following result, it seems unlikely that pursuing that column for matching is going to be fruitful:

508 – 144 = 364 NULL web addresses

364 / 508 * 100 = 71.7% NULL

However, consider the following revision:

```
SELECT
    COUNT(*) [Total Rows],
    COUNT(phone1) [Non-NULL Values],
    COUNT(DISTINCT phone1) [Unique Mobile #s]
FROM crm.Customer;
```

Total Rows	Non-NULL Values	Unique Mobile #s
508	505	502

Now:

508 − 505 = 3 NULL phone numbers

505 / 508 * 100 = 99.4% not NULL

Hence, mobile phone, or whatever we find *phone1* represents, looks like a good candidate, especially since the vast majority of them are unique.

On to the rest. We'll throw last name, first name, and company name in the scoring buckets because they are traditional. We will use at least part of the street address. I am going to be provocative, but if you remember the discussion in Chapter 10, I find most of the address fields to be unhelpful except postal code, so that's what we will use. Out of our original 13 columns:

- *first_name*
- *last_name*
- *company_name*
- *address*
- *city*
- *county*
- *state*
- *zip*
- *country*
- *phone1*
- *phone2*
- *email*
- *web_address*

we have decided to use these eight:

- *first_name*
- *last_name*
- *company_name*
- *address*
- *zip*
- *phone1*

- *phone2*
- *email*

This is a pretty good start, really. We may find in tuning that we need to add more columns or that we can remove a few (faster processing, smaller datasets), but typically you will discover about 5 to 10 columns that are meaningful and add to the score:

```
/*
    Only matching on our scoring columns.
*/
SELECT
    COUNT(*) [Total Matches]
FROM crm.Customer C
INNER JOIN dbo.PotentialMatches P ON
        C.first_name = P.first_name
    AND C.last_name = P.last_name
    AND C.company_name = P.company_name
    AND C.address = P.address
    AND C.zip = P.zip
    AND C.phone1 = P.phone1
    AND C.phone2 = P.phone2
    AND C.email = P.email;
```

First Pass: Naive Matching

Let's start with a naive first pass attempt at matching what we have:

Total Matches
0

Maybe we got lucky. Maybe.

Or maybe we forgot about NULL and how SQL handles them:

```
/*
    COALESCE out the NULLs.
*/
SELECT
    COUNT(*) [Total Matches]
FROM crm.Customer C
INNER JOIN dbo.PotentialMatches P ON
        COALESCE(C.first_name, '')   = COALESCE(P.first_name, '')
    AND COALESCE(C.last_name, '')    = COALESCE(P.last_name, '')
    AND COALESCE(C.company_name, '') = COALESCE(P.company_name, '')
    AND COALESCE(C.address, '')      = COALESCE(P.address, '')
    AND COALESCE(C.zip, '')          = COALESCE(P.zip, '')
    AND COALESCE(C.phone1, '')       = COALESCE(P.phone1, '')
```

```
      AND COALESCE(C.phone2, '')       = COALESCE(P.phone2, '')
      AND COALESCE(C.email, '')        = COALESCE(P.email, '');
```

Total Matches

0

Nope. Well, we hope by changing all the ANDs to ORs we'd get a hit on *something*; after all, that's going to be the basis of scoring:

```
/*
    COALESCE out the NULLs.
*/
SELECT
    COUNT(*) [Total Matches]
FROM crm.Customer C
INNER JOIN dbo.PotentialMatches P ON
        COALESCE(C.first_name, '')   = COALESCE(P.first_name, '')
    OR COALESCE(C.last_name, '')     = COALESCE(P.last_name, '')
    OR COALESCE(C.company_name, '')  = COALESCE(P.company_name, '')
    OR COALESCE(C.address, '')       = COALESCE(P.address, '')
    OR COALESCE(C.zip, '')           = COALESCE(P.zip, '')
    OR COALESCE(C.phone1, '')        = COALESCE(P.phone1, '')
    OR COALESCE(C.phone2, '')        = COALESCE(P.phone2, '')
    OR COALESCE(C.email, '')         = COALESCE(P.email, '');
```

Total Matches

13131

Hmmm...given we have only 508 rows in our CRM system and 34 in the import data, that isn't quite the number we were expecting. That join, even though it was an INNER JOIN, ended up creating "matched" rows out of every trivial match. It didn't do a complete Cartesian join (508 × 34 = 17,272), but it came close.

Let's go back to using ANDs for now and throw in some of our normalization magic:

```
/*
    Try and sprinkle some normalization on it.
*/
SELECT
    COUNT(*) [Total Matches]
FROM crm.Customer C
INNER JOIN dbo.PotentialMatches P ON
        LEFT(C.first_name, 1) = LEFT(P.first_name, 1)
    AND TRANSLATE(C.last_name, '.,', '  ') =
        TRANSLATE(P.last_name, '.,', '  ')
    AND REPLACE(C.company_name, 'L.L.C.', 'LLC') =
        REPLACE(P.company_name, 'L.L.C.', 'LLC')
    AND LEFT(C.address, 10) = LEFT(P.address, 10)
    AND LEFT(C.zip, 5) = LEFT(P.zip, 5)
    AND REPLACE(C.phone1, '-', '') =
```

```
        REPLACE(P.phone1, '-', '')
    AND REPLACE(C.phone2, '-', '') =
        REPLACE(P.phone2, '-', '')
    AND C.email = P.email;
```

Total Matches

1

That's actually sort of amazing when you think about it. We had to go through all
those gyrations to find even one row close enough to be called an "exact match,"
which obviously it is not, at least not from the literal data point of view. But from the
semantic point of view, probably "yes, it's a match." Let's change from COUNT(*) to
some attributes from the *Customer* table (alias *C*) and see who it is:

```
/*
    Who is our mystery match?
*/
SELECT
    'CRM Data' Source,
    C.first_name,
    C.last_name,
    C.company_name,
    C.address,
    C.zip,
    C.phone1,
    C.phone2,
    C.email
FROM crm.Customer C
INNER JOIN dbo.PotentialMatches P ON
        LEFT(C.first_name, 1) = LEFT(P.first_name, 1)
    AND TRANSLATE(C.last_name, '.,', '  ') =
        TRANSLATE(P.last_name, '.,', '  ')
    AND REPLACE(C.company_name, 'L.L.C.', 'LLC') =
        REPLACE(P.company_name, 'L.L.C.', 'LLC')
    AND LEFT(C.address, 10) = LEFT(P.address, 10)
    AND LEFT(C.zip, 5) = LEFT(P.zip, 5)
    AND REPLACE(C.phone1, '-', '') =
        REPLACE(P.phone1, '-', '')
    AND REPLACE(C.phone2, '-', '') =
        REPLACE(P.phone2, '-', '')
    AND C.email = P.email
UNION
/*
    And how did they look in the import data?
*/
SELECT
    'Import Data',
    P.first_name,
    P.last_name,
    P.company_name,
```

```
            P.address,
            P.zip,
            P.phone1,
            P.phone2,
            P.email
    FROM crm.Customer C
    INNER JOIN dbo.PotentialMatches P ON
            LEFT(C.first_name, 1) = LEFT(P.first_name, 1)
        AND TRANSLATE(C.last_name, '.,', '  ') =
            TRANSLATE(P.last_name, '.,', '  ')
        AND REPLACE(C.company_name, 'L.L.C.', 'LLC') =
            REPLACE(P.company_name, 'L.L.C.', 'LLC')
        AND LEFT(C.address, 10) = LEFT(P.address, 10)
        AND LEFT(C.zip, 5) = LEFT(P.zip, 5)
        AND REPLACE(C.phone1, '-', '') =
            REPLACE(P.phone1, '-', '')
        AND REPLACE(C.phone2, '-', '') =
            REPLACE(P.phone2, '-', '')
        AND C.email = P.email
    ORDER BY 1;
```

Source	first _name	last _name	company _name	address	zip	phone1	phone2	email
CRM Data	Mortimer	Snedley	Mortimer Snedley Estate	443 Arroyo Rd	87740	575-555-0956	575-555-0956	mortimer .snedley @example .com
Import Data	Mortimer	Snedley	Mortimer Snedley Estate	443 Arroyo Road	87740-0956	575-555-0956	575-555-0956	mortimer .snedley @example .com

We can see some subtle differences between the CRM and import data:

```
/*
    Let's do a "diff".
*/
SELECT
    C.address [Customer Address],
    P.address [Import Address],
    C.zip [Customer ZIP],
    P.zip [Import ZIP]
FROM crm.Customer C
INNER JOIN dbo.PotentialMatches P ON
        LEFT(C.first_name, 1) = LEFT(P.first_name, 1)
    AND TRANSLATE(C.last_name, '.,', '  ') =
        TRANSLATE(P.last_name, '.,', '  ')
    AND REPLACE(C.company_name, 'L.L.C.', 'LLC') =
        REPLACE(P.company_name, 'L.L.C.', 'LLC')
    AND LEFT(C.address, 10) = LEFT(P.address, 10)
    AND LEFT(C.zip, 5) = LEFT(P.zip, 5)
```

```
AND REPLACE(C.phone1, '-', '') =
    REPLACE(P.phone1, '-', '')
AND REPLACE(C.phone2, '-', '') =
    REPLACE(P.phone2, '-', '')
AND C.email = P.email;
```

Customer Address	Import Address	Customer ZIP	Import ZIP
443 Arroyo Rd	443 Arroyo Road	87740	87740-0956

That's good to know, but we're nowhere close to being done.

Second Pass: Normalizing Relations

We will assume that *dbo.PossibleMatches* is our first ETL—that is, the data came in from a file and was imported into that table. In this phase, we are going to do our first transformation, which is to get the data from both sides into a "normalized" format. We will be attacking punctuation and spaces in all the scoring fields, plus dealing with suffixes and "person-like entities." You've seen this technique used throughout the book, so we won't spend much time here except showing how to do it to get the data into a table for the next step.

Impossible Data

This is also where we can decide what to do about some "impossible data" in the import dataset. There are two cases I've planted in there:

Clive Snedley shows up from Canada!
> Do we want to simply treat him as new or send him down a different path since he is outside the United States?

There are some invalid email addresses.
> Do we want to drop the rows, try to fix them, or simply not match on that attribute (it is one of the scoring attributes, remember) and suffer a lower score on those records?

When Bad Things Happen to Good Data

Obviously, there are an infinite variety of bad data possibilities. You will find them all along the way:

During data imports
> Enforcing a schema on something from a CSV file will usually be your first line of defense. Of course, if we import everything to NVARCHAR(MAX), we won't see the errors there, but upon the first ETL to a table with a "real" schema—datatypes

---

that enforce specific values and ranges—you will probably see some data conversion errors pop up.

During EDA

The first time you receive a new dataset you should always (always) do a `SELECT * ` on it (unless it is huge, then something like `SELECT TOP 1000 *`) and simply scroll around, using your mind's beautiful pattern recognition circuitry to see things that "jump out" at you, like alphabetic characters in a column that is supposed to be numeric or columns where the data doesn't seem to have good consistency (remember those fields like *CustomField1* from Chapter 9?).

During analysis

To me, almost nothing is more powerful for finding outliers in data that is supposed to be consistent (either consistently unique or consistently clustered) than the following simple query pattern:

```
SELECT
    Foo,
    COUNT(*) Total
FROM Bar
GROUP BY Foo
ORDER BY 2 DESC, 1;
```

During scoring

Once you start trying to match a field in one data source with a field in another that are supposed to be "the same," you will find all kinds of surprises. ZIP code versus ZIP+4 comes to mind (and is it a valid ZIP+4 ZIP code if you have "65102-0000" in your data?). A lot of the normalization approaches in this book are to try to achieve some semblance of parity between the datasets for this step.

During reporting

Don't be surprised if after all that, you report the results to "the business" (the project owner) and find out "That column Foo with 399 values for 'ABC'? Yeah, 'ABC' is invalid there."

Back to our two impossible data examples. Let's take care of both of these first:

```
SELECT
    *
INTO staging.ImpossibleData
FROM dbo.PotentialMatches
WHERE state NOT IN (SELECT Abbreviation FROM ref.PostalAbbreviations)
    OR 0 IN (CHARINDEX('@', email), CHARINDEX('.', email));

SELECT
    *
INTO staging.PossibleData
FROM dbo.PotentialMatches
```

```
/*
    Yay for De Morgan's theorem! Negate the conditions and swap the OR with AND.
*/
WHERE state IN (SELECT Abbreviation FROM ref.PostalAbbreviations)
    AND 0 NOT IN (CHARINDEX('@', email), CHARINDEX('.', email));

SELECT
    last_name,
    first_name,
    company_name,
    state,
    email
FROM staging.ImpossibleData
ORDER BY last_name, first_name, company_name;
```

	last_name	first_name	company_name	state	email
0	Kines	Donte	NULL	MA	dkines@examplecom
1	Snedley	Clive	Pining Fjordlands Homeward, L.L.C.	NB	clive.snedley@example.com

As mentioned, it is not typically your job as a data analyst to know what to do with these. I often route such data back to "the business" either to clean (the email address, after verifying with the customer or prospect) or perhaps to route to another part of the company to handle the out-of-territory entries that inevitably show up. In our case, however, we eliminated the rows via the ETL into *PossibleData*:

```
SELECT
    COUNT(*) Total
FROM staging.PossibleData;
```

Total
27

Now Let's Normalize

Now that we have our "possible data," we can go ahead and normalize both sides of the data. We are also going to prune to just the scoring columns. First we will normalize our production customer data into a new table called *NormalizedCustomer*. In the following example, we'll also dump the first 10 rows just to see what they look like:

```
SELECT TOP 10 * FROM staging.NormalizedCustomer ORDER BY LastName, FirstName;
```

	LastName	First Name	Company	Address1	Postal Code	MobilePhone	HomePhone	Email
0	NULL	NULL	AcmeCorp	123SnellAv	65101	NULL	5735553256	NULL
1	NULL	NULL	FooInc	457Prairie	80301	NULL	3035555623	NULL
2	NULL	NULL	Snedley&SonsLLC	443ArroyoR	87740	NULL	5755550956	NULL

	LastName	First Name	Company	Address1	Postal Code	MobilePhone	HomePhone	Email
3	Abdallah	J	NULL	1088Pinehu	27514	9195559345	9195553791	johnetta _abdallah @example.com
4	Acey	G	NULL	7WestAve#1	60067	8475551734	8475552909	geoffrey@example .com
5	Acuff	W	NULL	73WBarstow	60004	8475552156	8475555866	wacuff@example .com
6	Adkin	B	NULL	4KohlerMem	11230	7185553751	7185559475	badkin@example .com
7	Agramonte	F	NULL	5HarrisonR	10038	2125551783	2125553063	fausto _agramonte @example.com
8	Ahle	D	NULL	65895S16th	02909	4015552547	4015558961	delmy.ahle @example.com
9	Albares	C	NULL	56EMorehea	78045	9565556195	9565557216	calbares @example.com

Similarly, we will normalize our input dataset into a table named *NormalizedImport* and again SELECT the first 10 rows for a quick sniff:

```
SELECT
    REPLACE
    (
        TRANSLATE
        (
            last_name,
            '.,-''()[]`',  /* From these                    */
            '         '    /* to spaces                     */
        ),
        ' ', ''           /* Replace spaces with empty strings */
    ) LastName,
    LEFT(first_name, 1) FirstName, /* Initial only           */
    REPLACE
    (
        TRANSLATE
        (
            company_name,
            '.,-''()[]`',  /* From these                    */
            '         '    /* to spaces                     */
        ),
        ' ', ''           /* Replace spaces with empty strings */
    ) Company,
    LEFT
    (
        REPLACE
        (
```

```
            TRANSLATE
            (
                address,
                '.,-''()[]`',
                '             '
            ),
            '  ', ''
        ),
        10                      /* Don't want too much!              */
    ) Address1,
    LEFT(zip, 5) PostalCode,
    REPLACE(TRANSLATE(phone1, '-()', '    '), ' ', '') MobilePhone,
    REPLACE(TRANSLATE(phone2, '-()', '    '), ' ', '') HomePhone,
    email Email
INTO staging.NormalizedImport
FROM staging.PossibleData;

SELECT TOP 10 * FROM staging.NormalizedImport ORDER BY LastName, FirstName;
```

	LastName	First Name	Company	Address1	Postal Code	MobilePhone	HomePhone	Email
0	Brideau	J	NULL	6SBroadway	07009	9735553423	9735555469	jbrideau@example.com
1	Chavous	R	NULL	63517Dupon	39211	6015559632	6015555754	roslyn.chavous@chavous.test
2	DegrootSmith	N	NULL	303NRadcli	96720	8085554775	8085551865	novella_degroot@degroot.test
3	Eroman	I	NULL	2853SCentr	NULL	4105559018	5554543	ilene.eroman@example.com
4	Galam	B	NULL	2500Pringl	19440	2155553304	2155558523	britt@galam.test
5	GarciaLopez	J	NULL	40Cambridg	53715	6085557194	6085556912	jgabisi@example.com
6	Hamilton	C	NULL	985E6thAve	95407	5551771	5558037	charlene.hamilton@example.com
7	Husser	S	HusserAssociates	9StateHigh	NULL	2015558369	2015557699	selma.husser@example.com
8	Layous	M	NULL	78112Morri	06473	2035553388	2035551543	mlayous@example.com
9	Maisto	R	NULL	9648SMain	21801	4105551863	5552667	reena@example.com

While teaching a course on this subject, I was asked, "Do you always look at the data?" That is, just scan it quickly. And my answer was, "Yes. Always." We can already see from our example that we are going to have some problems (the seven-digit phone numbers leap out). I will often SELECT TOP x * ... (where *x* is 10, 100, 1000) and then just quickly scroll up and down through the result set, looking for weird "shapes" in the data. Doing some SELECT x, COUNT(*) Total ... queries for some very quick and dirty EDA often shows problematic outliers as well.

Third Pass: Score!

Well, OK then! We have now done the following:

1. Filtered out impossible data versus possible data from the import via two ETLs

2. Normalized the scorable data attributes (columns) on both sides (our production customer data and the import data) via two more ETLs

We should be ready for a first real pass at matching. We had one row exactly match before. How many do we get now, remembering to compare both the mobile phone and home phones to both fields on the other side.

So even after normalization, we still have only one perfect match. But remember, we aren't doing one thing we said we'd do:

```
/*
   Let's try it again!
*/
SELECT
    C.*
FROM staging.NormalizedCustomer C
INNER JOIN staging.NormalizedImport I ON
        C.FirstName = I.FirstName
    AND C.LastName = I.LastName
    AND C.Company = I.Company
    AND C.Address1 = I.Address1
    AND C.PostalCode = I.PostalCode
    AND (C.MobilePhone IN (I.MobilePhone, I.HomePhone)
        OR C.HomePhone IN (I.MobilePhone, I.HomePhone))
    AND C.Email = I.Email
ORDER BY C.LastName, C.FirstName, C.Company;
```

LastName	First Name	Company	Address1	Postal Code	MobilePhone	HomePhone	Email
Snedley	M	MortimerSnedleyEstate	443ArroyoR	87740	5755550956	5755550956	mortimer .snedley @example.com

What? After all that—filtering, normalization, comparing multiple phone fields each to each—we still get only one row?

Now it is time to learn something harsh about SQL. Observe Python:

```
# Look, some Python!
print(None == None)
```

```
True
```

Now observe SQL:

```
SELECT CASE WHEN NULL = NULL THEN 'Equal!' ELSE 'Not Equal!' END [NULL Compare];
```

NULL Compare
Not Equal!

And so COALESCE (or ISNULL) to the rescue:

```
/*
    Now with no NULL comparisons.
*/
SELECT
    C.*
FROM staging.NormalizedCustomer C
INNER JOIN staging.NormalizedImport I ON
        COALESCE(C.FirstName, '') = COALESCE(I.FirstName, '')
    AND COALESCE(C.LastName, '') = COALESCE(I.LastName, '')
    AND COALESCE(C.Company, '') = COALESCE(I.Company, '')
    AND COALESCE(C.Address1, '') = COALESCE(I.Address1, '')
    AND COALESCE(C.PostalCode, '') = COALESCE(I.PostalCode, '')
    AND (COALESCE(C.MobilePhone, '') IN
        (COALESCE(I.MobilePhone, ''), COALESCE(I.HomePhone, ''))
        OR COALESCE(C.HomePhone, '') IN
        (COALESCE(I.MobilePhone, ''), COALESCE(I.HomePhone, '')))
    AND COALESCE(C.Email, '') = COALESCE(I.Email, '')
ORDER BY C.LastName, C.FirstName, C.Company;
```

	LastName	First Name	Company	Address1	Postal Code	Mobile Phone	Home Phone	Email
0	Brideau	J	NULL	6SBroadway	07009	9735553423	9735555469	jbrideau @example .com
1	Chavous	R	NULL	63517Dupon	39211	6015559632	6015555754	roslyn.chavous @chavous.test
2	Galam	B	NULL	2500Pringl	19440	2155553304	2155558523	britt@galam .test
3	GarciaLopez	J	NULL	40Cambridg	53715	6085557194	6085556912	jgabisi @example .com
4	Layous	M	NULL	78112Morri	06473	2035553388	2035551543	mlayous @example .com

	LastName	First Name	Company	Address1	Postal Code	Mobile Phone	Home Phone	Email
5	Maisto	R	NULL	9648SMain	21801	4105551863	4105552667	reena @example .com
6	Mirafuentes	B	NULL	30553Washi	07062	9085558409	9085558272	becky .mirafuentes @mirafuentes .test
7	Nunlee	G	NULL	2WMountRoy	46040	3175556023	3175558486	gary_nunlee @nunlee.test
8	OConnor	K	NULL	2SBiscayne	21230	4105554903	4105553862	kaitlyn.ogg @example .com
9	OConnor	K	NULL	2SBiscayne	21230	4105554903	4105553862	kaitlyn.ogg @example .com
10	Perin	L	NULL	6783rdAve	33196	3055557291	3055552078	lperin@perin .test
11	Rochin	X	NULL	2MonroeSt	94403	6505555072	6505552625	xuan @example .com
12	Schmierer	P	NULL	5161Dorset	33030	3055558970	3055558481	pamella .schmierer @schmierer .test
13	Snedley	B	NULL	443ArroyoR	87740	5755550956	5755550956	mortimer .snedley @example .com
14	Snedley	M	NULL	443ArroyoR	87740	5755550956	5755550956	mortimer .snedley @example .com
15	Snedley	M	MortimerSnedleyEstate	443ArroyoR	87740	5755550956	5755550956	mortimer .snedley @example .com
16	SnedleyJr	M	NULL	443ArroyoR	87740	5755550957	5755550956	mortimer .snedley @example .com

	LastName	First Name	Company	Address1	Postal Code	Mobile Phone	Home Phone	Email
17	Staback	M	NULL	7WWabansia	32822	4075556908	4075552145	martina _staback @staback.test
18	Timenez	L	NULL	47857Coney	20735	3015556420	3015556698	loreta.timenez @example .com

Much better! There are only 27 rows in the *staging.NormalizedImport* table, so we are already at 67% "perfect" matches! In many scenarios this would be considered a resounding success on its own. But can we do better? Let's score now and see. Remember this approach from Chapter 10, shown here as CTEs to bring it all together?

```
WITH AttemptToMatch
AS
(
    SELECT
        C.LastName CustomerLastName,
        C.FirstName CustomerFirstName,
        C.Company CustomerCompany,
        C.Address1 CustomerAddress1,
        C.PostalCode CustomerPostalCode,
        C.MobilePhone CustomerMobilePhone,
        C.HomePhone CustomerHomePhone,
        C.Email CustomerEmail,
        I.LastName ImportLastName,
        I.FirstName ImportFirstName,
        I.Company ImportCompany,
        I.Address1 ImportAddress1,
        I.PostalCode ImportPostalCode,
        I.MobilePhone ImportMobilePhone,
        I.HomePhone ImportHomePhone,
        I.Email ImportEmail
    FROM  staging.NormalizedCustomer C
    LEFT OUTER JOIN staging.NormalizedImport I ON
    (
        (
            COALESCE(C.LastName, '') = COALESCE(I.LastName, '')
            AND COALESCE(C.FirstName, '') = COALESCE(I.FirstName, '')
        )
        OR COALESCE(C.Company, '') = COALESCE(I.Company, '')
    )
```

```
        AND
        (
            (
                COALESCE(C.Address1, '') = COALESCE(I.Address1, '')
                AND COALESCE(C.PostalCode, '') = COALESCE(I.PostalCode, '')
            )
            OR COALESCE(C.MobilePhone, '') IN
                (COALESCE(I.MobilePhone, ''), COALESCE(I.HomePhone, ''))
            OR COALESCE(C.HomePhone, '') IN
                (COALESCE(I.MobilePhone, ''), COALESCE(I.HomePhone, ''))
            OR COALESCE(C.Email, '') = COALESCE(I.Email, '')
        )
),
ScoreMatches
AS
(
    SELECT
        CustomerLastName,
        CustomerFirstName,
        CustomerCompany,
        CustomerAddress1,
        CustomerPostalCode,
        CustomerMobilePhone,
        CustomerHomePhone,
        CustomerEmail,
        'LastName' Attribute,
        IIF(ImportLastName IS NOT NULL, 1, 0) Score
    FROM  AttemptToMatch
    UNION ALL
    SELECT
        CustomerLastName,
        CustomerFirstName,
        CustomerCompany,
        CustomerAddress1,
        CustomerPostalCode,
        CustomerMobilePhone,
        CustomerHomePhone,
        CustomerEmail,
        'FirstName' Attribute,
        IIF(ImportFirstName IS NOT NULL, 1, 0) Score
    FROM  AttemptToMatch
    UNION ALL
    SELECT
        CustomerLastName,
        CustomerFirstName,
        CustomerCompany,
        CustomerAddress1,
        CustomerPostalCode,
        CustomerMobilePhone,
        CustomerHomePhone,
        CustomerEmail,
        'Company' Attribute,
```

```
        IIF(ImportCompany IS NOT NULL, 1, 0) Score
FROM  AttemptToMatch
UNION ALL
SELECT
    CustomerLastName,
    CustomerFirstName,
    CustomerCompany,
    CustomerAddress1,
    CustomerPostalCode,
    CustomerMobilePhone,
    CustomerHomePhone,
    CustomerEmail,
    'Address1' Attribute,
    IIF(ImportAddress1 IS NOT NULL, 1, 0) Score
FROM  AttemptToMatch
UNION ALL
SELECT
    CustomerLastName,
    CustomerFirstName,
    CustomerCompany,
    CustomerAddress1,
    CustomerPostalCode,
    CustomerMobilePhone,
    CustomerHomePhone,
    CustomerEmail,
    'PostalCode' Attribute,
    IIF(ImportPostalCode IS NOT NULL, 1, 0) Score
FROM  AttemptToMatch
UNION ALL
SELECT
    CustomerLastName,
    CustomerFirstName,
    CustomerCompany,
    CustomerAddress1,
    CustomerPostalCode,
    CustomerMobilePhone,
    CustomerHomePhone,
    CustomerEmail,
    'MobilePhone' Attribute,
    IIF(ImportMobilePhone IS NOT NULL, 1, 0) Score
FROM  AttemptToMatch
UNION ALL
SELECT
    CustomerLastName,
    CustomerFirstName,
    CustomerCompany,
    CustomerAddress1,
    CustomerPostalCode,
    CustomerMobilePhone,
    CustomerHomePhone,
    CustomerEmail,
    'HomePhone' Attribute,
```

```
            IIF(ImportHomePhone IS NOT NULL, 1, 0) Score
    FROM  AttemptToMatch
    UNION ALL
    SELECT
        CustomerLastName,
        CustomerFirstName,
        CustomerCompany,
        CustomerAddress1,
        CustomerPostalCode,
        CustomerMobilePhone,
        CustomerHomePhone,
        CustomerEmail,
        'Email' Attribute,
        IIF(ImportEmail IS NOT NULL, 1, 0) Score
    FROM  AttemptToMatch
),
ScoredCustomers
AS
(
    SELECT
        CustomerLastName,
        CustomerFirstName,
        CustomerCompany,
        CustomerAddress1,
        CustomerPostalCode,
        CustomerMobilePhone,
        CustomerHomePhone,
        CustomerEmail,
        SUM(Score) Score
    FROM ScoreMatches
    GROUP BY CustomerLastName, CustomerFirstName, CustomerCompany,
             CustomerAddress1, CustomerPostalCode, CustomerMobilePhone,
             CustomerHomePhone, CustomerEmail
)
SELECT
    C.CustomerLastName,
    C.CustomerFirstName,
    C.CustomerCompany,
    C.Score
FROM ScoredCustomers C
LEFT OUTER JOIN ScoreMatches S ON
    C.CustomerLastName = S.CustomerLastName
    AND C.CustomerFirstName = S.CustomerFirstName
    AND C.CustomerAddress1 = S.CustomerAddress1
    AND C.CustomerPostalCode = S.CustomerPostalCode
    AND C.CustomerMobilePhone = S.CustomerMobilePhone
WHERE
    C.Score > 0
GROUP BY C.CustomerLastName, C.CustomerFirstName, C.CustomerCompany,
         C.CustomerAddress1, C.CustomerPostalCode, C.CustomerMobilePhone,
         C.CustomerHomePhone, C.CustomerEmail, C.Score
ORDER BY C.Score DESC, C.CustomerLastName, C.CustomerFirstName, C.CustomerCompany
```

	CustomerLastName	CustomerFirstName	CustomerCompany	Score
0	Snedley	M	NULL	36
1	SnedleyJr	M	NULL	36
2	Snedley	B	NULL	28
3	Snedley	M	MortimerSnedleyEstate	15
4	Snedley	M	MortimerSnedleyTrust	15
5	OConnor	K	NULL	14
6	Brideau	J	NULL	7
7	Chavous	R	NULL	7
8	Degroot	N	NULL	7
9	Galam	B	NULL	7
10	GarciaLopez	J	NULL	7
11	Hamilton	C	NULL	7
12	Husser	S	NULL	7
13	Layous	M	NULL	7
14	Maisto	R	NULL	7
15	Mirafuentes	B	NULL	7
16	Nunlee	G	NULL	7
17	Perin	L	NULL	7
18	Rochin	X	NULL	7
19	Schmierer	P	NULL	7
20	Staback	M	NULL	7
21	Timenez	L	NULL	7
22	Zurcher	J	NULL	7
23	Eroman	I	NULL	6
24	Waycott	K	NULL	6

Finally, some results that show what the human eye could easily see with two simple datasets: we have some matches! In this trivial example, it is easy to forget we are often dealing with millions of rows on both sides. Then it gets a bit harder to just glance at both sides and know you're on the right track. Scoring helps you know whether you are getting close.

What About Tuning?

Our first pass at scoring showed we have a really good "hit rate," with at least 24 rows out of 27 in the import showing a good match on six attributes or more. Typically, for something like a marketing list, I would just declare victory and go home, confident that the remaining three rows are new prospects. And that is what I am going to do here. We need to move on to Chapter 13, because there is still another interesting case study to consider.

If I were to tune something like this, I would start with the obvious duplicated entries that are a process of the scoring and try to get those whittled down to the same range as the others. For more thoughts on tuning, refer to Chapter 10.

Final Thoughts on Practical Matters

The approach I showed in this chapter is something I do quite often. To recap, we did the following:

1. Filtered out impossible data versus possible data from the import via two ETLs
2. Normalized the scorable data attributes (columns) on both sides (our production customer data and the import data) via two more ETLs
3. Matched the data and scored the matches
4. Tuned the scores, or in this case chose not to

Obviously, this is an iterative approach. You may find halfway through that you need more attributes for scoring and will need to go back and add them perhaps to the very beginning. This is why I try to make each ETL idempotent (able to be rerun repeatedly without side effects). I typically place `DROP TABLE IF EXISTS staging.ImportCustomer` and similar statements before conducting an ETL. The back and forth process will continue until you:

- Have data clean enough
- Can get matches good enough
- Can make actionable business decisions

That's it. That has been the whole point of this book: to help you find "Is *this* list of data related to anything in *that* table?" I hope you feel like you can now approach such an exercise with some new tools in your kit and an understanding of the challenges along the way. If so, then I have completed what I set out to do. I hope it helps!

But wait! There's one more chapter, because we have a few more "fuzzy" things to discuss, such as the use of metadata, plus handling other data formats besides pure SQL datatypes (including code as data).

CHAPTER 13

Code Is Data, Too!

This chapter is interesting for those who may not have any use for examples about customer data. It just might expand your concept of "data" and the kinds of fuzzy things we can do with it in SQL! It includes a second case study based on work I have done repeatedly for employers and clients over the years. We're going to approach it stepwise, all aimed at looking at code as data: data that can be read *and* written!

Working with XML Data

Often you get your import data as a CSV, tab-separated values (TSV), or Excel file. Sometimes there are other more esoteric delimiting schemes. Perhaps the most esoteric textual data format ever devised was XML. I won't go into the depths of how to deal with it with namespaces, entity encodings, all that. Once you understand the basics like XPath, the SQL documentation is easy enough to read. I just want to point out that if you get some XML data, via a file transfer, web service response payload, or whatever, the first thing you can do is import it into a SQL table and then ETL out of that. Let's check it out:

```
CREATE TABLE staging.XMLDemo
(
    ImportLine XML NULL
);

INSERT INTO staging.XMLDemo
VALUES
(
    '<Customer>
        <LastName>Snedley</LastName>
        <FirstName>Mortimer</FirstName>
    </Customer>'
);
```

```
SELECT * FROM staging.XMLDemo;
```

ImportLine
\<customer>\<lastname>Snedley\</lastname>\<firstname>Mortimer\</firstname>\</customer>

Note that in tools like SQL Server Management Studio (SSMS), the preceding result would actually be a hyperlink that when clicked would show the XML document in that column formatted and indented in a new window. Nice!

Here it comes, the big reveal:

```
SELECT
    ImportLine.value('(/Customer/LastName/node())[1]', 'NVARCHAR(MAX)') LastName,
    ImportLine.value('(/Customer/FirstName/node())[1]', 'NVARCHAR(MAX)') FirstName
INTO staging.XMLDemoImported
FROM staging.XMLDemo;
```

What dark magic did we just wield? The value function is available on XML datatype columns, and it allows you to use XPath expressions to query out XML values—node or attribute or both—and turn them into SQL values. Note that since we are wanting single values for each column in this SELECT, we use the subscript [1] in the XPath expression to return the first (if any) value only. That way, if the XML document had more than one *LastName* node, we get only the first one. Obviously you may have different needs.

Also note that even if we have an XML schema to validate against, we are treating the node values as "unknown" datatypes and converting each one to a Unicode-enabled NVARCHAR(MAX) value. As I joked in Chapter 11, you should handle all incoming data from text files like it's plutonium and can kill you if you touch it wrong. Bring it in "fuzzy" and then refine from there.

We used all that in our old ETL friend SELECT...INTO...FROM.... Let's look at the results:

```
SELECT * FROM staging.XMLDemoImported;
```

LastName	FirstName
Snedley	Mortimer

If you go down this path, you will have to get used to using XPath. There are plenty of good resources available, although I keep going back to Mozilla Developer Network (MDN) (*https://oreil.ly/GzRnV*) and Microsoft's documentation to XPath queries in SQL (*https://oreil.ly/cbfCa*). XPath is very powerful, but not something I keep "loaded in my skull" 24x7. I always have to look it up, and how to deal with namespaces in *this* language, and so on. But you need to be aware that this exists and is very powerful.

There is also native SQL functionality to produce valid XML documents without resorting to brute-force string concatenation, but that is beyond the scope of this book. If interested, read the documentation on `SELECT...FOR XML` (*https://oreil.ly/CAuYP*).

Working with JSON Data

What goes for XML data now goes for JSON, too. However you receive the JSON payload, if you can get it into SQL first, then you can extract it into SQL columns, perform comparisons, and so on:

```
CREATE TABLE staging.JSONDemo
(
    ImportLine NVARCHAR(MAX)
);

INSERT INTO staging.JSONDemo
VALUES
(
    N'{
        "customer":
        {
          "lastName": "Snedley",
          "firstName": "Clive"
        }
    }'
);

SELECT * FROM staging.JSONDemo;
```

ImportLine
{ "customer": { "lastName": "Snedley", "firstName": "Clive" } }

It would be better if we could get at the underlying data as SQL columns. To do that we use the `JSON_VALUE` SQL function and use a JSON path expression (*https://oreil.ly/PCihz*) to get to the JSON object properties. I tend to think of it as JQuery syntax:

```
SELECT
    JSON_VALUE(ImportLine, '$.customer.lastName') LastName,
    JSON_VALUE(ImportLine, '$.customer.firstName') FirstName
INTO staging.JSONDemoImported
FROM staging.JSONDemo;
```

And just like that, we have extracted the JSON data into SQL columns:

```
SELECT * FROM staging.JSONDemoImported;
```

LastName	FirstName
Snedley	Clive

In modern data environments, it is often best practice to ingest such "documents" into a documented-oriented, "No-SQL" data store that allows for direct querying of "ragged" or "nonrectangular" data represented in tree formats such as JSON or XML. Such systems can also search free-form text, proprietary document types, and, yes, even boring old tables of rows and columns. If you have such an environment, it will have tools that can take you beyond what we can do here with just SQL. Use it.

But often, either due to scale (too small or too large), maturity, time constraints, or whatever else, the majority of the data the business is interested in is already in a relational format, and the data to be matched must be brought to it instead of the other way around. If the amount of XML or JSON data to be ingested is relatively smaller than the production dataset—or more to the point, if you need only a few "columns" out of those tree-based datasets, then grab them using these techniques, jam them in a table with some SELECT * INTO ... ETL, and move on. Given the nature of fuzzy data matching projects, spending time pondering which platform to use for a one-off (but important!) project is often unproductive.

Extracting Data from HTML

A friend once sent me a request on how to parse HTML with SQL. Challenge accepted!

Here is the original request:

> I was wondering if you knew how to use SQL to parse a column and return multiple individual records where text in that column is started with This is a test. The column might have these tags multiple times.
>
> Sample column text...
>
> ```
> This is a test
> Test
> How is it going
> Get this Text Also
> ```
>
> It should return...
>
> ```
> Test
> Get this Text Also
> ```

Here was my initial reply:

> You're going to hate me, but you can do this with SQL's XML functionality. I have built a test case that works on your sample set.

 It's important to remember that all XML function names are case-sensitive (lowercase), even though SQL in general is not.

Consider the following table, which represents the existing table, which I presumed had the HTML stored as a VARCHAR:

```
CREATE TABLE dbo.ParseExample
(
    HTMLText VARCHAR(4000) NULL
)
```

Now we insert the test case into it:

```
INSERT INTO ParseExample VALUES('This is a test
<B\b>Test</b>
How is it going
<b>Get this Text Also</b>')
```

SELECT * will bring back what you'd expect.

So, we can convert the HTML into XML (even though it's not valid XML) on the fly using a common table expression:

```
WITH Converted
AS
(SELECT CAST(HTMLText AS XML) AS X FROM ParseExample)
SELECT * FROM Converted
```

Now you can do fun things with XPath and XML functions. For example, to just get the <b> elements and their values (the XPath //b will look for bold elements wherever they are in the XML DOM), you can use the query function:

```
WITH Converted
AS
(SELECT CAST(HTMLText AS XML) AS X FROM ParseExample)
SELECT X.query('//b') FROM Converted
```

But this isn't useful, because the result still has the <b> tags and also returned everything in one row and column, which isn't what you want. So then you use the nodes function to get individual rows for each node that matches the XPath query, and then the value function to extract just the text (and not the tags) from that:

```
WITH Converted
AS
(SELECT CAST(HTMLText AS XML) AS X FROM ParseExample)
SELECT nref.value('.', 'nvarchar(max)') BoldText
FROM Converted
CROSS APPLY X.nodes('//b') AS R(nref)
```

The preceding code returns exactly what we are looking for.

Of course, there was one more wrinkle: his actual live data had   entities in it, so the XML parser was choking on that with:

```
XML parsing: line 1, character 9, well formed check: undeclared entity
```

In follow-up discussions he decided to just do this in the common table expression:

```
(SELECT CAST(REPLACE(HTMLText, ' ', ' ') AS XML) AS X FROM ParseExample)
```

I personally would prefer something more like this, which would have left the entity as is in the results:

```
(SELECT CAST(REPLACE(HTMLText, ' ', ' ') AS XML) AS X
  FROM ParseExample)
```

All of this was a trivial example, but remember that if you get data in XML format (or HTML format!), you can load it into an XML datatype column in SQL and with a moderate learning curve (if you don't know XPath already) can extract useful data from it with SQL queries! Then I would of course load that data into a staging table using the SELECT * ... INTO ... statement and move forward from there.

Code-Generating Code

This is a technique I have loved since college (a long, long time ago) and used in almost every language I've worked in. Sooner or later you find a use for code-generating code. And we can use SQL to generate SQL (or any other code), for sure!

Why is this of more than just esoteric interest? For one, it is how I generated some of the INSERT statements to use as test data for this book. Sometimes you have data in one SQL database and need to get it to another—perhaps from a different vendor, so backup and restore won't work. Perhaps there is no direct database connectivity between the two. Then you can send the dataset as a file containing generated INSERT statements, like this (getting only the first 10 rows for brevity):

```
SELECT TOP 10
    'INSERT INTO staging.CodeGeneratingDemo ' +
    '(LastName, FirstName, Company) VALUES(''' +
    COALESCE(last_name, '') + ''', ''' +
    COALESCE(first_name, '') + ''', ''' +
    COALESCE(company_name, '') + ''')' [SQL]
FROM staging.PossibleData
ORDER BY last_name, first_name, company_name;
```

	SQL
0	INSERT INTO staging.CodeGeneratingDemo (LastName, FirstName, Company) VALUES('Brideau', 'Junita', '')
1	INSERT INTO staging.CodeGeneratingDemo (LastName, FirstName, Company) VALUES('Chavous', 'Roz', '')
2	INSERT INTO staging.CodeGeneratingDemo (LastName, FirstName, Company) VALUES('Degroot-Smith', 'Novella', '')
3	INSERT INTO staging.CodeGeneratingDemo (LastName, FirstName, Company) VALUES('Eroman', 'Ilene', '')
4	INSERT INTO staging.CodeGeneratingDemo (LastName, FirstName, Company) VALUES('Galam', 'Britt', '')

SQL	
5	INSERT INTO staging.CodeGeneratingDemo (LastName, FirstName, Company) VALUES('Garcia Lopez', 'Janey', '')
6	INSERT INTO staging.CodeGeneratingDemo (LastName, FirstName, Company) VALUES('Hamilton', 'Charlene', '')
7	INSERT INTO staging.CodeGeneratingDemo (LastName, FirstName, Company) VALUES('Husser', 'Selma', 'Husser Associates')
8	INSERT INTO staging.CodeGeneratingDemo (LastName, FirstName, Company) VALUES('Layous', 'Ma', '')
9	INSERT INTO staging.CodeGeneratingDemo (LastName, FirstName, Company) VALUES('Maisto', 'Reena', '')

You can save the results to a text file and email it to someone around the world, and as long as they had created the *staging.CodeGeneratingDemo* table correctly, it would work regardless of which relational database management system the sender or the recipient uses, even if they are different.

There's a bug in the preceding code; can you find it? It can be fixed with a simple REPLACE or better, the SQL function QUOTENAME (*https://oreil.ly/gEjsv*), which gives away the problem: it doesn't handle embedded single quotes correctly; check out the 'O'Connor' entries. Those would cause a syntax error because the single quote in the name needs to be doubled in the generated string constant.

However, with a couple of tweaks you can quickly generate not just INSERT statements, but UPDATE, DELETE, and SELECT statements, too. Why would you want to generate SELECT queries? Let's say you're handed a new database of a couple of hundred tables containing some structure of CRM data from a company your company is taking over. Maybe the first thing you want to do is lift the lid of each table and see what's in there. You have the CRM manuals. You have a documented schema. But you're a data person and you want to look at, you know, some data. How about going to the database catalog and simply generating a SELECT TOP 100 * FROM x for each table in the database? Copy and paste the results into a new query window, hit Execute, and go get some liquid caffeine. When you come back, you will probably have some interesting things to look at while you sip it.

By the way, "a couple of hundred tables" could be a small CRM system, if it is a mature one with many customizations and orbiting applications added over time.

Impact Analysis: The Second Case Study

Looking at all the previous sections—XML (and HTML), JSON, code-generating code—it quickly becomes apparent that code is just data, too (for both input and output), and we're going to use both! Because all of our fuzzy techniques can be applied to code, not just boring old customer data!

Why would you do this? One example is work I have done multiple times: automated impact analysis. Consider the following real-world scenario:

A legacy system is going away.
Because of obsolescence, merger, or whatever, a "back-end" system is getting retired, perhaps after 30 years or more. It happens.

There are ties everywhere.
As with most legacy systems there is no clean "layer" that isolates the legacy system from "everything else." Instead, there are hundreds of code bases and other artifacts containing thousands of references into the database that represents the data for this system. And remember, it isn't just code:

SQL objects
The SQL database will have references back to itself in the form of views, stored procs, and user-defined functions (UDFs). There are probably other databases on the same server or other servers accessing that database, too, through three-part (*SalesDB.dbo.Customer*) and four-part (*DBSRV01.Sales DB.dbo.Customer*) names. You may have to look through a lot of databases and servers! In one place it was around a dozen databases where either references to the legacy database or replicas of its data could be found.

Reports
There will be reports...so many reports...from tools such as Power BI, Crystal Reports, SQL Server Reporting Services (SSRS), Excel, or Access files with direct database connections (this one is "complicated"), and legacy platforms like DocumentDirect. These are often the hardest artifacts to chase down, since in many organizations reporting is not a centralized function. For each type of reporting software you have, you may have to ask Security or Finance for a list of licensed users for that software and then ask each of those users to "Give me all your reports, please."

Homegrown applications
The references will be buried in code—Java, C#, C, C++, Python, JavaScript, HTML, SQL, PowerShell, and other scripting languages, config files, and on and on, are all places where I have seen such references squirreled (because I buried those nuts myself in many cases).

Integrations
Of course there will be all kinds of integrations pushing copies of the data around, especially if you have a data warehouse.

Even the data warehouse doesn't protect you.

You may bring all that data into the data warehouse, give it nice column names, and translate the obscure mainframe codes into English. But if the data contains user-defined fields (Duh-duh-dun—remember Chapter 9?), then it is rare those values get translated. So there are "legacy-isms" right there in your shiny data warehouse. Bummer. And if they're in there, you're probably reporting off them somewhere, so now we have to track down at least the user-defined field usage from the data warehouse, as well, unless you're moving those legacy user-defined fields as is to the new system—"like moving garbage into our shiny new house," as I've heard one person say it. It happens because of time and budgetary constraints. It's sad.

"Wow, Jim," you exclaim, "that's a lot! Besides panic, what can I, a mere data person, do to help?" Some analysis based on fuzzy data matching, of course! What if you could answer the following questions for management?

What are we using?

Which data attributes in the legacy system are you actively using?

Where are we using them?

Where are all the places in our "code" (source, SQL, reports, integrations, etc.) that touch the legacy system?

This allows two types of analysis by management and BAs:

What applications are affected?

The answer to this question is useful for scoping, budgeting, resource planning, and so on.

Where is "xyz" being used?

As analysis moves on, there will be a need to identify everywhere a specific "object" or "attribute" (table, column) is used. There will likely be phased data and application migrations, and this helps put boundaries around each and helps people "map" between the old and new systems.

These are the problems this chapter is going to show you how to solve, with SQL! We will look at a simplified example, and in the following sections we're going to deal with the approach in bite-sized pieces.

Gather Together Every Code "Artifact" You Can

Code artifacts to be gathered include the following:

Source code

Java, C#, C++, Python, JavaScript, HTML, SQL, so many others—whatever "source code" means in your shop. Basically if it's a file in your source code control system that could conceivably hold a reference to anything in that database, grab it. Don't go checking first, though; that's what we're going to automate here! If you think it could at all, just grab it and everything around it. Basically, depending on the criticality of the database to your business processes and its tenure in your organization, "All the organization's source code, everywhere" is a fine starting place. For those reading this working with legacy Microsoft stack applications, note that not only your *.cs* and *.vb* files can contain SQL references, but so can *.asmx* and *.aspx* files. (Remember those? If you are migrating from a legacy app I bet you do!)

Config files

Really, I've put SQL in them and seen others do it, too (where do you think I learned it from?). It supposedly added a layer of indirection to keep the SQL out of the compiled code so it could be maintained separately. You see this pattern in places where the developer-to-DBA communications have broken down, so the developers can't get views and stored procedures created (or don't have the ability to update them) as that layer of indirection. Microsoft programmers, this means *web.config, app.config, .sln, .csproj,* and *.vbproj* files should all be examined.

SQL DDL

Script out into separate files every SQL view, stored proc, and user-defined SQL function, not just on the target database but on any that you know or think reference it (or every database to be safe). This step may be iterative as you discover new references based on this exercise. Do not go looking through them by hand to check; automating that is why we're here! If you suspect there may be references to the legacy database in another database, just generate that database's DDL, too, at least for views, stored procedures, and user-defined SQL functions. I usually just use SSMS's *Tasks>Generate Scripts* on each database for this step. When set to generate one file per database object, SSMS places the object type as part of the file name, e.g., *crm.NormalizedCustomer.View.sql*, which can come in handy later (you know how to parse it out of the file path with SQL now).

Report source

SSRS RDL files are just XML. Note you can pull this XML right out of the SSRS database; there's no need to ask anyone for anything other than *db_reader* access to the SSRS database. Even though XML loading it into an XML datatype column doesn't really buy us much, we will just treat it as a big string like the rest of the files. Power BI and Crystal Reports do not succumb to this technique, but there are other approaches for them outside a book on pure SQL (hint: APIs).

Integration source

SQL Server Integration Services (SSIS) DTSX files are just XML, too! Again, we will just load it as VARCHAR, however.

Whatever else

One would note an executable notebook like the one used to generate this chapter is just a JSON file containing Markdown and code cells, all of which is "just text" like all the preceding.

 Earlier I argued to just grab everything and filter later. That may depend on the situation and timing. Many projects of this scale are visible coming from afar, slowly approaching the village like a glacier of internal meetings, RFPs, sales presentations, demos, more internal meetings, maybe a proof of concept, and so on. *You know the impact is coming even before you have to estimate it.*

This is a good time to spend some smart college intern resources and get that source code control system (SCCS) of yours cleaned up. You know what I am talking about: varied naming "standards" that reflect software fads of the previous decades, branches used as filesystem directories instead of proper SCCS labels, "Temp" and "DELETE_ME" and "FooProj_20170401" directory names. Don't look away when I'm lecturing you, because it happens to all of us. If you can get all that cleaned up (obsolete code pared off and deleted or placed in cold storage, proper "Release" branches easily identifiable, application naming standards, at least at the repo level), then everything that follows will be quicker and easier. And you will have a good idea of your current software inventory! Winning!

Import Artifacts into SQL

Put the artifacts into a meaningful directory structure. For things like source code, they may come out of the source code control system (like git) in a well-defined directory structure already. For other artifacts you gather from "the business" or elsewhere, you may have to come up with your own directory structure. This will help you remember where everything came from and help avoid name collisions when you end up getting two different *Customer.rdl* files.

This will also help you filter as you find you are given directories with subdirectory names containing words like *Backup* or *Archive* or *Obsolete*. Many people don't have access to source code control systems and so keep multiple copies of their report files or similar around "just in case." Many people with access to source code control systems don't use them properly and re-create the same patterns there. That's why we capture the full path to each file as a column, as shown here.

First, create a table that will hold at least the following:

Artifact name
> *Customer.rdl.*

Full path
> *F:\Data\Reports\SSRS\Sales\Customer.rdl.* This could be enough; you could manufacture the filename out of it on the fly, but I find it better to have that data duplicated.

Artifact text
> The full contents of each file or artifact; code, XML, SQL, etc. The contents of the file should be loaded uninterpreted into something like a VARCHAR(MAX).

The DDL for my artifact table often looks as simple as the following code. Note that you may have to increase your *FileName* and *FilePath* VARCHAR sizes if your filesystem supports longer paths, or you can just make all three columns VARCHAR(MAX) and be done with it:

```
CREATE TABLE impact.CodeArtifacts
(
    FileName     VARCHAR(260) NULL,
    FilePath     VARCHAR(260) NULL,
    FileContents VARCHAR(MAX) NULL
);
```

Using PowerShell (shown next) or your favorite import tool, integration platform, or programming language, for each source add a row to the above table with the appropriate content for each column—name, full path, and file contents. Like this:

```
# Load all SQL artifacts (views, stored procs, user-defined functions) into the
# SQLArtifacts table.
Install-Module -Name SqlServer -Scope CurrentUser

foreach ($artifact in Get-ChildItem -Recurse \
        "C:\Users\me\Documents\SQLArtifacts\*.sql")
{
    $row = [PSCustomObject]@{
                            Name=$artifact.Name;          \
                            FullName=$artifact.FullName; \
                            Artifact=Get-Content -Raw $artifact.FullName
                    }
        Write-SqlTableData -Passthru -ServerInstance "MyDBSrv" \
            -DatabaseName "TestDb" \
            -SchemaName "impact" -TableName "CodeArtifacts" -InputData $row
}
```

The preceding PowerShell is slow, but you can be accomplishing the following tasks while it runs, and it is typically easier to use PowerShell or another shell in many places than to get access to import tools or, even harder, a development environment to write some custom import code. Besides, while we want this to all be repeatable and expandable as we work through this replacement project, the code we write here will ultimately be a bespoke "one-off" and retired once the migration is complete, so it doesn't have to be perfect. Just "good enough." If you are in another programming stack, all I am saying here is that for impact analysis you don't have to get fancy; often a simple script in the shell of your choice is enough.

For the purposes of this book, I preloaded some fake "code artifacts." These in no way represent anything real and aren't even syntactically valid. But they show that given a series of files or "artifacts" considered as long strings, we can basically search through them for other strings of interest. Let's look:

```
SELECT
    FileName,
    FilePath,
    LEFT(FileContents, 50) FileContents
FROM impact.CodeArtifacts
ORDER BY FilePath, FileName;
```

	FileName	FilePath	FileContents
0	InventoryDataLayer.cs	/Apps/Inventory/DataLayer.Gateway.cs	Nothing to see here, folks!
1	InventoryLogicLayer.cs	/Apps/Inventory/LogicLayer.Controller.cs	Nothing to see here, folks!
2	InventoryPresentationLayer.cs	/Apps/Inventory/PresentationLayer.ViewModel.cs	Nothing to see here, folks!
3	MarketingDataLayer.cs	/Apps/Marketing/DataLayer.Gateway.cs	SELECT * FROM crm.Customer
4	MarketingLogicLayer.cs	/Apps/Marketing/LogicLayerController.cs	Nothing to see here, folks!
5	MarketingPresentationLayer.cs	/Apps/Marketing/PresentationLayer.ViewModel.cs	Nothing to see here, folks!
6	web.config	/Apps/Marketing/web.config	SELECT * FROM Customer -- It's always Marketing!
7	SalesDataLayer.cs	/Apps/Sales/DataLayer.Gateway.cs	SELECT * FROM crm.Customer
8	SalesLogicLayer.cs	/Apps/Sales/LogicLayer.Controller.cs	Nothing to see here, folks!
9	SalesPresentationLayer.cs	/Apps/Sales/PresentationLayer.ViewModel.cs	Nothing to see here, folks!
10	crm.NormalizedCustomer.View.sql	/DDL/CRMDatabase/crm.NormalizedCustomer.View.sql	SELECT * FROM crm.Customer
11	CustomerIntegration.dtsx	/Integrations/SSIS/CustomerIntegration.dtsx	SELECT * FROM crm.[Customer]; SELECT * FROM [crm].
12	InventoryIntegration.dtsx	/Integrations/SSIS/InventoryIntegration.dtsx	SELECT * FROM [prod].[Inventory]
13	MarketingIntegration.dtsx	/Integrations/SSIS/MarketingIntegration.dtsx	SELECT * FROM crm.Customer; SELECT * FROM crm.Norm

	FileName	FilePath	FileContents
14	InventoryReport.rdl	/Reports/Inventory/InventoryReport.rdl	Nothing to see here, folks!
15	MarketingReport.rdl	/Reports/Marketing/MarketingReport.rdl	SELECT * FROM Customer; SELECT * FROM ref.PostalAb
16	SalesReport.rdl	/Reports/Sales/SalesReport.rdl	SELECT * FROM Customer

Even in our tiny loaded dataset of fake "artifacts," we can do some preliminary statistics on what could be potentially impacted. The file paths had the project or "type" of artifact as its first directory, and the project or database name as its second, e.g., */Apps/Marketing/PresentationLayer.ViewModel.cs*. Given that info, let's see what we can do. First, what projects or databases might be impacted? Instead of a lot of highly embedded function calls, we will "unroll" this into a series of chained CTEs to see what happens at each step:

```
WITH StripLeadingSlash
AS
(
    SELECT DISTINCT
        RIGHT(FilePath, LEN(FilePath) - 1) Remainder
    FROM impact.CodeArtifacts
),
RemoveProjectType
AS
(
    SELECT
        RIGHT(Remainder, LEN(Remainder) -
                        CHARINDEX('/', Remainder)) Remainder
    FROM StripLeadingSlash
),
GrabProjectName
AS
(
    SELECT
        LEFT(Remainder, CHARINDEX('/', Remainder) - 1) Project
    FROM RemoveProjectType
)
SELECT DISTINCT
    Project
FROM GrabProjectName
ORDER BY Project;
```

	Project
0	CRMDatabase
1	Inventory
2	Marketing
3	Sales
4	SSIS

What types of files do we have in our trivial example, and how many of each? Remember this trick?

```
WITH GrabFileType
AS
(
    SELECT
        RIGHT(FilePath, CHARINDEX('.', REVERSE(FilePath))) FileExtension
    FROM impact.CodeArtifacts
)
SELECT
    FileExtension,
    COUNT(*) Total
FROM GrabFileType
GROUP BY FileExtension
ORDER BY 2 DESC, 1;
```

	FileExtension	Total
0	.cs	9
1	.dtsx	3
2	.rdl	3
3	.config	1
4	.sql	1

Look! We have a config file in the mix. Where is that?

```
SELECT * FROM impact.CodeArtifacts
WHERE
    RIGHT(FileName, LEN('.config')) = '.config';
```

FileName	FilePath	FileContents
web.config	/Apps/Marketing/web.config	SELECT * FROM Customer -- It's always Marketing!

Throughout this book, we have talked about boring business constructs like "customer" and "CRM" and "import data." In this case we are going to be doing something that may not make sense to the average business user but is going to make executives looking for good estimates sit up and take notice. We're going to treat these source code artifacts as our production data (it is), and the legacy system objects as the import data to be matched. Why? And why does your CIO care? It's because now you will be able to answer two questions with real numbers:

- If the legacy system went away tomorrow, how bad would it hurt? (How much of it are we using?)

- Where would it hurt the most? (Which systems are we going to have to rewrite versus perhaps find another source for some simple data needs?)

You may not even know the new system's schema yet to even know where the new data is going to come from, but you will be able to provide hard numbers for the preceding questions. Even this limited data allows for some early prioritizations. For example, if something is sourcing just a few columns from the legacy system, perhaps that data can be found in the data warehouse instead. For some marginal legacy systems, maybe the impact estimate is enough to argue to make the *business decision* to finally retire it, because the cost of rectifying it will exceed its profitability. This approach also allows you to start making budget estimates to bring on full-time or contract resources for the upcoming project. Look at you being all proactive! You rock.

The point being that now you will have data about the impact of the system replacement beyond hand-gathered, anecdotal evidence. That will be needed, too! But in your case you can have everything scripted, repeatable, and tunable; people may challenge your assumptions, and you can tweak your parameters as you need in response, but no one will be able to challenge your approach.

And Now, for My Next Trick

We are ready to do some analysis.

"But wait!" you exclaim. "The legacy database that is going away has hundreds, nay, *thousands* of tables! We can't look for all those tables, through the thousands of artifacts we've collected!"

No, *you* can't. But *code* can!

"But we can't write all that code! We can't copy and paste and change it all in time and without too many errors!" you argue back, getting a little flushed in the face (didn't you, just now?).

No, *you* can't. But *code* can!

The following code describes how we will do it. First, for the affected database(s), gather the table, view, stored procedure, and user-defined SQL function names out of the database(s) catalog(s). Let's say we don't care about anything in the *staging* schema, since those are integration tables and we know they will be going away or changing anyway:

```
SELECT
    s.name [Schema],
    o.name ObjectName,
    o.type_desc ObjectType
FROM sys.objects o
INNER JOIN sys.schemas s ON
    o.schema_id = s.schema_id
WHERE
    s.name <> 'staging'
```

```
        AND o.type_desc IN
        (
            'USER_TABLE',
            'VIEW',
            'SQL_TABLE_VALUED_FUNCTION',
            'SQL_STORED_PROCEDURE',
            'SQL_INLINE_TABLE_VALUED_FUNCTION',
            'SQL_SCALAR_FUNCTION'
        )
    ORDER BY 1, 2;
```

	Schema	ObjectName	ObjectType
0	crm	Customer	USER_TABLE
1	crm	CustomerCountByState	VIEW
2	crm	NormalizedCustomer	VIEW
3	dbo	PotentialMatches	USER_TABLE
4	dbo	USFakeDemoData	USER_TABLE
5	impact	CodeArtifacts	USER_TABLE
6	ref	PostalAbbreviations	USER_TABLE

This is purposefully a trivial example. I have run this for literally thousands of objects in this table.

How do you get results like this from multiple servers? Using OPENQUERY and linked servers on SQL Server is one way:

```
SELECT * FROM OPENQUERY(RmtServer, '
    SELECT
        SERVERPROPERTY(''MachineName'') Server,
        ''SomeDatabase'' [Database],
        s.name [Schema],
        o.name ObjectName,
        o.type_desc ObjectType
    FROM SomeDatabase.sys.objects o
    INNER JOIN sys.schemas s ON
        o.schema_id = s.schema_id
    WHERE
        s.name <> ''staging''
        AND o.type_desc IN
        (
            ''USER_TABLE'',
            ''VIEW'',
            ''SQL_TABLE_VALUED_FUNCTION'',
            ''SQL_STORED_PROCEDURE'',
            ''SQL_INLINE_TABLE_VALUED_FUNCTION'',
            ''SQL_SCALAR_FUNCTION''
        )
') A; -- Mandatory sub-query alias, I usually use "A"
```

OPENQUERY passes along a SQL string (which can be dynamically created, by the way) to another server to be executed. In the previous example, it is a linked server with the name *RmtServer*. When gathering statistics like this remotely, it is good to include the remote server and database names in the result set, as the preceding query does with the first two columns. More discussion of OPENQUERY is beyond the scope of this book, but now you know it exists and can be used to access remote database *catalog* metadata as well as simple application data. There are other ways to solve this problem, but this is the easiest.

Now for each object we're going to generate some SQL to search our artifacts table looking for that object name. This process has many nuances to discuss. The first is the heavy use of LIKE in all the following code examples, so we know it will be slow. But that's OK. We are going to run the scan only once, or whenever we reload all the artifacts to catch any changes. In real life this scan can run for days depending on the number of objects being searched for multiplied by the number of search patterns we will define next multiplied by the number of artifacts to be searched. Again, though, we will save the statistics, the "hits," so the expensive scan has to be run only once.

First let's create the table that will store the hits:

```
CREATE TABLE impact.CodeArtifactHits
(
    SearchTerm VARCHAR(255) NOT NULL,
    FileName VARCHAR(255) NULL,
    FilePath VARCHAR(255) NULL
);
```

Let's write some code to write some code:

```
WITH SqlObjectInfo
AS
(
    SELECT
        s.name [Schema],
        o.name ObjectName,
        o.type_desc ObjectType
    FROM sys.objects o
    INNER JOIN sys.schemas s ON
        o.schema_id = s.schema_id
    WHERE
        s.name <> 'staging'
        AND o.type_desc IN
        (
            'USER_TABLE',
            'VIEW',
            'SQL_TABLE_VALUED_FUNCTION',
            'SQL_STORED_PROCEDURE',
            'SQL_INLINE_TABLE_VALUED_FUNCTION',
            'SQL_SCALAR_FUNCTION'
        )
```

```
)
SELECT
    'INSERT INTO impact.CodeArtifactHits ' +
    'SELECT ''' + ObjectName + ''' SearchTerm, ' +
    'FileName, FilePath FROM impact.CodeArtifacts ' +
    'WHERE ' +
    'FileContents LIKE ''%' +
    REPLACE(ObjectName, '_', '\_') +
    '%'' ESCAPE ''\'''
FROM SqlObjectInfo;
```

0	INSERT INTO impact.CodeArtifactHits SELECT 'CodeArtifacts' SearchTerm, FileName, FilePath FROM impact.CodeArtifacts WHERE FileContents LIKE '%CodeArtifacts%' ESCAPE '\'
1	INSERT INTO impact.CodeArtifactHits SELECT 'CodeArtifactHits' SearchTerm, FileName, FilePath FROM impact.CodeArtifacts WHERE FileContents LIKE '%CodeArtifactHits%' ESCAPE '\'
2	INSERT INTO impact.CodeArtifactHits SELECT 'USFakeDemoData' SearchTerm, FileName, FilePath FROM impact.CodeArtifacts WHERE FileContents LIKE '%USFakeDemoData%' ESCAPE '\'
3	INSERT INTO impact.CodeArtifactHits SELECT 'Customer' SearchTerm, FileName, FilePath FROM impact.CodeArtifacts WHERE FileContents LIKE '%Customer%' ESCAPE '\'
4	INSERT INTO impact.CodeArtifactHits SELECT 'PostalAbbreviations' SearchTerm, FileName, FilePath FROM impact.CodeArtifacts WHERE FileContents LIKE '%PostalAbbreviations%' ESCAPE '\'
5	INSERT INTO impact.CodeArtifactHits SELECT 'NormalizedCustomer' SearchTerm, FileName, FilePath FROM impact.CodeArtifacts WHERE FileContents LIKE '%NormalizedCustomer%' ESCAPE '\'
6	INSERT INTO impact.CodeArtifactHits SELECT 'CustomerCountByState' SearchTerm, FileName, FilePath FROM impact.CodeArtifacts WHERE FileContents LIKE '%CustomerCountByState%' ESCAPE '\'
7	INSERT INTO impact.CodeArtifactHits SELECT 'PotentialMatches' SearchTerm, FileName, FilePath FROM impact.CodeArtifacts WHERE FileContents LIKE '%PotentialMatches%' ESCAPE '\'

This is the simplest way to do it. There are nuances you can provide for if you think you are going to have a lot of false positives. For example, "Customer" may be a word that shows up in form names, field labels, and so on, and doesn't just denote our table *Customer*. To help eliminate some (not all) false positives, you can more add LIKE clauses, at the cost of slowing the resulting queries down more. For example:

```
WHERE FileContents LIKE '% Customer%
```

Note the leading whitespace before Customer. Of course, this still doesn't get rid of false positives like "This field holds the customer name" in hover text or whatever else may be found in your source files. Note you can't add trailing whitespace because that will miss SELECT * FROM Customer.

```
WHERE ArtifactText LIKE '%dbo.Customer%
```

Adding the schema as an additional LIKE will pick up those missed by the preceding text, and really lowers the likelihood of this being a false positive.

```
WHERE ArtifactText LIKE '%[crm].[Customer]%
```
Of course, both can have square brackets around them.

```
WHERE ArtifactText LIKE '%crm.[Customer]%
```
Or just the object name itself can (you will see this in SSIS *.dtsx* files sometimes).

For now, we're keeping it simple with a single LIKE and accepting any false positives we may get.

What is that ESCAPE '\' on the generated LIKE clauses? If the SQL object names have underscores in them (mine don't), then the REPLACE in the code generator "escapes" the underscore character with a leading \ so that LIKE doesn't treat the _ as a single-character wildcard.

Now we can save the preceding results as a file or copy and paste them into a new query window and run them:

```
INSERT INTO impact.CodeArtifactHits
SELECT 'USFakeDemoData' SearchTerm, FileName, FilePath
FROM impact.CodeArtifacts
WHERE FileContents LIKE '%USFakeDemoData%' ESCAPE '\';
INSERT INTO impact.CodeArtifactHits
SELECT 'Customer' SearchTerm, FileName, FilePath
FROM impact.CodeArtifacts
WHERE FileContents LIKE '%Customer%' ESCAPE '\';
INSERT INTO impact.CodeArtifactHits
SELECT 'PostalAbbreviations' SearchTerm, FileName, FilePath
FROM impact.CodeArtifacts
WHERE FileContents LIKE '%PostalAbbreviations%' ESCAPE '\';
INSERT INTO impact.CodeArtifactHits
SELECT 'NormalizedCustomer' SearchTerm, FileName, FilePath
FROM impact.CodeArtifacts
WHERE FileContents LIKE '%NormalizedCustomer%' ESCAPE '\';
INSERT INTO impact.CodeArtifactHits
SELECT 'CustomerCountByState' SearchTerm, FileName, FilePath
FROM impact.CodeArtifacts
WHERE FileContents LIKE '%CustomerCountByState%' ESCAPE '\';
INSERT INTO impact.CodeArtifactHits
SELECT 'PotentialMatches' SearchTerm, FileName, FilePath
FROM impact.CodeArtifacts
WHERE FileContents LIKE '%PotentialMatches%' ESCAPE '\';
```

Did we get any hits?

```
SELECT * FROM impact.CodeArtifactHits;
```

	SearchTerm	FileName	FilePath
0	Customer	SalesDataLayer.cs	/Apps/Sales/DataLayer.Gateway.cs
1	Customer	SalesReport.rdl	/Reports/Sales/SalesReport.rdl
2	Customer	CustomerIntegration.dtsx	/Integrations/SSIS/CustomerIntegration.dtsx

	SearchTerm	FileName	FilePath
3	Customer	MarketingIntegration.dtsx	/Integrations/SSIS/MarketingIntegration.dtsx
4	Customer	MarketingDataLayer.cs	/Apps/Marketing/DataLayer.Gateway.cs
5	Customer	web.config	/Apps/Marketing/web.config
6	Customer	MarketingReport.rdl	/Reports/Marketing/MarketingReport.rdl
7	Customer	crm.NormalizedCustomer.View.sql	/DDL/CRMDatabase/crm.NormalizedCustomer.View.sql
8	PostalAbbreviations	MarketingReport.rdl	/Reports/Marketing/MarketingReport.rdl
9	NormalizedCustomer	CustomerIntegration.dtsx	/Integrations/SSIS/CustomerIntegration.dtsx
10	NormalizedCustomer	MarketingIntegration.dtsx	/Integrations/SSIS/MarketingIntegration.dtsx
11	CustomerCountByState	MarketingReport.rdl	/Reports/Marketing/MarketingReport.rdl

That's it. Now in the hits table you know every SQL object that is actually found somewhere in a source code artifact (with some possible false positives around "customer," perhaps). This allows you to quickly answer those two questions:

Which legacy objects are actually in use?

Presumably these need to be mapped in existing or new artifacts (code, reports, integrations) with the new source names when you get them. Which are the most used? Which are the least? (Maybe the latter can be re-sourced from different data already?)

How many artifacts are affected?

Which ones? Which are the most affected? Which are the least? (Maybe the latter can be retired?)

The first is easy enough:

```
SELECT
    SearchTerm,
    COUNT(*)
FROM impact.CodeArtifactHits
GROUP BY SearchTerm
ORDER BY 2 DESC, 1;
```

	SearchTerm	
0	Customer	8
1	NormalizedCustomer	2
2	CustomerCountByState	1
3	PostalAbbreviations	1

To which then management will ask, "Where are we using them?"

```
WITH StripLeadingSlash
AS
(
```

```sql
SELECT DISTINCT
    FilePath,
    RIGHT(FilePath, LEN(FilePath) - 1) Remainder
FROM impact.CodeArtifacts
),
RemoveProjectType
AS
(
    SELECT
        FilePath,
        RIGHT(Remainder, LEN(Remainder) -
                        CHARINDEX('/', Remainder)) Remainder
    FROM StripLeadingSlash
),
GrabProjectName
AS
(
    SELECT
        FilePath,
        LEFT(Remainder, CHARINDEX('/', Remainder) - 1) Project
    FROM RemoveProjectType
)
SELECT
    G.Project,
    COUNT(*) Total
FROM impact.CodeArtifactHits C
INNER JOIN GrabProjectName G ON
    C.FilePath = G.FilePath
GROUP BY Project
ORDER BY 2 DESC, 1;
```

	Project	Total
0	Marketing	5
1	SSIS	4
2	Sales	2
3	CRMDatabase	1

You could also do this by crawling the filesystem with grep or PowerShell, but you'd still have to gather and analyze the results, and it is slow to open and search through that many files repetitively. Whereas once they are all loaded into a SQL table, they may be repeatedly searched quickly without repeatedly navigating directories and opening, reading, and closing each file. Many online source code control systems allow the ability to search across all the code repositories, but it is hard or obscure to *script* those searches and extract the results. You will still want the results in SQL or similar anyway, for easy analysis.

You can get fancy by loading RDL and DSTX files and other XML into a column with an XML datatype and then use XPath queries to search only through the elements or attributes that you have found are likeliest to have the SQL object names in them. I have done this myself. But at the end of the day, just treating them as text and searching all artifacts in the same way is usually acceptable, if marginally slower.

Some people object to this approach, complaining about potential false positives: "We have tables called *Loan* and *Customer* that will get way too many false hits." Maybe. Probably not. First go back and look at the discussion of generating a bunch of different LIKE statements to minimize them. They have a few guards built in, but you may get a few false positives around those types of table names. But in my experience most object names are pretty unique in terms of clashing with any simple "English" words in source code. Tables names like *CustomerAddress* and *LoanCollateral* are not words that come up in most conversations—or code, unless it is accessing those tables. In other words, you'll get false positives, maybe, but they're worth the insights you will gain from this technique.

Also, you can expand this technique and search for column names, too; it is just another "layer" of metadata extraction from the database catalog. This can be helpful when you have the replacement system's schema and are trying to build some sort of mapping where you can find all the *CUST_NO* fields in your code and know you have to replace them with *CustomerNumber*. That can be helpful, but often just knowing which files are impacted when *crm.Customer* goes away is enough.

Final Thoughts on Code As Data

I may not be a "10x programmer," but if I am any "x" above "1," it is probably from using techniques such as reading metadata to write code-generating code. It can seem a bit *Sorcerer's Apprentice*-like at times, trying to keep track of all the different layers. But the payoff is large.

We dealt a lot in the earlier chapters with parsing strings by hand with SQL functions. But it is important to remember that SQL can do some of that for us. Look at the wide variety of date representations it can parse. And consider how it now understands XML and JSON. Using the SQL function techniques in this book would not be fruitful for parsing an XML payload, but you don't have to. Just extract what you need with XPath. You now have more tools in your toolbelt!

There are data lineage vendors that offer products that can do some of what we looked at in this chapter. Typically, they are good at answering questions like this:

> If we change table *Foo*, what projects are impacted, and which source artifacts?

This is good stuff, because most day-to-day maintenance is not of the "rip out an entire system" variety but instead are quiet changes here and there to applications.

What these tools usually can't answer easily, because they often only offer a point-and-click user interface, is a way to easily answer these questions:

> Given this list of 469 tables and views and stored procedures are going away, what projects are impacted, and which source artifacts? How many are impacted per distinct database object? How many are impacted by the most database objects? Which projects will be hurt the most, perhaps requiring rewrites or replacements?

It is these latter questions I started to show how to answer here. With those answers, management can start to prioritize and plan for the upcoming disaster system replacement. It will be fine. Really. And you can help! Impact analysis could be the subject of a whole other book. Stay tuned!

Searching human-generated text—any text, including code—is the ultimate "fuzzy" matching exercise. The sheer variety of ways something can be represented is vast. The second case study detailed in this chapter breaks down as a combinatorial problem above a certain size. The number of files or other artifacts to be searched times the number of objects in the database being retired times the number of patterns each object name can take in the source code rapidly grows. In a recent gig, there were a few thousand objects being searched across a quarter million files, and it took over a week. However, that search only needed to happen once, since all the statistics were saved off of it, allowing querying by project managers to start calculating impact to their hearts' content. I simply did other things while the SQL job executed—like eat and sleep.

Final Thoughts on All of It

In the end, it comes down to if all data was perfectly represented, perfectly "normalized" in a data modeling sense (e.g., third normal form), perfectly entered each and every time, and perfectly transmitted and stored without error, then everything would be precise, and there would be no need to be "fuzzy" to get what we want out of it. Some nights I dream of that world and then wake up, sadly realizing I live in this one, where data is often messy, but we still have to use it to get answers. Data quality problems will always exist. This book gave you some tools to not be a victim of them.

Again, if you think your data warehouse protects you, you should probably first go ask some probing questions of the data warehouse team:

Does the data warehouse cover all our data?
> Does it represent every attribute from every application or data source you have? Not just from all the new, cleanly architected and implemented apps, but your legacy ones as well?

Does the data warehouse truly insulate us?
> Or are there fields, perhaps renamed, that still represent untranslated *Custom Field1* values? Do you have "legacy bleedover" in your data? Poke real hard at data coming from mainframe applications. Are *all* the one-byte code fields being translated to real words, or are they still in there as "A" (meaning "Active" or "All" or "Archive" or only the users know what)? And will report writers know to translate that to "All" (for example), or simply leave it untranslated because the report consumers know what "A" means and have for decades?

One thing any honest data warehouse architect will tell you is there is never a point where the data warehouse is "done." There are always more data sources waiting to be added (and translated), always data quality problems waiting to be dealt with "upstream" in the integrations to the data warehouse, always "legacy-isms" floating in there, sometimes very subtly. Those complex multi-use custom fields are almost never completely mapped to a nice list of restricted values. How about *ModifiedBy* fields holding mainframe user IDs that need to be retained for audit and forensic purposes? Are you going to map those to the user's network ID? What if that network ID changes when they get married? Does remapping it to their new ID violate "time, person, and place" audit connections? And on and on.

Want an example? Take names. Names are hard, as we know, and that includes in computer science. I know of one legacy system many decades old that is at the core of a large group of companies. The identifier for customers is not called *Customer Number* (or since it's a mainframe app, more likely *CUST_NUM*). No. It is something akin to *CEFKey* (name changed to protect the guilty), pronounced by one and all as "seef-key." "CEF" stands for "Customer Entry File" and is literally a VSAM file used by the legacy CICS mainframe application. No one knows that but the techies, but over the decades, the business users have universally taken to calling it "CEFKey" in lieu of a corporate-defined generic "customer identifier," and it is referenced in policy and procedures, service desk documentation, and casual business conversation.

Guess what? The legacy application is being replaced, and in the bright new application being migrated to, it is going to be called *CEFKey* as well. Why? Because the cultural change is too large to make the leap to "Customer number" in the midst of a huge systems migration. Therefore, that legacy name will outlive the people moving it to the new system. There will be people in those organizations asking "What's that customer's *CEFKey*?" long after the legacy system and the VSAM file to which it indeed was a key is gone. So, you just got a dirty legacy-ism embedded in your shiny new data warehouse and application! Happens every day. Data is data, but people are people, and changing them is beyond the scope of this book.

I hope this book has helped you understand the challenges that arise when given two or more datasets to match, the approaches to use to make the problem tractable, and now, with something like code-generating code, a way to make your tools scale beyond what you could ever type. I was (in)famous at one job for always answering, "Easy. It's a simple matter of code." Now you can say that and sincerely mean the "Easy" part, too.

May the scores be with you!

The Data "Model"

I put "model" in quotes because it is so simple I am almost embarrassed. Almost. But I dislike those tech books that build some huge, fake application that you have to understand as well as the subject itself, so I chose to go simple to keep the actual topic in the forefront:

Customer Table

Customer is the main "production" table in our *crm* system (see Table A-1):

```
SELECT TOP 10 * FROM crm.Customer;
```

NormalizedCustomer View

This view implements some of the data normalization techniques used in the book (see Table A-2):

```
SELECT TOP 10 * FROM crm.NormalizedCustomer;
```

PotentialMatches Table

This is an "import" table that is used in various examples to attempt to match against the CRM data (see Table A-3):

```
SELECT TOP 10 * FROM dbo.PotentialMatches;
```

Table A-1. Customer

	id	first_name	last_name	company_name	address	city	county	state	zip	country	phone1	phone2	email	web_address
0	1	NULL	NULL	Acme Corp	123 Snell Ave	Jefferson City	Cole	MO	65101	U.S.A.	NULL	573-555-3256	NULL	www.acme.test
1	2	NULL	NULL	Foo, Inc.	457 Prairie View St	Boulder	Boulder	CO	80301	US	NULL	303-555-5623	NULL	www.foo.test
2	3	NULL	NULL	Snedley & Sons, L.L.C.	443 Arroyo Rd	Raton	Colfax	NM	87740	U.S.	NULL	575-555-0956	NULL	www.snedley.test
3	4	Johnetta	Abdallah	NULL	1088 Pinehurst St	Chapel Hill	Orange	NC	27514	United States	919-555-9345	919-555-3791	johnetta_abdallah@example.com	NULL
4	5	Geoffrey	Acey	NULL	7 West Ave #1	Palatine	Cook	IL	60067	USA	847-555-1734	847-555-2909	geoffrey@example.com	NULL
5	6	Weldon	Acuff	NULL	73 W Barstow Ave	Arlington Heights	Cook	IL	60004	U.S.A.	847-555-2156	847-555-5866	wacuff@example.com	NULL
6	7	Barbra	Adkin	NULL	4 Kohler Memorial Dr	Brooklyn	Kings	NY	11230	US	718-555-3751	718-555-9475	badkin@example.com	NULL
7	8	Fausto	Agramonte	NULL	5 Harrison Rd	New York	New York	NY	10038	U.S.	212-555-1783	212-555-3063	fausto_agramonte@example.com	NULL
8	9	Delmy	Ahle	NULL	65895 S 16th St	Providence	Providence	RI	02909	United States	401-555-2547	401-555-8961	delmy.ahle@example.com	NULL
9	10	Cammy	Albares	NULL	56 E Morehead St	Laredo	Webb	TX	78045	USA	956-555-6195	956-555-7216	calbares@example.com	NULL

Table A-2. The NormalizedCustomer view

	LastName	First Name	Company	Address1	City	County	State	Postal Code	Country	Mobile Phone	HomePhone	Email	Web
0	NULL	NULL	Acme Corp	123 Snell Ave	Jefferson City	Cole	MO	65101	U.S.A.	NULL	5735553256	NULL	www .acme.test
1	NULL	NULL	Foo, Inc.	457 Prairie View St	Boulder	Boulder	CO	80301	US	NULL	3035555623	NULL	www.foo .test
2	NULL	NULL	Snedley & Sons, L.L.C.	443 Arroyo Rd	Raton	Colfax	NM	87740	U.S.	NULL	5755550956	NULL	www .snedley .test
3	Abdallah	Johnetta	NULL	1088 Pinehurst St	Chapel Hill	Orange	NC	27514	United States	9195559345	9195553791	johnetta _abdallah @example.com	NULL
4	Acey	Geoffrey	NULL	7 West Ave #1	Palatine	Cook	IL	60067	USA	8475551734	8475552909	geoffrey @example.com	NULL
5	Acuff	Weldon	NULL	73 W Barstow Ave	Arlington Heights	Cook	IL	60004	U.S.A.	8475552156	8475555866	wacuff @example.com	NULL
6	Adkin	Barbra	NULL	4 Kohler Memorial Dr	Brooklyn	Kings	NY	11230	US	7185553751	7185559475	badkin @example.com	NULL
7	Agramonte	Fausto	NULL	5 Harrison Rd	New York	New York	NY	10038	U.S.	2125551783	2125553063	fausto _agramonte @example.com	NULL
8	Ahle	Delmy	NULL	65895 S 16th St	Providence	Providence	RI	02909	United States	4015552547	4015558961	delmy.ahle @example.com	NULL
9	Albares	Cammy	NULL	56 E Morehead St	Laredo	Webb	TX	78045	USA	9565556195	9565557216	calbares @example.com	NULL

Table A-3. *PotentialMatches*

	first_name	last_name	company_name	address	city	county	state	zip	country	phone1	phone2	email	web_address
0	NULL	NULL	Acme Corp	123 Snell Ave	St. Martins	Cole	MO	65101-3256	U.S.A.	NULL	573-555-3256	NULL	www.acme.test
1	NULL	NULL	Foo, Inc.	457 Prairie View St	Boulder	Boulder	CO	80301-5623	US	NULL	303-555-5623	NULL	www.foo.test
2	NULL	NULL	Snedley & Sons, L.L.C.	443 Arroyo Road	Raton	Colfax	NM	87740-0956	U.S.	NULL	575-555-0956	NULL	www.snedley.test
3	Janey	Garcia Lopez	NULL	40 Cambridge Ave	Madison	Dane	WI	53715-7194	United States	608-555-7194	608-555-6912	jgabisi@example.com	NULL
4	Kaitlyn	O'Connor	NULL	2 S Biscayne Blvd	Baltimore	Baltimore City	MD	21230-4903	United States	410-555-4903	555-3862	kaitlyn.ogg@example.com	NULL
5	Blanche	Snedley	NULL	443 Arroyo Road	Raton	Colfax	NM	87740-0956	U.S.A.	575-555-0956	575-555-0956	mortimer.snedley@example.com	NULL
6	Mortimer	Snedley	NULL	443 Arroyo Road	Raton	Colfax	NM	87740-0956	US	575-555-0956	575-555-0956	mortimer.snedley@example.com	NULL
7	Mortimer	Snedley	Mortimer Snedley Estate	443 Arroyo Road	Raton	Colfax	NM	87740-0956	U.S.	575-555-0956	575-555-0956	mortimer.snedley@example.com	NULL
8	Mortimer	Snedley	Mortimer Snedley Trust	443 Arroyo Road	Raton	Colfax	NM	87740-0956	United States	575-555-0956	575-555-0956	NULL	NULL
9	Mortimer	Snedley, Jr.	NULL	443 Arroyo Road	Raton	Colfax	NM	87740-0957	USA	575-555-0957	575-555-0956	mortimer.snedley@example.com	NULL

CustomerCountByState View

This is a hokey view used in some early SQL primer examples:

```
SELECT TOP 10 * FROM crm.CustomerCountByState;
```

	State	Total
0	AK	6
1	AR	1
2	AZ	9
3	CA	72
4	CO	9
5	CT	5
6	DC	1
7	FL	28
8	GA	7
9	HI	4

PostalAbbreviations Table

This is a simple cross-reference table:

```
SELECT TOP 10 * FROM ref.PostalAbbreviations;
```

	StateOrProvince	FIPS	Abbreviation
0	Alabama	1	AL
1	Alaska	2	AK
2	Arizona	4	AZ
3	Arkansas	5	AR
4	California	6	CA
5	Colorado	8	CO
6	Connecticut	9	CT
7	Delaware	10	DE
8	District of Columbia	11	DC
9	Florida	12	FL

Glossary

customer dataset

Also known as *production data*, as *CRM data*, and by other similar terms in this book. This is the production dataset you are going to be comparing the incoming data against for matches.

data quality

Data represented in a way that minimizes error while maximizing utility. This includes having consistency in encoding, abbreviations, spelling, punctuation, and more.

dataset

A "rectangular" collection of one or more rows (i.e., with a fixed number of columns). Each column is named and optionally typed. A dataset can be stored and accessed via a SQL table, comma-separated value (CSV) or tab-separated value (TSV), Excel file, XML, JSON, or whatever.

EDA

"Exploratory data analysis." This is a fancy term for running some really simple queries and statistics against a dataset to see what's there. I often informally call it "sniffing the data" to look for patterns, errors, data distributions, and the like.

ETL

"Extract, transform, and load." That is, extract data from somewhere (table, flat file, wherever), transform it by applying various filters and alterations to the data, and load the results into a new location, which in the SQL world is typically a(nother) table.

fuzzy

Attempting to match between heterogeneous datasets that represent the "same data" in differing data entry formats, schemas, datatypes, encodings, conventions, and locales—and sometimes even different semantics (see Chapter 9).

import dataset

Also known as "incoming data." This is the dataset given to you by Marketing to compare against the production/customer/CRM/patient/subject dataset.

impossible data

Values allowed by the underlying data schema but semantically impossible. My favorite and repeated example is always "Birth dates in the future."

normalized

A data value translated in such a way that all irregularities when comparing it to another normalized value are ideally removed.

orthogonal

Formally, "of or involving right angles; at right angles" or "statistically independent." Informally, this means using the same data field for multiple purposes, often at the same time. Calm down. It happens. Again, there's a whole chapter on it, Chapter 9.

person-like entity

My term for business organizations (entities) that share a tax ID/Social Security number and/or other demographics with an actual human being, living or deceased. Estates, trusts, guardianships, and the like apply in certain jurisdictions. Being able to tell "Is this a human?" can be important.

score

A simple number that implies the strength of a given match based on the sum of the matching attributes (columns). Given it is one of the core points of the book, the topic has its own chapter, Chapter 10.

scoring

The process of determining the score, including picking which attributes (columns) are relevant and material to the disambiguation process.

tuning

Adjusting the inputs to the scoring process such that the most material attributes are chosen and that a suitable cutoff point (for your local business requirements) between "Match!" and "No Match!" is found.

Index

Symbols

% (percent sign) wildcard, 38
* (asterisk) wildcard, 38
+ operator (see add operator)
- (minus) sign, 53
0-relative strings, 38
1-relative string, 38
1:n matches, 170
@ (at) sign, 100
^ (caret), 105

A

Active Directory, 61
add (+) operator
    adding to email address, 101
    as numeric datatype, 53
    overloading, 31
addresses, 77-90
    causing duplicate data, 167
    cities, 86
    counties, 86
    countries, 88-89
    overview of, 77-78
    parsing, 136-138
    states, 86
    street addresses, 78-85
    ZIP and postal codes, 87-88
ADS (Azure Data Studio) import wizard, 112-114
aggregate functions, 28-31
    AVG, 30
    COUNT, 29-30
    MAX, 29
    MIN, 29

    SUM, 30
aliases, for tables, 16
AND condition, 196
anonymous (lambda) function, 190
ANSI_NULLS setting, 18
apartment numbers, 80
APO codes, 87
articles, 72
asterisk (*) wildcard, 38
at (@) sign, 100
AT commands, 104
AttemptToMatch view, 147, 151-152, 162-164
attribute-based matching
    deduplicating data by, 165-170
    overview of, 143-151
automated impact analysis, 219-235
    code-generating code, 228-235
    gathering code artifacts, 222-223
    importing code artifacts into SQL, 223-228
    real-world scenario of, 220-221
automated processes, 170
AVG function, 30
Azure Data Studio (ADS) import wizard, 112-114

B

backup tables, 186
bad characters, 111-124
    cleaning up input data, 120-123
    collation, 117-120
    data representations, 111-114
    whitespace, 115-117
BIGINT value, 157
birth dates, 91-95, 178, 193

About the Author

Jim Lehmer has spent a career of more than four decades doing two things: systems integration and data integration. This book is the result of some of the experience he's picked up over the years trying to work with "heterogeneous datasets" and get some meaningful results out of their intersection.

His extensive experience with SQL started in the late 1980s with DB2 v1.2 on MVS (now z/OS), moving then to Sybase and Microsoft SQL Server in the early and mid-1990s. Jim worked on database connectivity and "middleware" products for various software vendors before moving over to "industry" as a software architect and consultant. He also wrote a book called *Ten Steps to Linux Survival: Bash for Windows People*, which was then condensed and published as a small ebook by O'Reilly.

Jim currently lives in the mountains of northern New Mexico with his wife Leslie. When not consulting or writing, he is usually out playing somewhere in the Rocky Mountains there or over the border in Colorado—hiking, climbing, backpacking, snowshoeing, and other things much more fun than dealing with data!

Colophon

The animal on the cover of *Fuzzy Data Matching with SQL* is the Galapagos penguin (*Spheniscus mendiculus*), a species of banded penguin endemic to the island archipelago from which it gets its name.

The Galapagos penguin is the smallest South American penguin and the only penguin found north of the equator. Its small size is, in fact, a key adaptation for remaining cool in a warm climate, allowing the bird to squeeze into small caves or crevasses to escape the sun. Bare patches on its face and behaviors such as panting and standing with flippers extended also help it to release heat.

Galapagos penguins are thought to have been originally brought to the Galapagos islands by the Humboldt Current, which brings cold waters north from Antarctica. Unfortunately, today Galapagos penguins are considered endangered, with a population numbering no more than a few thousand individuals. Many of the animals on O'Reilly covers are endangered; all of them are important to the world.

The cover illustration is by Karen Montgomery, based on an antique line engraving from Dover. The cover fonts are Gilroy Semibold and Guardian Sans. The text font is

Adobe Minion Pro; the heading font is Adobe Myriad Condensed; and the code font is Dalton Maag's Ubuntu Mono.

Tech Stack

The technology stack used to author this book includes the following:

Jupyter (https://oreil.ly/iTyHe)
  The computational notebook environment, running Python3.

Jupyter Book (https://oreil.ly/DmeHy)
  A method of collecting Jupyter notebooks and building the output for publication (PDF, HTML). Note that the final publication output was built by O'Reilly's Atlas, but it ingested the Jupyter Book files directly. The following two libraries are used by Jupyter Book:

  Sphinx (https://oreil.ly/MN_IG)
    A Python library for generating documents used by Jupyter Book.

  MyST (https://oreil.ly/DV5qT)
    A Markdown processor and series of extensions used by Jupyter Book but frustratingly not Jupyter (so you have to build the book to see the output correctly).

pandas (https://oreil.ly/IsX-G)
  A Python library for manipulating and rendering all things data.

Microsoft SQL Server (https://oreil.ly/3P5tu)
  A powerful relational database management system, in my case running on Linux.

Microsoft ODBC Driver for SQL Server for Linux (https://oreil.ly/MK7vV)
  Yes, ODBC is still alive. One of my first software engineering jobs was working for an ODBC driver company.

ipython-sql (https://oreil.ly/O4KED)
  A notebook extension for enabling %%sql magic methods used throughout this book. It relies on the following:

  pyodbc (https://oreil.ly/uNL21)
    A Python library overlaying ODBC. In other words, an "open" Python abstraction layer on top of the *Open* Database Connectivity Layer...because one layer of indirection was not enough!

  SqlAlchemy (https://oreil.ly/NDeLW)
    A Python library for abstracting operations against SQL-based databases.

Printed in the USA
CPSIA information can be obtained
at www.ICGtesting.com
JSHW050739141023
50189JS00006B/13